KINGDOM FINANCING

THE HEART OF THE KING IN HUMAN HANDS

THE GAME SERIES

A BIBLE NOVEL BY

MILTON MAYE

Creative Ministry Resources Publishing
Email: creativeministry_music@gmail.com

ISBN: 978-1-955809-46-7 (sc)
ISBN: 978-1-955809-47-4 (hbk)
ISBN: 978-1-955809-48-1 (ebk)

Rev 2/17/2022

CONTENTS

PREFACE

In the hustle and bustle of everyday life, millions, considered poor, are in a fight for survival, the middle class is occupied getting rich, and the rich are getting bored and wasteful, while still greedy for more. With the reality of the end times passing the ordinary believer by on the silent wind, the kingdom is calling for administrators.

The apostle Paul is still crying out for us to redeem the time because the days are evil. With this cry a profound truth has been dislodged from heaven, searching for hearts to inhabit. This truth is an open secret that many will hear but only a few will receive.

The secret is being whispered with the wind this very minute and tugging at your heart. Will you receive it?

THE BIG SECRET:
1. Anyone can be a Kingdom administrator, rich or poor; strong or weak… anyone.
2. You must understand who owns the resources you will be given to administer, what He desires for His resources, His laws that govern His resources and His rewards from good administration.
3. And… you must obtain His heart for His people above the resources you administer.

This book Kingdom Financing takes us into the belly of the end time beast to rescue a world that is being devoured. It mobilizes you to understand and deploy the financial design of the Kingdom so you can access the supply necessary for enhanced success…Kingdom Success…Good Success…Whatever you do shall prosper success.

INTRODUCTION

"**L**ucifer is cast down from Heaven to earth. He has taken one-third of the angels with him," said the first Voice of authority.

"Yes We must replace them all," the second Voice of authority said.

"We will create beings in Our image," they spoke together. "And in Our likeness," the third Voice of authority spoke. It was as if these three deities were thinking the same thing concurrently and they were in perfect agreement with each other even before a word was uttered.

"We will place them on the earth, where Satan is." The first Voice of authority said. (Now Satan is that same Lucifer, the archangel who rebelled and was cast out of heaven).

"We will not create this being in Heaven. Let Us create them on earth," the first Voice spoke.

"Yes, test them for their faithfulness there first," the third Voice said.

"Then take them to Heaven," the second quipped. "Let Us give them authority over the earth," the Voice continued.

"Satan will be angry with them, he will attempt to steal that authority from them," the second Voice of authority spoke as a joint proponent.

"And he will succeed," the third Voice said.

"Blood will have to be shed to redeem them." The first Voice spoke.

"The blood of man. It must be a man who has not fallen prey to Satan," the first Voice said. "Someone has to rise to destroy the works of the Devil."

"I will become that man, and die and offer My blood," the second Voice spoke up. "Consider Me slain," He continued.

"I now sacrifice You for the redemption of man. I would rather consider You resurrected, though," the first Voice said, pained.

"I will stay with mankind to teach them the ways of God and help them to prepare for the kingdom of Heaven," the third Voice spoke up. "I will help them overcome their tests. There will be ongoing resis-tance of Satan to their redemption."

"You will prepare My bride." The second Voice said.

"Only giving, Our giving, man's giving, can make it possible," the first Voice concluded. "The principles of Our redemption plan are:

>Giving constantly
>Giving the very best
>Giving freely and selflessly;
>Giving of self
>Giving generously
>Giving in obedience
>Giving as an act of Worship
>Giving extravagantly

Preparation of the gift in advance, You My Son! Love: The giving that love compels as love has compelled Me to offer You My Son. Considering the gift sacrificed, slain, once it is dedicated; never to be withheld or withdrawn. I consider You sacrificed. The gift will continue to give until purpose is fully accomplished, yes every gift perpetuates. You will bring many sons to glory. Every gift is personal to Me, to honor Me as You have done."

The second Voice spoke up, "For the Kingdom to be expedited, these principles must be replicated by mankind. My covenant will be established through giving."

"As with God, so with man! You will initiate the redemption

plan, man must promulgate and perpetuate it," the first Voice added.

"I will give man the power to get wealth. Sadly only a few will understand its purpose. Only a few will remember the Lord their God. The cattle on every hill is Mine. ***Grievously many will build private pens for the cattle and even deny Me access. They will attempt to put bars and gates on our redemption plan.*** Man must be taught to give, to let go," He continued.

"Just as You have done Father," the second Voice picked up.

"You will be recalled to Heaven, but I will go to earth," the third Voice spoke up, addressing the second Voice. "I will not have a body so I cannot take this salvation to man in person."

"You will live in man," the second Voice said.

"That will make them gods like Us," the first Voice quipped. "The real power is to those who understand this and take on Your character," the second Voice asserted.

"Only a few will really understand this." the third Voice said almost lamenting.

"Mankind will have to continue where I leave off," the second Voice said. "They will have to give as I gave and much more."

The first Voice spoke, "They will have need of travel, com-munication, labor, materials, buildings and expenses. Mankind must be taught the principles of giving. It will be a struggle against their selfish sinful nature, but it is necessary for true success. The expediting of the salvation of mankind will be measured by the generosity of mankind. ***It is on giving that the redemption plan of mankind is anchored.***"

The second Voice concluded then, "Man will be gods like Us. They will have to adopt Our nature of love, selflessness, and generosity to save mankind."

"And replace the angels who have fallen, whom We have lost forever," the first Voice added. And so it happened, God created a world that would perpetuate by repro-duction. God placed the seed of the plants in themselves. He placed the seed of the animals and mankind in the males. There would have to be interaction, communication, and exchange to facilitate procreation. The very existence of life was based on giving. When Adam fell, the principle of sowing and reaping and reproduction became very apparent to mankind. Adam had to sweat in order to sustain himself. Man's continued existence depended on his knowledge and engaging of these principles of giving, and of sowing and reaping. Adam understood that life in any form could only continue to exist by giving.

The human race had to produce and reproduce. This would be the setting in which the redemptive plan of God would be placed. It would enter the earth as a seed, as small as the grain of a mustard seed. It would enter the earth as a little leaven. ***The plan of redemption would be dependent on the principle of giv-ing, receiving and reproduction.*** This is how it was packaged and given to mankind.

The Voices of the deity in heaven, all three as one, echoed together in chorus, "Except a grain of wheat falls to the ground and die, it abides alone!"

GIVING IS NOT AN AFTER-THOUGHT; THE GIFT WAS PREPARED, PRESENTED AND SLAIN IN HEAVEN BEFORE MAN WAS CREATED. AS HE HAS DONE; SO WE DO!

CHAPTER

1

PREPARATION OF THE GIFT

He sat on the hill overlooking his flock. His heart was satisfied. God had really blessed him. "That one," he said to himself. "No, that one! Mmmm…" he chuckled. It seemed as if all of his sheep were fat alike and very healthy. Ever since he started giving his very best to God it seemed all his flock was competing to be the very best.

This had now become an entertaining game for him. He had just offered his offering to God and he could not wait to begin the process all over again. He would select his next offering well in advance and get it ready for the offering time.

He held on to a sheep and stroked its head. He soon let it go to dash after another one who appeared to be stronger and fatter. He was doing this for almost two hours now and each time he selected an offering he always saw a better one. He could not resist. As he held on to a lamb he said, "I love You God. My daddy failed You but I will not."

He grabbed hold of another he felt was bigger and he said, "You deserve something better my God." He laughed as he acknowledged, "As if they all do not belong to You in the first place."

He humored himself with the thought, "Am I really chasing sheep or chasing God?" He then looked up and whispered, "Lord I will chase You with my offering."

The sun was beginning to set when this ardent lover of God settled on his offering. It was not the fattest but the one he considered to be the strongest. It was the one he felt would respond best to care and special attention and preparation. When the time for offering came he would ensure that no other sheep in the land could compare to the one he would prepare for God. He had done this every time and he never failed to present the best.

He had satisfied God every time with his thoughtful and generous offering. This time would be no different. In his heart, he could not wait to see how God would respond to him. This was not about his brother Cain. Certainly not! He was competing with his last offering. He wanted to find better and better ways of telling his God these three words, "I love You."

His brother could not understand what all the fuss was about. "It is only God," he would say. Abel would simply shake his head. His brother's perception of God was so poor...so poor!

> *GIVE TO MEN AS YOU WOULD HAVE MEN GIVE UNTO YOU; GIVE TO GOD AS IF NOTHING ELSE MATTERS.*

TEMPLE PREPARATION

It was years later. David the son of Jesse was king of Israel. He looked around satisfied. He gazed with pleasure at the cache of gold and silver that he had dedicated to be used in the temple of God. They were to be used to make the articles of silver and gold. It was even more pleasing for him that he had weighed the exact measurement needed.

David had set his heart on building a temple for the Lord and for the Ark. He wanted to build it himself but the Lord had restrained him. As he sought the Lord and set his heart on building the temple, the Lord had made him understand the plans for the temple. It was as if the hand of the Lord was upon him, writing the plans in his heart.

David had earlier called Solomon, his son and given him a detailed outline of the plan. He had also given him the plans in writing. Now it pleased David to give the gold by weight for the articles for every kind of service in the tabernacle. It pleased him also to give silver by weight for every silver article. He weighed the gold by weight for each lamp, for each lampstand, and for the altar of incense. He weighed the gold for the forks, the basins, the pitchers, the bowls, and the tables. His servants looked on amazed as they whispered among themselves at his giving. It was prophetic, and it was preparation; it was prophetic preparation.

For David however, it was very simple. ***If God reveals His plans for His house and for His tabernacle, everyone who loves***

God should want to be a part of it; should lay aside for it; should position themselves and their resources to contribute to it.

When God outlines His plan of redemption, everyone who has a heart for God should want to get involved. Everyone who can, should be ready to participate. The best response to God is to prepare in advance, to get the offering ready. *The heart's best reaction is to select the best and let it rest. To say, "Yes Lord, how do I allocate Your resources today?"*

David called the assembly together. They came to hear what the king had to say. Everyone loved their king dearly. He was wise, he was impartial, he was generous, and greatest of all, he loved the Lord Jehovah with public affection. God was with him and had blessed David considerably in every way.

They heard him speak of how he prepared for the tabernacle. They knew that he would not build this tabernacle in his time, and they received it as a public testimony of David's devotion to God. A devotion that propelled him to do everything he could, in every way that he could for the work of the Lord.

They knew their king would rather spend one day in the courts of the Lord than a thousand days elsewhere. They knew that although David was king and had a preferred place in the tabernacle, he would rather be an ordinary usher, keeping the doors of the tabernacle, than to be numbered among wicked men. When David said that he prepared for the house of the Lord with all his might, it resonated with everyone. They knew that everything their king did for God, he did with all his might.

He spoke of his offering of gold, silver, bronze, iron, wood, onyx, and other precious stones and marble for their various assignments. David's attention to the offering of God, his excitement and fuss over the things of God, and the way he prepared well in advance reminded them of...of Abel.

They heard him say, "I have set my affection on the house of God." This too resonated with everyone. *Affection prompts attention. Attention prompts thoughtfulness. Thoughtfulness prompts generosity. Generosity prompts preparation.*

It was then that King David made a call to action. He turned to the assembly and asked, "Who is willing to consecrate themselves to the Lord?" This was a call for others to give. ***To David, giving was an act of consecration. Releasing a gift is saying, "Lord I am totally Yours. I have, and own money, but money does not have nor own me. You have and own me and my money."***

The captains over the king's work responded. Each captain dedicated gold, silver, bronze, and iron. The people looking on were happy. They rejoiced because, above all things, the captains offered willingly. They had the right attitude. Their hearts were faithful. David rejoiced with tears in his eyes to see the response of his captains. He had a good set of men that he could trust.

Then David blessed the Lord spontaneously with a glad heart, saying:

> You are blessed, Lord God of Israel, Our Father, forever and ever. Yours, O Lord, is the greatness, The glory and the power, The victory and the majesty. Everything in heaven and in earth is Yours; The kingdom is Yours, O Lord, And You are exalted as Head over all. Both riches and honor come from You, Over everything, You reign. In Your hand is power and might; Your hand has the power to make great And to give strength to all. Now, therefore, our God, we thank You And praise Your glorious name. But who am I, and who are my people, That we should be able to offer so willingly? For all things come from You, And of Your own, we have given You. For we are strangers and pilgrims before You, As were all our fathers too. Our days on earth are as a shadow, And with no hope at all. O Lord our God, all

this abundance that we have prepared To build You a house for Your holy name, Is from Your hand, and is all Your own. You test the heart and have pleasure in righteousness. As for me, in the uprightness of my heart I have willingly offered all these things; And now with joy, I have seen Your people, Who are present here offer willingly to You. O Lord God of Abraham, Isaac, and Israel, our fathers, Keep this forever in the intent of the thoughts of the heart of Your people, And fix their heart toward You.

David in blessing the Lord made some very salient points and acknowledgments:

God owns everything in Heaven and earth Whatever is given to God actually belongs to Him already The kingdom is God's God reigns over everything Riches and honor come from God Offering directs the heart towards God;

David knew that by placing the treasure, you place your heart; it fixes the heart on God.

The three Personalities of the deity in Heaven smiled at David. He had followed the principle of the offering that was dedicated in Heaven before time. The offering prepared long before man was created. This offering was not yet offered in the natural but He was presented and offered in eternity as the foundation for the redemption plan. David was truly a man after God's own heart. "Honey, it's our anniversary today," Sarah said excitedly. This was their first anniversary and she was expecting something very special from her husband, perhaps a big surprise.

"Our anniversary?" he said, surprised himself. "Let me run and get you a present!" he continued. Sarah felt depressed.

"How could he forget our most important date?" she agonized. "I will not accept his gift."

Zoe woke up to the sound of a band playing love songs. The soothing beat of Happy Anniversary serenaded her heart. This was her first anniversary and Zoe was swept off her feet. Her husband had taken the time to employ a playing band to wake them up on their anniversary day. She pulled her husband close and gazed in his eyes speechless for a few minutes. As the tune played, she kissed him with the most passionate kiss imaginable.

For her husband, this was just the beginning of what would be her most memorable day. He had planned and provided for this all year, every day of which he spent loving her.

Sarah had tasted how it is received in Heaven when giving is an afterthought and not an overflow of thoughtfulness. Zoe had experienced how Heaven feels when giving is done with much cheerfulness, thought and passion. ***When there is preparation in advance and the presentation is perfect, the womb of Heaven opens, and the windows of Heaven release.***

The husband of Zoe experienced how Heaven reacts when giving is generous and is done with thoughtfulness. Abel, the brother of Cain, lived the experience, for in his heart, he lived to create an experience for Heaven.

The Apostle Paul would later document one of the most important principles of Kingdom Financing. It was not long after the offering which was prepared in Heaven before time was finally offered on earth. Paul was a convert to Christianity. He had met the offering Himself. He had received the gift personally and he would ensure that through his own giving and sacrifice the gift would perpetuate. He placed his life on the line and became an offering himself for the propagation of the gift.

Now he was sending instructions to the church at Corinth, one of the many testaments of his illustrious work. It was with these instructions that he reiterated this profound principle. A principle that Abel, and later David, understood and practiced.

This principle is the principle of Advance Preparation. In his first letter to the Corinthians, Paul wrote, "Let everyone give in accordance with what he has purposed in his heart."

Paul was admonishing the believers that ***preparation should always precede giving. For Paul, the heart must get involved before the gift is selected.*** The heart must also be engaged before the offering is given. His continuation of this charge appropriately summed it up. Paul said, "Do not give grudgingly or because you feel obligated to give, because God loves a cheerful giver."

Paul realized that ***the attitude of giving, essentially determines how the gift is received.*** Both Zoe and Sarah and their respective husbands can attest to this. Cain and Abel can also add their voices to this testimony. It is clear from Paul's revelation that this attitude of giving must be displayed in the level of preparation of the gift. The attitude of giving is the amount of thought that goes into the gift before the time of offering. It is the conversation and sacrifice in Heaven long before the cross at Calvary. When the giver takes time to purpose the gift in his heart, and to prepare it in advance, he is called a cheerful giver. God loves him!

> *1. THE THOUGHT IS ALWAYS MORE WEIGHTY THAN THE GIFT SINCE GIVING IS ESSENTIALLY A COMMUNICATION OF THE THOUGHT.*
>
> *2. GIVING IS NOT AN AFTER-THOUGHT; IT IS the PRODUCT OF THOUGHTFULNESS evidenced by preparation. AS IN HEAVEN, SO on EARTH!*

CHAPTER

2

TEMPLATE OF GIVING

"**I** do not belong here! I do not belong here!" He said to himself, pacing the floor. "I really do not belong here!" He could smell the smoke of the incense coming from his father's bedroom. His father was offering his daily sacrifice to his idols. Everyone in his nation, Ur, worshipped idols. He remembered when he himself participated in these rituals.

He remembered the time he became very uncomfortable with this practice. It was a rainy evening. He had gone with his brother to the goldsmith shop to have one of his uncle's idols repaired. As the goldsmith worked, it became clear to him, something was wrong. He asked his brother then, "Why is it that we worship something that we make and repair? We pray for blessings and help from our gods but see, it is our gods that need our blessings and help. They cannot even repair themselves." Day after day his discomfort continued. He was so confused, or rather liberated, that he refused to participate in the worship of the idols anymore.

His father noticed and challenged him. "Why son? We are kept and preserved by our gods. They provide for us and protect us. Why then do you refuse to worship?"

"Do they really protect us father?" he replied. "Can they really hear you when you pray? Can they smell the incense you offer to them? Can they see your devotion? Can they repair themselves?"

His father heard him and could not find an appropriate

answer. His boy was very logical. He knew his worship of idols was to maintain a tradition and to keep his stature in this pagan world. He could not give it up while living in this country, he would become an outcast. He would not force his son however. He hugged him and stepped away, not responding to his logics. It was very profound.

It was after this that this man, Abram, heard from God. He was out in the field with his father's livestock and he felt a presence. He was alone yet he knew someone was there. He could not see a figure but someone was there. There was that feeling of fear and authority mixed with a feeling of purity and joy. He fell to his face. Abram heard a voice then. It was as if it spoke right through him and yet directly to him. As if his body had ears from head to toe and the voice spoke to every part of him. It may not have been audible but it was loud. He heard the voice say, "I am God!"

As soon as it began, it was over. The Presence was gone and everything was back to normal. Abram went home hastily. He could not wait to tell this to his father. Now he knew for a fact that there is a God out there and it was not these idols. There is a God who could communicate.

His father listened patiently. He was very skeptical but his son Abram was very responsible and trustworthy. He pondered his son's experience and said, "If this God you speak about desires to reveal Himself to you, perhaps He will come again." Abram held on to that conversation as he stepped out of his father's presence that evening.

Abram came back to the place where he heard from God every day from then. He always went to his favorite spot, the spot at which he had heard the voice of God. He wanted another encounter. Not very long from then, he broke tradition. He began to worship and offer incense to this God that his fathers did not know, to this God he did not know, but whom he was determined to discover.

A few years had passed. Abram had developed a relationship with God. Although he did not hear that voice again, he felt the presence every time he made an offering and he knew his offering was accepted. His worship became very frequent and more pas-sionate. His expectation increased. He was almost becoming an outcast among his people. He had broken with tradition in worshiping a God that was not visible. It was as if he was mocking the tradition of his people.

The morning sun was rising in the sky. The light filtered through the leaves of the tree and formed a pattern of oval shad-ows all around Abram and upon his head. He was enthused by its magic. He played a game with the patterns. The wind caused them to dance all over. The freshness of the morning was fragrant and he drank it in like the ocean.

He was close to the place of his first encounter with God. He felt an excitement every time he came close. He lifted his voice in praise. It was then that he heard that voice again. The words had the same effect as at first. It spoke to him, at him, and right through him. He felt the words from head to toe. Abram was mesmerized by the voice and the presence as he listened transfixed. This time the words were instructional. It also contained an awesome promise.

The voice said, "Abram, get out of your country, from your family and from your father's house, to a land that I will show you. I will make you a great nation. I will bless you and make your name great, and you shall be a blessing. I will bless those who bless you, and I will curse those who curse you. In you all the families of the earth shall be blessed."

Abram fell on his face and cried. It would be a difficult decision to make but he would not hesitate. Nothing ever felt so right to him before. He did not know to which land he would be going, but God would show him. A God he hardly knew would show him, but that was enough for him. He knew the gods in this country. He could touch them, handle them, drop them accidentally, and repair them. Yes, he knew them very well, that they were no gods. He would definitely move to the command of a God who could actually speak, and who could move him in this way.

The days following were very busy. Abram's excitement was enough to convince everyone he was serious about this crazy idea. His wife Sarai had no reservation about going with her husband. Her commitment was to the ends of the earth. Abram also had foster responsibility for his nephew, Lot, after his brother Nahor's death. Lot would come along also. His father Terah decided he would go. He was sure this crazy idea would wear off. He wanted to be there to bring his son back when he became disenchanted. When the excitement wore off and disillusionment set in, he would be there. He would be ready to rescue Abram and lead him back.

They set out on the journey. It was a journey that would see Abram becoming very rich and influential. His nephew Lot would also become extremely rich at the time they separated. Abram would have favor with kings and with all the people. This journey would see this ordinary man defeat kings in battle. He would live a life of devotion and sacrifice. God had met with him and spoken to him many times. At one such time, God promised Abram that his descendants would be as numerous as the stars of Heaven. God had changed his name to Abraham, which means father of many nations. He would father a son when it was impossible to do so and would offer his son to God in unreserved obedience.

As for his father Terah, his heart was not in the mission. He realized Abram had no intention of changing course, but instead was even more excited every day. His father became disillusioned in the land of Ur of the Chaldees, his native land. He realized that there would be no going back, but he refused to go forward. Abram stayed with him in the land of Ur, until he died there.

Abram lifted his eyes to God as the gentle breeze ruffled his clothes. Sarah was dead and buried. Her memory was alive in his heart but no longer painful. His thought took him back to the promises God had made him. This was some of his favorite meditation:

In blessing, I will bless you.
I will make you a great nation.
I will bless you and make your name great,
You shall be a blessing.
I will bless those who bless you,
And I will curse those who curse you.
In you, all the families of the earth shall be blessed.

Time had passed. Abraham had received every blessing imaginable in his time and he knew it. God had fulfilled his promise to him in every way. Abraham smiled and lifted his eyes to God. He was fully satisfied. Every time he had a moment like this he always thought of a sacrifice. He called a servant and sent him to prepare. His gratitude intensified. Although God had done so many things for him, he could not help but ask himself, "Has God really fulfilled all His promises?" His descendants were not yet as the stars. He was not yet a nation. He had won a battle and restored a nation. "Amazing!" he reflected to himself. But even then, he was sure that the promise of being a blessing was not fully actualized. The families of the earth were not yet blessed in him. ***He was blessed so that he could be a blessing. He was a riverhead that would distil pure living water to the earth. This he had fully received by faith.***

Yet Abraham was sure in that moment that the fulfillment of this promise was not for his time. It would not be for his son, Isaac's, time either; it was too extensive. Somewhere in the future, the nations of the earth would be blessed. Nations would rejoice in the blessings of Abraham, but he did not know when, or how, or by whom.

His servant came to him at that time and said, "Master Abraham, the altar is prepared." Abraham rose up and went to sacrifice. He was satisfied, very satisfied. God had been faithful to him from the very first day.

God had fulfilled every promise He made to him. His children had not yet inherited the land he lived in, but he had no doubt, it was his. ***He was sure of this one thing, his descendants would be blessed with one purpose: to be a blessing in the earth.***

> *1. GOD's FOCUS IS SINGULAR, THE REDEMPTION OF THE EARTH; HIS BLESSINGS DO NOT FACILITATE INDEPENDENT FOCUS.*
>
> *2. GET WITH IT SO YOU CAN GET FROM IT.*

THE BLESSING OF ABRAHAM

The first Voice in heaven, received the offering of Abraham. It was a very sweet perfume to Him. It was not the smell of burning flesh, but the smell of faith. It was the savor of a heart that was rightly aligned to Him. It was the sweet-smelling aromatic taste of righteousness, as it were, on His taste buds and in His nostrils. He turned to the second Voice and said, "Our plan of redemption is progressing perfectly. Just as Abraham offered his son because he loved Me, I have offered You because I love the world. He does not know it, but You are the fulfillment of My promise to him. His blessing was never to establish his plans, it was always meant to establish My plans. It was never about Isaac, it was always about You, Jesus. It was never about Isaac's seed, it was always about Your seed. The blessing was never for his consumption, it was always for the redemption of all mankind. Through him, or rather through his offspring, You Jesus, all families of the earth will be blessed."

The second Voice looked down from Heaven. Time had passed. He had obeyed His Father and sacrificed Himself for mankind. He had returned to Heaven, to that place where time has no place. He was looking down at one of His apostles who was trying to explain this complication to the Galatians. The third Voice intercepted His thoughts and redirected the conversation the apostle was having. This apostle Paul, began writing. He was surprised himself at what he had written. The apostle was in tears. He felt the inspiration of God as he sat there. He was overcome as he read his own statement, "He did not say, 'And to seeds,' as of many, but as of one, 'And to your Seed,' who is Christ." This astounded him. "Where did that come from?" he thought.

He paused to read, and to reflect on all he had just written in this letter to the Galatians. He needed time to digest it as if he was seeing and hearing it for the first time. "…Just as Abraham believed God and it was credited to him as righteousness, only those who are of faith are sons of Abraham," he continued. This would pierce the hearts of the religious people he lived among, but it was the truth. The truth may hurt but it also heals and prospers. He read his explanation, satisfied, "The Scripture records God's intention to bless the Gentiles by faith, and so He preached the gospel to Abraham in advance." What was that gospel? "In you all nations shall be blessed." That was a Wow moment for Paul. It was an amazing revelation for him, although it was he who had just written it. The blessing was not for the nation that blossomed from Abraham's children. This was not limited to Abraham's offspring although God had promised to make of him a great nation. The promise was for 'all nations'. It was much bigger than Abraham. The first and second Voice smiled as Paul deliberated. He had caught up with a conversation that was held a long time ago in Eternity. The third Voice had opened up the oracles of God to him.

Paul continued reading and reflecting. His understanding flowed like a river from then and he had just kept writing and writing. He was being blessed tremendously by what he had written. He read as a spring of joy exploded in his heart. "So those who are of faith are blessed with faithful Abraham. Those who seek justification by the law are under a curse. For the Scripture says, 'Cursed is everyone who does not continue in the book of the law to do them…'" As he read he transitioned from thinking to meditation. "This is what the word of God says, 'The just shall live by faith.' Help me. It is very obvious. The law is not by faith.

Under the law, you live only by performance of the law. With faith there is no performance, just belief. But how do we transition? We do not need to." Paul laughed to himself. "Christ had redeemed us from the curse of the law!"

The Voices in heaven smiled, "The redemption plan." Paul continued his meditation, "They will ask, 'How did He do it?' Well, He became a curse Himself. Is it not the law which says that everyone who hangs on a tree is cursed? But what is the purpose of His redemption?" Like a chorus, all three Voices joined Paul's meditation at this point. They all said together, "That the blessings of Abraham may come unto the Gentiles, through Christ." "Through You," the first and third Voice said.

"Through Me," the second Voice echoed. "That they may receive the promise of You living in them," He continued addressing the third Voice.

"All of this is through faith." Paul would conclude. His sum-mary of this revelation would be forwarded to the Corinthians and to the Galatians:

> "For you are all sons of God through faith in Christ
> Jesus. For as many of you as were baptized into
> Christ have put on Christ. There is neither Jew nor
> Greek, there is neither slave nor free, there is neither
> male nor female; for you are all one in Christ Jesus.
> And if you belong to Christ, then you are Abraham's
> children, and heirs according to the promise."

Paul would continue to write some salient points on the matter in his letter to the Galatians and to the church. He would present reasoning and revelations that would be hard to ignore, hard to dispute, and impossible to dismiss.

The Voices in heaven had 'connected the dots' for all mankind. The blessing of Abraham was for everyone who received Jesus Christ by faith. ***The blessing had an effect and the blessings had a purpose.***

1. Heaven, having sacrificed, released its blessings in the earth in a template; it was a package to one man who was prepared to do what heaven had done, sacrifice his son.

2. The blessing was intended to be received centuries later by the one man who would complete the sacrifice on earth, (the blessing can only be received through a completed sacrifice.) This person would do on earth what He had done before time, in heaven, sacrifice Himself. He was the only Person who could truly understand, fulfill and appropriate the blessing.

3. The blessing was intended for all people.

4. The template for the blessing is sacrifice. As in heaven, so on earth.

THE EFFECT OF THE BLESSING

The king clapped his hands at the performance of his singers. Their voices were excellent and their performances were sensational. Above all this, they were his. He looked around at the luxury of his palace. His palace was a mix of colors and expensive draperies. Precious metals and precious stones of all kinds were everywhere. They were so craftily woven into the design that everyone found the palace magical.

Every vessel that the king and his servants drank from, were made of gold. He had twelve lions craftily made and placed on either side of the six steps of his throne. They too were gloriously created from precious metals and stones. The kings of the nations all around were simply amazed when they came and saw the magnificence. And his throne, wow! His throne was made of ivory, overlaid with gold. They had never seen anything like it.

His servants were smartly dressed in expensive attire. Their conduct was very orderly and dignified. Everyone was happy in his presence and had an abundance of everything in this palace. Above all the king was full of counsel.

The king had everything he could ever desire. Everything that he desired he acquired. Kings would give to him freely and there was no price too high that he could not pay.

A servant came in and sought audience with the king just then. "Your highness, your envoy from Ophir is here." The king commanded, "Send them in!" They came in with pomp and paraded some of the treasures before the king with which they had returned. He received them and blessed them and gave orders for the captain of his army to provide an escort for the shipment to one of his treasure cities. His wealth was so much that he placed them in treasure cities carefully guarded by his armies. Sometimes he wondered why he bothered to guard them so carefully.

All the nations around respected and feared him. No one dared to attack him. Instead, they brought him more and more gifts every year. It seemed they all competed to see who could give the most precious and rarest treasure to this king. His treasure houses were filled with gold and precious jewels of all types, size, and shape. Just a glimpse into one of these stores would leave the wealthiest person bewildered. This king was so rich that silver became common as stone in his kingdom.

It was getting late. The day's activities and entertainment had left the king very drained. His thoughts wandered to his wives for a brief moment. They too had become a collection to him. He had so many wives that his palace had become a place of wedding ceremonies. He had a minimum of two to three wedding ceremonies every month. They were his own weddings to his new wives. His own marriages had become one of the main entertainment parties of his kingdom.

In addition to his wives, seven hundred of them, he had three hundred concubines. These were beautiful women whom he did not get to marry. He could not fit their marriage into his schedule.

As he walked down the elaborate corridors to his exquisite bedroom, he knew he was too tired to see any of his wives today. The king undressed and went to bed. His mind was occupied with the treasures and magnificence of his kingdom. He was satisfied, very satisfied. The king said to himself as he drifted off to sleep, "The blessing of the Lord makes one rich, and He adds no sorrow to it."

> *1. The blessing of Abraham would be nailed to the cross with heaven's offering so it could be received by everyone who would embrace the cross and heaven's offering.*
>
> *2. THE blessings of Abraham, blessed to be a blessing, received, stewarded, preserved and passed on to its original intended target...us!*
>
> *3. The template for the blessing is sacrifice!*

SON OF GOD, ABUNDANT LIFE

"**I**s there anyone like King Solomon?" King Hiram spoke to his counselors. "Absolutely no one!" he answered himself as they listened and nodded in agreement. The king of Tyre was pleased with himself for his long association with Solomon. King Hiram had always loved King Solomon's father, David, with all his heart. When he heard that Solomon was anointed king, he initiated contact immediately.

This had begun a longstanding relationship that benefited Solomon in many ways. King Hiram had supplied him with cedars from Lebanon, and with skilled laborers for the building of the temple and his other buildings. King Hiram had also partnered with him in his ventures to Ophir for gold annually. Hiram smiled as he said to his counselors, "I feel very much a part of everything King Solomon has accomplished, but I still cannot help but mar-vel at the magnitude of his achievements."

"The wealth just keeps pouring in," one of his counselors responded. "Kings from all over bring him riches."

"Yes," Hiram responded. "But the magnificence of everything he has built is amazing. The precision is stunning. I have never seen or heard of anything like this."

"What makes him stand out like this? What do you believe is his big secret?" Another of his servants asked. The king was silent for a while. He was about to answer but one by one his counselors began offering answers before he could respond.

"His wisdom," one said.

"Must be his diligence," another responded.

"His father

counselors began offering answers before he could respond. "His wisdom," one said.

"Must be his diligence," another responded.

"His father David is fully responsible for his success," another said.

At this point Hiram, the king responded. He had listened quietly as his counselors, one after another, offered fabulous deductions about the cause of Solomon's distinguishing wealth and success.

King Hiram said, in a very slow, yet deliberate tone. "I have heard that the God of Heaven, his father's God, had promised his father David, the king, to make Solomon, His son. The only explanation I see is that King Solomon is a son of God. What I have heard about the God of Israel is that He created the heavens and the earth and everything in it. His father David contended that the earth is His and everything in it: gold, precious jewels and people including us.

If this God made Solomon His son then it is no wonder that silver in Jerusalem is common as stones. His wisdom is noth-ing less than the wisdom of God Himself. Do you see how King Solomon operates with confidence as if he owns everything? Do you see the way kings and people gravitate to him?"

"He is living the abundant life!" One of his counselors joked.

"Abundance in life and abundance of life," King Hiram agreed.

"But I have never heard of any human being born of human parents becoming a son of God," a close friend of the king inter-jected. "How is that possible? How can I become a son of this God?" The king responded.

"King David's, and King Solomon's God is supreme. He does whatever He pleases. He made Israel His people by selection. He made Solomon His son by election."

It would be centuries later that Paul would get a picture of the truth. Paul was an apostle of Jesus Christ who was truly the Son of God. Many would know Him as man and some religions still see Him as a man, just a mere prophet.

The truth is some-times too wonderful to grasp and too confusing to untangle. He was God, who was all God, and yet He was man who was all man. What everyone seems to agree on is that He came to bridge the gap between God and man. He came to make men gods.

The Apostle Paul documented his revelation. "You are all sons of God through faith in Christ Jesus. As many of you who are baptized into Christ have put on Christ. There is neither Jew nor Greek, slave nor free, male nor female; for you are all one in Christ Jesus. And if you belong to Christ, then you are children of Abraham, and inheritors of the promise."

King Hiram and his counselors could never conceive how close they were to the truth. God would one day elect many sons, as many as accepted Christ. All of these sons would inherit the blessings of Abraham. This blessing would make them rich. The riches were eternal. The blessing of God is blessings with a purpose. This knowledge was so close and yet so far. Asaph captured this revelation in a moment of inspiration in Psalm 82.

YOU are gods; I have said it;
You are gods!
All of you are sons of the Most High,
But just like men you shall die
And fall like one of the princes.
But you are gods; will you receive it?
You are gods!

Arise, O God, and judge the earth,
For You shall inherit all the nations.
Arise, O 'gods,' and judge the earth,

For you shall inherit all the nations. You are gods!

@CWDSBible

God stands in the congregation of the mighty;
He judges among all the gods.
How long will you judge unjustly,

And show partiality to the wicked man?
For you are gods!

Defend the poor and fatherless;
To the needy and afflicted do justice.
Deliver the poor and needy;
Free them from the hand of the wicked.
They do not know nor do they understand;
In darkness they walk around;

They know not nor do they understand,
But you are gods.
All the foundations of the earth are out of course.

You are gods! I have said,
"You are gods,
And all of you are children of the Most High,
But just like men you shall die,
And fall like one of the princes."

Arise, O God, judge the earth,
For you shall inherit all the nations.
Arise, O 'gods,' and judge the earth,
You are gods!

@CWDSBible

Hiram and his servants may not have received this revelation but they could certainly see and associate the blessings of Solomon with his God. It was wrapped up in the promise for sons. ***Solomon, however, would go through a dilemma... the dilemma of having wealth without a definite purpose.***

*1. THE GLORY OF THE SON SHOULD BE A REFLECTION
OF THE GLORY OF THE FATHER, OTHERWISE,
THE FATHER LOSES HIS GLORY IN HIS SON.*

*2. IF GOD CALLS YOU SON HE HAS EVERY
MOTIVATION TO MAKE YOU BECOME JUST LIKE
HIM. AS HE IS SO ARE WE IN THIS WORLD.*

*3. JESUS AUTHENTICATED YOUR DIVINE NATURE: "IF DAVID
CALLED YOU GODS TO WHOM THE WORD OF GOD CAME..."*

BLESSINGS WITHOUT PURPOSE

Solomon woke up to the sweet sound of music from instruments his father had invented. There was nothing he liked more than to smell the fragrance of the morning, to capture the golden beauty of his private garden dripping with dew, and to hear the sound of the pipes all at the same time. It was mesmerizing.

He had slept late and he felt rested and re-energized. He had a busy day ahead of him but he was in no hurry. He wanted a few moments to savor the morning and to enjoy the beauty of life. He was happy that he did not see any of his wives or concubines last night. If he were to see one of his wives or concubines each day it would take three years before each would have a turn with him again. The thought of this alone would leave him totally burnt out. Many of his wives experienced the king on their wedding night only. The pain of these women had become somewhat of a burden to him. He knew this made them just as common animals.

For him to fully enjoy the morning he had to keep these thoughts at bay. To satisfy his conscience and to occupy them in his absence, he allowed them to maintain their traditional customs. He even dropped into their ceremonies and worship of their native gods when he had the time. This was the best he could do as a husband to please them. He knew it was totally wrong. He should not allow this in the city of David and of God. He hoped God would understand the complications of his wealth.

These thoughts were too expensive and too condemning. He quickly dismissed them and refocused on the morning. Somehow the glory and the magic had faded. It happened every time he thought about the dark side of his success.

He slammed his right fist in his left hand and cursed, saying, "Vanity, all is vanity!"

Solomon quickly refreshed himself and dressed in his royal robe. He left his bedroom and headed for his dining hall. He knew everyone would be waiting on him. As his servants bowed to him, he took his seat at the table. It was the usual banquet of delicacies, pastries and fruits. He had always said, "If a king is to pay attention to the food he will be useless to his kingdom." This too is vanity, he thought. He had success, there was no doubt about it, but it was becoming a burden to him.

Today he was unusually quiet at the dining table. He seemed oblivious to the fact that he had three kings dining with him today. For a few minutes, he drifted into his own private world of thoughts. His reflections took him back to his father David. He said in his thoughts:

I was my father's son. I was protected and the only one in the sight of my mother. My father David taught me and said to me, "My son Solomon. Let your heart retain my words. Keep my commands and live. I charge you, get wisdom; get understanding. Do not forget nor turn away from these instructions I give you. Never forsake wisdom and she will preserve you. If you love her, she will keep you. Wisdom is the best thing that exists. You must get wisdom. Among everything you acquire, get understanding my son. If you exalt her, she will promote you, if you embrace her, she will bring you honor. She will place an ornament of grace on your head. She will give to you a crown of glory." Solomon laughed at his father's sense of humor as he remembered how his father presented wisdom as a woman. "Love her, never forsake her, exalt her, embrace her," he chuckled silently. His thoughts then reflected on his harem for a brief second and the laughter faded in his thoughts. This pursuit of women was not his wisest decision, and he knew it.

As he reflected on his father's instruction, he could remember… he remembered it as if he was in the moment now. He was at the high place at Gibeon. He had just finished offering one thousand burnt offerings to the Lord. It was an exhilarating day. He was intent on picking up where David his father had left off, in his generosity towards God.

As he went to bed that night the Lord God visited him. The Lord was about to test his heart and to prove to Solomon that he could never out-give God. He had just drifted off to sleep when the vision appeared to him. In his dream, the Lord said to him, "Ask and I will give it to you!" God really told him to ask for anything he desired, anything!

To respond to God appropriately he knew he needed a vision of God. What was God's capacity? What would please God the most? Why would God be this generous to man? He could ask for angels for his protection; God could give it. He could ask not to ever die; God could give it. He could ask for all the riches of the world; God could give it. *He knew however that the gift of God was to accomplish the purposes of God.* He was happy that although he was young, he could align God's giving to His purposes.

His father had instructed him well. The word of his father was very loud in his ear in that moment. It was like alarm bells. "I charge you, get wisdom; get understanding. Do not forget nor turn away from these instructions I give you. Never forsake wisdom and she will preserve you. If you love her, she will keep you. Wisdom is the best thing that exists. You must get wisdom. Among everything you acquire, get understanding my son. If you exalt her, she will promote you, if you embrace her, she will bring you honor. She will place an ornament of grace on your head. She will give to you a crown of glory."

Solomon responded to God then, "Lord my God. You have made me king instead of my father David. I am in the middle of Your people whom You have chosen. They are great and too many to be counted. Give me an understanding heart to judge Your people. That I may also discern between good and evil. For who is able to judge this great people of Yours?" ***Solomon recognized that he was elected by God for the work of God among God's people. He requested understanding with a mission; to make him effective in fulfilling God's purpose for him.***

Solomon knew that most people if given this opportunity would go directly for wealth and riches without a purpose or a vision of God. He felt in his spirit that one day, the world would be given this opportunity. Somehow he could not shake the feeling that one day God wanted to make more people His sons, as he had promised David he would do for Solomon. ***Giving generously to sons is what a father does.*** This opportunity was in no way inappropriate or out of place.

Solomon also learned from his father David, that a son who has his father's heart and pleases his father gets control of his father's wealth. He himself was instructed at David's feet. He pleased his father David in everything. He was entrusted with his father's business. He had the kingdom. ***He wanted to be a student of God, as his father David was, so he could manage the kingdom of Israel for the God of Israel.***

Solomon remembered God's response to him then. Every time he remembered this it endeared God to him. It also was vivid proof of the accuracy of his father's counsel. His father David was always so on-point about everything. He had the heart of God. God had said, "Because you have asked for this and not for long life, or riches for yourself, or for the life of your enemies, I have given you what you asked. I give you a wise and understanding heart so there has not been any like you before you and no one like you after you."

This is why the kings keep coming. I have something they want; something very rare, my wisdom. God had also said, "I have given you also what you have not asked for: riches and honor, so no king can measure up to you all your days."

Well, well, they never come empty. Each king carries with them the best of the treasures of their kingdom. The kings want to impress me of the magnificence of their own kingdom. I just collect them all and magnify my kingdom. God had also promised me long life, but this time with a condition: that I follow His ways just as my father David.

Solomon sighed. He had a vision for understanding, he would put it to use in leading and judging God's people. He remembered the two women who came to him not long after his encounter with God. "Surely the sword shall test the heart. Surely the heart that is tested shall raise the child," he chuckled. He sighed again, God made him extremely rich but he did not have a vision for wealth. He did not ask God for riches and it was accumulating. "How do you keep riches from being a contagious disease?" he muttered.

Although he had so much, the people felt burdened and slightly oppressed under his leadership. He did not use his wealth to ease their burdens. Instead, he burdened them to increase his wealth. This was not so difficult to bear for them as they were happy to bask in his glory. He felt ashamed of himself. He had become preoccupied with the provision and had forsaken the purpose. He never had a vision for wealth. His wisdom was for the people but the wealth was for himself. He could not shake the feeling that he was making a big mistake.

A gold fork fell to the ground, and the noise awakened King Solomon from his deep meditations. He realized he was not alone and he felt a little selfish. He would definitely continue his reflections later. For now, he would focus on the task at hand. He began immediately to engage his guests in conversation. He became once more the consummate host. The kings at his table had many questions for him. Some of these questions were calculated simply to test his wisdom. They marveled at his answers. The meal was very pleasurable for them.

The rest of the king's day was very normal and routine, but his heart was troubled. The first Voice in heaven had spoken. He had troubled Solomon's spirit. Today Solomon was to summarize for the world what happens to wealth without purpose. What happens when the blessing of Abraham does not abound to the blessing of the families of the earth!

Solomon called his chief servant to him and told him, "Cancel all my evening sessions. I must retire early." The king had many things to think about. He wanted time to reflect. He went into his private quarters and reclined. As he began to ponder all his accomplishments, the mystery of his heart began to unfold. He had many questions. He had many disappointments. He was frustrated by his limitations. ***It was the dilemma and frustration of blessing without purpose. Solomon began writing as he poured out his heart.***

1. ABUNDANCE, OVERFLOW, RUNNING OVER, MORE THAN YOU CAN ASK OR THINK, YOU WILL NOT have ROOM ENOUGH TO CONTAIN, EXTRAVAGANCE, THAT IS THE LANGUAGE OF A FATHER TO A SON. IT WAS THE LANGUAGE OF GOD TO SOLOMON IN REALTIME.

2. "WHAT IS YOUR HEART? I WILL DO IT." THAT IS THE LANGUAGE OF A SON TO A FATHER.

SOLOMON'S DILEMMA

"It is all a waste of time; vanities of vanities. I have seen everything that is done under the sun. I have greatness. I have wisdom. It is all a waste of time, vanity. Just as grasping the wind in your fist. I have tried to gratify myself with wine. I made great things. I built houses and planted vineyards. I have gardens and orchards with every type of fruit trees. I made aqueducts to water my plants. I have many male and female servants. I took for myself whatever my eyes desired. I did not restrain myself from any pleasure. Then I looked on it all and concluded, it was all a waste of time, vanity."

As Solomon reflected and wrote, he said in his heart, "I hate life! Everything that I have done on earth is distressing me. I hate everything I have worked for. I am going to die, just like the common animals. Who can tell if the person who succeeds me will be wise or foolish? What was I really working for?" I am in despair because of everything I have accomplished. I do all the work and leave it to someone who does not work at all. A person works hard, day and night, and bears the sacrifice, the sun, and burden and what then? This is all a waste of time.

Solomon came to this conclusion very early in his reflections, "There is nothing better for a man to do than make his soul enjoy all he has worked for. This is from the hand of God."

"Wrong conclusion," the Voices in heaven said in chorus.

"His wisdom will settle the matter in the end," the first

Voice resounded. "Wisdom is from God."

Solomon would come to the same conclusion many times before he found the heart of God. He had lived his life for pleasure and for women, but fulfillment had eluded him. The truth was never far away. He continued his meditation: "Who can eat or have enjoyment and pleasure more than myself? God gives wisdom and knowledge to a person who is righteous in His sight, but He let the sinners sweat and collect to hand over to the righteous. All of this is a waste of time."

Solomon reflected on his years and was confronted with one glaring reality, his time was almost at an end. He reflected, "There is a time for every purpose under heaven: A time to be born a time to die, a time to gain, a time to lose, a time to speak, a time to be silent." He realized that there are just fleeting moments between each period marked by time markers. He was concerned about the worker who will find that his labor is just a waste of time. Then he became concerned about what eternity will record about our time. He spoke softly, "God has made all things beautiful in its time. He has put eternity in our hearts."

For a fleeting moment, Solomon focused on a higher pur-pose for time. He accepted that no one can figure out what God is doing from start to finish. He knew within himself that God is doing something. God has a purpose for every time allocated. He knew that there is a finish, perhaps already completed, yet to manifest in time. He summarized the moment by stating that the best thing for man to do is to rejoice and do good in his life. His reflection on eternity brought him close to a God reality. It was the aspect of giving, time or resources. Doing good! He reverted to his situation and concluded that man should eat and drink and enjoy the fruits of his work. He wrote, "This is the gift of God!"

Solomon was getting close to the mind of God, but he was still not there yet. The reflection on heaven made him wonder if the spirit of man really goes up. Does this have anything to do with the purpose for wealth? Again Solomon concluded that man should just eat and enjoy his wealth since he does not know what will happen when he dies. Solomon had reached the wrong conclusion once more. With all his wisdom he could not see a purpose for his wealth beyond himself.

As Solomon continued his reflection, he began to see the futility in many things. He reflected on the tears of the oppressed, the person who is always working hard to accumulate riches yet he has no purpose for it. He also reflected on the strength of collaboration.

Solomon had some instructions for those who were rash with their words. He noted that those who love silver will never be satisfied with silver or with their increase. He reminisced on those who have riches but were destroyed for it. Then he concluded again that to enjoy the good of your labor all the days of your life is your heritage. He asserted then that this was good and fitting and the gift of God. He was right about this but it was not the conclusion, fulfillment should provide the enjoyment.

Many centuries later, the Apostle Paul would assert that everyone should work hard that they may have to give to those who are in need. While not disagreeing with Solomon's assertion, he felt the purpose should be others and the pleasure will be realized. It is clear that Paul believed that blessings, fulfillment and enjoyment accompany the pursuit of purpose.

Solomon continued the expression of his disappointment with life. He agonized over all those who have wealth but do not have the power to enjoy it. Then he made an important notation. He wrote. "All the labor of a man is for his mouth yet his soul is not satisfied." Solomon in that moment acknowledged that pursuit of personal gratification cannot satisfy the soul. It was at this point that the king expressed his doubts about all his previous conclusions. He wrote, "Who knows what is good for a man in this life? All the days of this vain life passes as a shadow. Who can tell a person what will happen after him on the earth?"

Solomon then began to contradict himself. He wrote, "It is better to go to the house of mourning than feasting. The heart of the wise is in the house of mourning, the heart of fools in the house of mirth." Solomon then hinted on a place for purpose in everything. He wrote, "A good name is better than precious ointment."

The king's reflections took him to kingdom government and the power of the king. He was saddened at the thought that wicked men are getting the reward of the righteous and the righteous getting the reward of the wicked. This he felt was another waste of time. At this point, the king reverted to his previous conclusion. It justified the way he lived. He wrote, "Therefore I recommend enjoyment. A man has nothing better to do in the earth than to eat and drink and have pleasure." But then he admitted, "A human being cannot find out or understand God's purposes in the earth. Even though he had given himself to discover it, even wisdom cannot unseal God's secrets."

Solomon reflected, "One event happens to the righteous and the wicked, the clean and the unclean, and to everyone. They all die." He felt this too was a waste of time. "You accumulate, you make yourself a distinction, you are honored, then you die, what next?" He wrote humorously, "A living dog is better than a dead lion." He did not realize then that wrapped up in this thought was the engine of the redemption plan, life after death. He did not know that wrapped up in this thought was the purpose for wealth. No matter how much a person eats and enjoys, he will be confronted with that event of Solomon's dilemma. There will also be the accounting for time and resources, for which he did not get a picture of.

Solomon had some advice for everyone, "Go eat your bread with joy, and drink your wine and make your heart glad; for God has already accepted your works." At this point, Solomon began to put things into perspective. "Eat and enjoy because your works are accepted. Perform acceptable works, then eat and enjoy."

He continued, "Let your garments be white and your head lack no oil." His wise men would say:

"The chickens are coming home to roost." They would then interpret, "The king is closing in on the truth." They would applaud to hear him say.

"Live joyfully with the wife of your youth." This for them would be the summary of the futility of pursuing women in Solomon's own words. He said, "wife", not "wives".

His wisdom became very clear and instructional. Whatever you are doing, do it with all your might, for you have no oppor-tunity in the grave where you are going. It became clear that the futility of life necessitates purposeful occupation and preoccupa-tion. The right attitude to approach purposeful occupation was: with all your might.

The king began thinking. As he engaged his thoughts, he wrote a statement, "Money answers everything." He understood that money was necessary for kingdom financing, for the financing of his kingdom and for his lavish lifestyle. He never understood the purpose of money in the redemption plan designated from Heaven. If he had, he would have understood the purpose of wealth.

The king, however, had no doubt about this principle; the principle of sowing and reaping. He wrote, "Cast your bread upon the waters and you will find it after many days. He who observes the wind will not sow. He who regards the clouds will not reap." He continued, "A person does not know which way the wind will blow, or how the bones of a child grow in the womb. Be generous, sow your seed. Do not restrain yourself."

It was at this point that Solomon began to put pleasure and a life of self-gratification into context. He wrote: "Rejoice in your youth, young man, walk in the ways of your heart and according to your sight. You must know however, that God will judge all of these."

The king was reflecting a long time. It was already after midnight and he was about to conclude his reflections. He had come to the realization that everything was a waste of time except for one thing. He could see that his father, David's, life was no waste of time. The Voices in heaven cheered him on. He was beginning to demonstrate true wisdom. He was engaging the true purpose for life and wealth.

The king wrote, "Remember your Creator now, while you are young, before hard times come, and you get to that age where you begin to lose pleasure in your days. Remember your Creator before the silver chord is loosed or the golden bowl is broken. Before the pitcher is shattered at the fountain or the wheel broken at the well."

The king was coming to the conclusion that wealth and prosperity are not forever. To Solomon, it was becoming clear that the wheel will be broken at the well and the golden pitcher will lose its glory. He embraced the reality that the dust will return to the earth from which it was taken and that the spirit will return to God.

Life for him seemed even more pointless because of this revelation. It was all a waste of time. Then he remembered what his father David had taught him. The futility of his own life had brought him back one hundred and eighty degrees to that conclusion. He wrote, "Let us hear the conclusion of the whole matter: Fear God and keep His commandments. This is the duty, the absolute duty of man." He further continued, "God will judge every work, including every secret thing, whether good or evil."

The king had concluded that life without purpose is futility, an absolute waste of time. Pursuing self-gratification is futility, an absolute waste of time. ***Wealth without purpose is futility, an absolute waste of time.*** If we fear God and discover what He desires for our lives, if we give our lives to work worthy of His judgment and approval, then there will be some value in life. His father David was the perfect example.

The deity in Heaven looked on. King Solomon's dilemma was a demonstration of what happens when wealth is pursued without a vision. His conclusion was a summary of the heart of God for man and for the appropriation of His wealth. In the next generation the kingdom would go on to lose everything Solomon had acquired. The earth, however, would record Solomon's experience as a demonstration of the lack of value and longevity of wealth used for self-gratification alone.

> *1. REMEMBERING YOUR CREATOR MUST BE THE VISION THAT DRIVES EVERYDAY LIFE AND PERSONAL PURSUITS, NOT THE EXHAUST OF A LIFE DRIVEN BY GREED AND SELFISH PURSUITS.*
>
> *2. WHEN LIFE IS ONLY ABOUT WHAT YOU CAN GET FROM IT YOU IMPLODE (AND IT DIES WITH YOU); WHEN LIFE IS ALL ABOUT WHAT YOU CAN GIVE TO IT YOU EXPLODE (AND CREATE A LASTING UNTAINTED LEGACY; IT GOES BEYOND YOU).*

GONE WITH THE WIND

"Everything, they have taken everything?" Rehoboam said to himself as he stared at the main treasuries of his father. "Shishak has stripped the kingdom. My father must be turning in his grave to see what I have done with his legacy."

"Not you," one of the wise men who had been around King Solomon interrupted. "Your father did this all by himself." For such a young man, in the early years of his kingdom, Rehoboam felt as if he was a complete failure. Firstly he had lost ten of the twelve tribes of Israel to an independent kingdom of Israel led by his rival Jeroboam. Now King Shishak had defeated Judah and stripped the nation of all the wealth King Solomon had accumulated.

Rehoboam did not know where to turn. In these trying times, wisdom told him to turn his heart back to God and he humbled himself. Rehoboam could recall what happened at the very beginning of his reign. All the tribes of Israel had come to him requesting one thing. That he made their burden lighter.

Solomon in his relentless pursuit of wealth had made life burdensome for his people Israel. ***He did not recognize that God's true intention for the appropriation of His wealth is to ease burdens and to free captives.*** Solomon had increased the burdens of the people of God instead in order to satisfy the thirst for more. He himself had said that anyone who loves riches will never be satisfied with it. His life was a perfect testimony.

The people desired to serve his son and to remain faithful to the house of David but they wanted Rehoboam to ease their burdens. Rehoboam had asked them to go and come back. He wanted to get counsel on the matter. The old men who had counseled with Solomon advised him to listen to the people. The young men he grew up with advised him to take the opposite approach. They told him to speak roughly to the people and threaten them to increase the burdens instead.

Solomon's greatest fear and dread had come through. His son was just like him. He wanted wealth but he had no vision for it. He did not have the people in his heart. The people went away from him.

Rehoboam remembered the hurt he felt as he put the army together to fight for his kingdom. He felt helpless when God sent a prophet to warn him not to fight. Rehoboam began serving God until he became strong in his kingdom. He then decided to follow Jeroboam and his father Solomon and worship other gods. He turned from the God of Israel, David's God. This was when it happened.

King Shishak of Egypt with a confederate of nations came up against Israel. Rehoboam was defenseless. ***He was to learn that God only defends what is submitted to His control and yielded to His purpose.*** "If we make what is His ours, we will have to defend it ourselves," a wise old man whispered inaudibly.

King Shishak took away everything Solomon had stored up. He left with every valuable treasure that Solomon gloried in. The life work of his father was gone in just a few moments. It was a massive store of wealth. It was sitting there without purpose or appropriation. It was sitting there while the people of the land felt oppressed and burdened. It was all taken; all of it, gone! Even the golden shields that would be displayed when the king entered the temple were taken. King Rehoboam replaced them with bronze shields. The golden days of glory were gone, now bronze defined the new order of Judah. This will always happen whenever purpose does not define wealth. ***God's promise to Abraham was not blessings in isolation, but blessings with intention, blessings with a purpose. Abraham was blessed to be a blessing.***

King Rehoboam sighed, his father could not take all the blame. He had all the information his father had. He had the benefits of the instruction of David in writing. He knew about Solomon's experiences with God. He knew he would have to accept some of the blame himself. He was the one who refused to ease the people's burdens. What was he trying to prove? Was he trying to compete with his father?

He was the one who turned from God and served idols. He knew the difference between the right and wrong and he chose to do the wrong. "I am at fault very much myself," he said. "It is sad that I had to suffer so much to learn. From now on I will pursue the Lord God of my father David. I will pursue His purpose for my life and for this kingdom only."

> *1. THE GIVER OF WEALTH IS THE SUSTAINER AND PRESERVER OF WEALTH. YOU NEED HIM AS MUCH WHEN YOU HAVE IT, AS BEFORE YOU DID.*
>
> *2. YOUR LIFE IS WRAPPED UP IN GOD, NOT IN POSSESSIONS; YOU LOSE HIM YOU LOSE EVERYTHING!*

CHAPTER

3

THE PLACE OF RICHES

t was long after the time of Rehoboam. A Teacher was teaching the people daily with wisdom and with the demonstration of power as was never seen before. He was a marvel and many people followed Him. It was on one such occasion that this scene took place.

They saw him coming from a distance. He was a stoutly built man with small eyes. His walk was brisk. He wore a frown on his face that seemed to have carved out its own lines and built a nest for itself. It appeared that laughter had long gone from his heart as water from the desert. Life for him was a battle and he could find no better person to pull into this battle than this Person. He was celebrated, He was respected, He had many followers. Everyone listened to Him and did whatever He told them.

This man did not introduce himself. He came directly into the crowd and shouted to the Teacher, "Teacher, tell my brother to divide the inheritance with me." From the moment these words escaped his lips it was clear to everyone that this man was out of place. He did not want what the Teacher had. He wanted to lower this Teacher to the role of an ordinary judge. He wanted to use the influence of the Teacher to coerce his brother to give up what was rightfully his by inheritance. He did not want the pure wealth of the word of the Teacher for his corrupt heart. He wanted the Teacher to corrupt His message to illegally help him to acquire a part of his brother's wealth.

The Teacher would have none of it. He said to this man, "Who made Me a judge over you?" The second Voice of the deity from Heaven was among men. He would take this opportunity to teach a very important lesson from the redemption plan decided in Heaven before the earth was formed.

It was the principle of wealth and its role in the Redemption plan of God. He turned to the crowd following Him and said, "Be careful to avoid covetousness. A person's life is not made up of the abundance of possessions he has." In this one statement, the second Voice communicated a strong conclusion and a rebuke for all those who live to pursue abundance. He strongly asserted that man was not created for this purpose, to pursue wealth. The people could not possibly appreciate the authority of His words then. No one really fully understood that nothing was created without Him and that He understands the real purpose of all creation.

He then told them a very weighted story that solidified His message. He said, "The field of a certain rich man yielded an abundance of produce. This man thought to himself, 'What am I to do? I have no room to store my crops!' He then concluded, 'I will do this: I will pull down my barns and build bigger ones. I will store all my crops and my goods there. I will say to myself, "My dear, you have many goods in store for many years. Enjoy yourself; eat, drink, and be happy."'"

God responded to him, 'You fool! Your life will be taken from you tonight. Who will possess these things you have provided?' Amazingly, this was also one of Solomon's foremost dilemmas.

The Teacher was not finished. He was yet to make His most cogent statement. This statement captured the very essence of life. It is the very heartbeat of Heaven. It answered the question of redemption. It also answered the question of the second Voice coming to earth to manifest His sacrifice. Solomon stated that money answers all things, but this statement answered the question of money and wealth.

The Teacher said, "*So is everyone who lays up treasure for themselves, and is not rich toward God.* They are just as this man." It was clear He meant they were just as foolish as this rich man. That they were living life in futility as this man had done. They were living and acting contrary to their creation design. Solomon understood it from experience. He said all of his gains for him was futile, a waste of time, vanity.

In years to come, the theologians would grapple with the question: If Jesus died so we could inherit the blessings of Abraham, surely He has no problem with wealth. They would all come to the same conclusion: The key is 'not to hold on to the wealth for selfish and personal reasons. The key is to be rich towards God.' *The purpose of wealth is to make it accessible to the purposes of God.* It is clear God disapproves when we take the cattle He places on our hills and build private pens for them, then restrict His access to it. Some would dare to ask, how much of your wealth does God want access to?

> *God likes rich people dearly; or rather, God likes people, rich or poor, who hold Him dear by being rich towards Him!*

EVERYTHING

He came to the Teacher with great pomp. He was young but it was clear from his attire and his entourage that wealth was dripping from him like honey. He had everything he desired in life, everything that money could buy him. Yet, he was very concerned because somehow he felt he did not have a life. He had heard many things about Jesus. He had heard how He was respected for His authoritative sermons on the truth. He knew if Jesus justified him he would be justified.

He had set out with one mission, to buy life. This was his opportunity. He came to Jesus and said, "Good Teacher, what good thing shall I do that I may have eternal life?"

Jesus had to set something straight immediately. He could see through this rich man that he was more concerned with being good than being Godly. Jesus realized that by calling Him good, this man was try-ing to place himself in a bracket of goodness that would make Him feel justified. He did not desire to live a life of goodness, he wanted that one good thing he could do to settle the matter.

Jesus excluded Himself from the company the man sought immediately. He also eliminated man from that company. He said to him, "Why do you call Me good? There is no one good but One, that is God." Now He could drive home the fact that life only exists in God and comes out of God and His word. He said, "If you want to enter into life, keep the commandments."

The rich man said to Him, "Which ones?" He had something to boast about and Jesus had just made it easy. He was sure he would return to his home more justified than ever. He was being endorsed by Jesus Himself.

Jesus said, "'You shall not murder; You shall not commit adultery; You shall not steal; You shall not bear false witness; Honor your father and your mother; and love your neighbor as yourself.'"

The young man was beaming. He could not hide the pride in his voice as he retorted triumphantly, "I have kept all these commandments ever since I was a child. Is there anything that I still lack?" He was never ready for the response of Jesus. If there ever was a day he wished he had someplace to hide it was today. If there ever was a conversation he wished he had not initiated, it was this one. If there ever was a time he wished he had not persisted, it was now.

He could not hide his shock when Jesus said to him, "If you want to be perfect, go and sell what you have and give to the poor. You will have treasure in Heaven; and come, follow Me."

Jesus had the answer for how much Heaven desired and He was very blunt about it, "All you have." Heaven wants everything. ***God wants to be able to put His hand on anything or, rather, everything He appropriates to man, without objection or resistance.***

The young man dropped his head immediately. He did not dare to look around. He had done everything to ensure he was heard before. His posture was, as one could say, dignified boisterous. Now he wished no one else had heard the conversation. He certainly would not give up his treasure on earth for treasure in Heaven.

He certainly had no desire to follow Christ. He loved the words and wisdom of Jesus. He believed in Him, at least enough to seek his justification. He just did not believe enough to trade his lavish lifestyle. These were his treasures and they were where he wanted them, here on earth. This rich young man had wealth but the wealth also had him. He did not realize that everything he had was Heaven's treasures assigned to him as its administrator. He never acknowledged or surrendered his wealth to Heaven. He refused to surrender his wealth to the assignment on earth of the true owner, God. He would hang on to it for his own personal gratification.

The second Voice of Heaven had just revealed to man God's great secret but He was not yet finished. He would speak to one dividing boundary that man would set up between himself and Heaven: money.

Jesus said to His disciples, "I tell you, it is hard for a rich man to enter the kingdom of Heaven. It is so much easier for a camel to go through the eye of a needle than for a rich man to enter the kingdom of God."

This stunned His disciples. Almost everybody they knew strived to be rich. There is hardly any person on this planet who would refuse wealth if given. They began to express their thoughts, "Master, who can be saved then?"

Jesus saw their dismay. He realized He needed to clarify His statement. He said to them, "How hard it is for those who trust in riches to enter the kingdom of God!"

Jesus had made a distinction. He was speaking specifically about those who refuse to submit their wealth to God. They instead submit themselves to their wealth. They make their riches their trust and their god. These people seek to enter the kingdom of God hanging onto their wealth without submitting the wealth to the kingdom. The problem is that anything that enters a king-dom is under the authority of the King. It is physically impossible to keep the wealth separate from the kingdom, just as it is for a camel to go through the eye of a needle.

When Shechem the son of King Hamor the Hivite, had raped the daughter of Jacob, Dinah, the sons of Jacob gave them one condition to approve a marriage which he requested. He and all his people would have to be circumcised. To justify this sacrifice and imposition of this new custom on the people, Hamor and Shechem said to the people: "The men will only dwell with us and be one with us on this condition alone, if every male is circumcised as they are. Will not their property, their livestock, and all their animals be ours?" So physically impossible is the proposition of keeping the wealth separate from the kingdom, that Jesus compared it with a camel trying to go through a needle's eye.

But what happens to those who submit everything to the kingdom of God? Peter wanted to know. He said to Jesus, "Lord we have left all and followed You. Therefore what shall we have?"

Jesus then spoke to assure all His disciples. He wanted them to know that their special assignment had a special reward, a throne in glory. He also had a message for everyone who is obedient and willing to sacrifice for Heaven's redemption plan. Jesus said, "Everyone who has left houses, or brothers, or sisters, or father, or mother, or wife, or children, or lands, for My name's sake, shall receive a hundredfold, and inherit eternal life."

The leaving was not necessarily physical, He was speaking of positioning the heart. He was speaking about prioritizing. He was speaking about willingness to give up.

The blessings of obedience to the redemption plan and of submitting your wealth to the kingdom is multifaceted. Jesus wanted everyone to know obedience did not come without reward. The reward was both for this life: houses, lands and abundance of wealth with persecution. The reward was also for the life to come: eternal life in a place where abundance cannot be defined, and peace is forevermore.

---

1. If we are not our own because we were bought with a price, then we have not our own. This is the reality, nothing we have belongs to us!

2. Every employer frowns on an employee who gets possessive with the Employer's property.

HOW TO LAY UP TREASURES

"**S**ell what you have and give to the poor. You will have treasure in Heaven."

The rich young ruler kept turning this over in his head late that night on his bed. "Sell what you have and give to the poor. You will have treasure in Heaven…" He could not forget his encounter with Jesus earlier that day. His face still flushed red at the memory. He wished he had never set out in the first place. In the cloud of the heat waves that kept him emotionally unbalanced the memory of one phrase from Jesus kept bothering him, "Treasure in Heaven?" He was a very diligent student of the Torah and it was his nature to seek and find answers.

"What did He mean? How can you have treasure in Heaven? Why would you want treasure in Heaven?" The rich young ruler pondered. "What was that He said I needed to do to have treasure in Heaven, 'Sell everything I have and give to the poor'? There must be a key in this somewhere. Is it about selling everything I have, or is it about giving to the poor?"

As he lay there, tired and distressed, he remembered a con-versation that he had with one of his servants about this same Jesus. Jesus had taught them they were to lay up treasures in Heaven. He had said that in Heaven the rust will not corrode the treasures, the moth will not corrupt it, and the thieves will not steal it.

"It is very clear that the main benefit of treasures in Heaven is that they are durable." He did not remember his servant saying anything about accessing those treasures. "This for me is the most important part. I must maintain my lifestyle," he agonized.

Jesus had said something about where your treasure is, your heart will be also. Now he understood why Jesus had said to him, "…and come follow Me."

"Placing the treasure positions the heart to follow," he thought. "It is all about taking the heart off the trea-sure and placing it on the kingdom. It is all about surrendering the treasure to the kingdom," he thought.

A faint smile crossed his lips as he thought, "Perhaps God does not require me to give up everything physically." The smile quickly disappeared as his thoughts progressed, "He only requires me to…to give up everything. To remove my heart from my trea-sures and place it on Him only." This would be hard.

It did not answer his question though, "How do you access these treasures? If the treasure is placed in a normal bank, there is safety, interest and access." He fell asleep from sheer exhaustion, his mind still very actively contemplating all these issues. He had no idea when his eyes closed that night. It was in the wee hours of the morning.

The rich young ruler jumped up from his sleep startled. The night was still very dark. He could not have been asleep very long. He looked around and his eyes adjusted. There was no one else in the room. He had a dream and the only thing he could remember from it was a line from the Proverbs. "He who gives to the poor lends to his Maker." A flood of revelation entered his mind then. "This is what Jesus means by treasure in heaven," he thought. "It is very simple in fact. ***When you give to the poor you lend to God. God is in heaven. If the loan is with the borrower, the treasure is with God in heaven.***"

A flood of Scriptures about giving to the poor entered his heart. The rich young man lit a lamp and began to search the

Scriptures. He called upon his memory and the Scriptures he had marked previously as he began his search for answers.

> *You lay up treasures in heaven by giving to the poor!*
> *This is a very practical principle: you give to the*
> *poor, you lend to God. Heaven has your loan!*

THE KINGDOM AND THE POOR

The rich young ruler began his study: For the poor will never cease from the land; therefore I command you, saying, 'You shall open your hand wide to your brother, to the poor and needy, in your land.'

This Scripture spoken by Moses in the book of Deuteronomy chapter 15 came alive to the rich young ruler in that moment. His heart began to race as he remembered the Teacher's words to him, "Sell all you have and give to the poor…" He would search for a Scripture that would provide a way out.

He went to the book of Job. Job was speaking of his own righteousness in chapter 29. He said, "I delivered the poor who cried out, the fatherless and the one who had no helper. I was a father to the poor."

He was confronted from all angles as he examined the Psalms: This poor man cried out, and the Lord heard him, and saved him out of all his distresses, Psalm 34:6. Blessed is he who considers the poor; The Lord will deliver him in time of trouble. The Lord will preserve him and keep him alive, and he will be blessed on the earth, Psalm 41.

He will bring justice to the poor of the people. He will save the children of the needy, and break in pieces the oppressor, Psalm 72.He raises the poor out of the dust and lifts the needy out of the ash heap, Psalm 113.I will abundantly bless her provision; I will satisfy her poor with bread, Psalm 132.

God's love and affection for the poor had never been as apparent to him as in this moment. It became very clear to him that God took it as His personal responsibility to take care of the poor and to deliver them. He also could see that God had wrapped up a package of blessings that is delivered whenever anyone considered the needs of the poor.

His thought took him back to the kingdom of Israel in its former glory, and all the kingdoms he was familiar with. He could see that it was the duty of the king and his government to satisfy the needs of all his subjects. Special attention was always placed on taking care of the poor and creating conditions for them to survive and succeed. He could understand why the administration of the kingdom of God made this its priority.

He wanted to stop there for fear of what else he would uproot. The desire to find just one Scripture of justification took him into the Proverbs of Solomon. He read:

> He who despises his neighbor sins; But he who has mercy on the poor, happy is he. Whoever shuts his ears to the cry of the poor will also cry himself and not be heard. He who has a generous eye will be blessed, for he gives of his bread to the poor. He who oppresses the poor to increase his riches, And he who gives to the rich, will surely come to poverty. He who gives to the poor will not lack, but he who hides his eyes will have many curses. The righteous considers the cause of the poor, but the wicked does not understand such knowledge. Open your mouth, judge righteously, and plead the cause of the poor and needy. She extends her hand to the poor, yes, she reaches out her hands to the needy.

Tears came to his eyes. There were so many blessings wrapped up in taking care of the poor. This was the route to righteousness he was searching for. He wept, not because of the truth he discovered, but because of the price he was not prepared to pay.

The rich young ruler sighed as he read the prophecies about the Messiah from the book of Isaiah:

> But with righteousness, He shall judge the poor, and decide with equity for the meek of the earth, Isaiah 11. The Spirit of the Lord God is upon Me, for the Lord has anointed Me to preach good tidings to the poor. He has sent Me to heal the brokenhearted, to proclaim liberty to the captives, and the opening of the prison to those who are bound. Isaiah 61.

Many persons were saying that this Teacher was the Messiah. Was He? He certainly has the heart for the poor. He even carries a money bag to distribute to them.

As he continued reading his face was emotionless, his heart turned to rock. ***It was clear to him that the poor were very dear to the heart of God.*** It became self-condemning for him as he read more from Isaiah and Jeremiah.

What will they answer the messengers of the nation? That the Lord has founded Zion, and the poor of His people shall take refuge in it, Isaiah 14. For You have been a strength to the poor, a strength to the needy in his distress, a refuge from the storm, a shade from the heat. Isaiah 25.

Sing to the Lord! Praise the Lord! For He has delivered the life of the poor from the hand of evildoers, Jeremiah 20. He judged the cause of the poor and needy; Then it was well. "Was not this knowing Me?" says the Lord, Jeremiah 22.

As the rich young ruler read from the books of Ezekiel and Daniel, he could see that it was not only the right thing to look after the poor, it was sinful not to do so. He read:

> Look, this was the iniquity of your sister Sodom: She and her daughter had pride, fullness of food, and

abundance of idleness; neither did she strengthen the hand of the poor and needy, Ezekiel 16. "Therefore, O king, let my advice be acceptable to you; break off your sins by being righteous, and your iniquities by showing mercy to the poor. Perhaps there may be a lengthening of your prosperity." Daniel 4.

This young man was a rich man, but he was a man of fasting. He really loved God. He followed the commandments just as the religious leaders of his day. As he read the book of Isaiah he was confronted by what God really considered to be a pleasing fast.
This is the Scripture he read from Isaiah 58:

DO YOU WANT your light to be as the dawning?
To have it break forth as the morning?
Health and righteousness to be your adorning?
Then let God's chosen fast be known.
It is to loose the bonds of wickedness,
Undo heavy burdens and free the oppressed;
Give the hungry bread and let the poor have rest;
This fast will satisfy your soul!

ISAIAH 58

They say, 'Why have we fasted and You have not seen?
We have afflicted our soul and You take no notice.'
But, you find pleasure in the day of your fast,
And exploit all your laborers.
Behold, you fast for strife and debate
And to strike with the fist of the wicked.
But you will not fast as you do this day
To make your voice heard on high.
"Is it such a fast that I have chosen,

A day for a man to afflict his soul?
Is it to bow down his head like a bulrush
And to spread out sackcloth and ashes under him?
Will you call this a fast?
An acceptable day to the Lord?
Is not this the fast I have chosen?
This is the fast you must bring to Me:
"To loose the bonds of wickedness,
To undo heavy burdens, to set free the oppressed,
And to break every yoke from the necks;
Is it not to give the hungry some of your bread;
To bring the poor and outcast to your house;
When you see the naked, that you cover him with clothes,
And not hide from your own flesh?
This fast is good, for it is then
That your light shall break forth as the morning,
Your health shall spring forth speedily;
Your righteousness shall go before you,
And the glory of the Lord shall guard you from behind.
Then you shall call and the Lord will answer;
You will cry and He will say, 'Here am I.'
If you take away the yoke from your
midst, the pointing of the finger,

And also the speaking of vain words,
"If to the hungry you extend your soul
And satisfy the afflicted,
Then your darkness shall be as the noon,
And in obscurity, your light will rise.
The Lord will guide you continually.
And in times of drought, He shall satisfy you,
And make your bones strong;

Like a watered garden you will be blooming with life,
"Like a spring of water whose waters do not fail.
Those from among you shall rebuild the old waste places;
You shall raise up the foundations of many generations.
You will be called the 'Repairer of the Breach,
The Restorer of Paths to Dwell In.'"

@CWDSBible

The rich young ruler was torn in many pieces with emotions that kept him awake. Every fiber of his body screamed at him in physical exhaustion. This added to his mental anguish as he meditated, ***"The heart of a king is on his subjects. His duty is provision for all. A righteous king will oversee appropriation and distribution of wealth to the needs of the poor. This is what God has done!"***

The rich man had no doubt that God required people to consider the poor and to serve them. He had no doubt that this is what Jesus meant when He said, "Then you will have treasures in Heaven."

He was filled with a low feeling of emptiness as his thoughts centered on this question, "But how do I access my treasures in Heaven?" It was then that he remembered the rest of the Scripture from Proverbs 19, "…and the Lord will certainly repay what He is given. The Lord is no man's debtor," he thought. This was very consistent with the Scriptures he had just revised. Many of them held a similar promise of blessings and abundance.

The thought of this became more agonizing for this ruler. Access to his own treasures would be based solely on faith. It was all about his confidence in knowing God is taking care of him and would meet all his needs according to His riches. It was all about his confidence in walking in the blessings of Abraham. It was all about his confidence in knowing God would respond to his call at all times. It was all about his confidence in God to give back to him abundance in this life, so God could have His hand on it.

He fell back to sleep even more drained and distressed. He could hear himself mutter in his distant comatose, "It is all about my confidence in the money I have now and nothing else. I cannot surrender this."

> *The poor will always be among you, therefore the opportunities to make investments of a lifetime that yield significant gains and favor in this life and perpetuate well beyond this lifetime are limitless.*

CHAPTER

4

KINGDOM FIRST, KING'S TREAT

As the rich young ruler grappled with his personal encounter, or as some would say, confrontation with Jesus, another man was grappling with another statement Jesus made.

He was middle-aged and counting his years. He came from a background where poverty was the norm. His conversations oftentimes centered upon his lack, and his thoughts always engaged his emotions on the matter. This brought to him much anger, frustration and headaches. His health had deteriorated. He was worried because he could not adequately meet the needs of his family. His worries brought him poor health and his poor health added to his worries. His sicknesses were costing him, and in addition to this, it increased his woes. There were long periods when he could not work due to illness, and he watched as his children starved. He sank deeper into poverty. This caused him to worry even more and his problems were spiraling out of control.

He was standing there in the crowd that gathered around Jesus. He was wearing what could have been considered near rags. He did not have the resources to replace his clothing. Everything he earned went to feed his family. Everyone around him seemingly jostled for any space available to allow them to see and to hear the Teacher clearly.

This was a place where the rich had no privilege; they jostled everyone just as the poor did. They came because they too were hungry for what this Teacher was sharing. In this forum, the teachers of the law and the priests had no special rights or VIP treatment. They were given passage because of the respect and honor of the people only.

The words of the Teacher held a certain effect, a certain authority. His teachings were very strange but it went deep within, into the inner soul and resonated. The miracles He performed were simply awesome. They were also magnetic. Many people were drawn to Him because of this.

This man was there in the midst of the crowd, hot, sweating and uncomfortable. He strained his ears to listen and sought to focus over the noise and constant movements around him. It was at that moment that he heard the Teacher speak words that were the most refreshing he had ever heard. It seemed to meet him just where he was.

The Teacher said, "I say to you, do not worry about your life, what you will eat or what you will drink; nor about your body, what you will put on. Is not life more important than food, and the body more important than clothing? Look at the birds of the air, for they do not sow nor reap nor gather into barns; yet your heavenly Father feeds them. Are you not of more value than they?"

This caught his attention and had him focused as if he was a part of a guard of honor being inspected. He begged the person next to him to be very still so he could hear properly. The person complied and began to listen. The person, too, was quickly captivated by what Jesus was saying. The crowd became still as Jesus continued. "Which of you by worrying can add one inch to his stature?

So why do you worry about clothing? Consider the lilies of the field, how they grow. They do not work or spin, and yet I say to you that even Solomon in all his glory was not arrayed in beauty like one of these. Now if God so clothes the grass of the field, which today exists, and tomorrow is thrown into the oven, will He not provide clothes for you with more diligence and enthusiasm, O you of little faith?

Therefore do not worry and say, 'What am I going to eat?' or 'What will I have to drink?' or 'Where will I get clothes to wear?' For after all these things the Gentiles seek. Your Father in heaven knows that you need all these things. Instead seek first the kingdom of God and His righteousness, and all these things will be added to you."

Days had passed. The Teacher had moved on but these words refused to leave this man. He had fasted while he prayerfully analyzed this message, word by word, line by line, phrase by phrase, to get the full meaning. The more he considered it, the more confused he became. This speech was too loaded for him to digest it all at once. The real confusion came when he considered how to apply it to his present situation. The contrast was too pronounced. The Teacher had said, "Do not worry about what you eat, or drink, or wear." This was very easy to say. Anyone can say anything until they are in the real situation as he was. As his thought progressed he said to himself, "The Teacher appears to believe that these basic needs are not our responsibility but God's who is in Heaven. Was He really teaching that this is what God does naturally, take care of people just as he decorates the flowers? Why then am I in such a state of poverty?" he lamented.

Then his thoughts converged on this closing phrase, "Seek first the kingdom of God, and all his righteousness, and all these things will be added to you." Jesus was offering him the solution to his problems, or was He? He had turned this phrase over in his head a thousand times in the past days. He was convinced this was the solution the Teacher was giving. But…he did not know just how to seek the kingdom of God.

He had many questions, "What is the kingdom of God? How do you seek the kingdom of God? What does He mean by 'first'? Are all these things I am concerned about just additives, things that will be added, and not the main priority of life? Is it that God requires me to shift my focus?"

These thoughts bothered him every moment he was awake, it also tormented his sleep. He needed answers. He knew a kingdom in simple terms was the domain of a king, but the kingdom of God…? Hmmm… His domain? In Heaven perhaps. Has to be much more. The Teacher had said, "It is among you, it is in you, it is with you."

"This is too big for me," he thought. "How do you seek the kingdom?" he asked himself. As his meditation continued he settled on some possible answers. To seek the kingdom you must seek the interest of the kingdom. The interest of the kingdom is the interest of the King. What is the main interest of God: Keeping the law? Obedience to God? The Teacher had said love was the greatest commandment and all the law and the prophets were hinged on love. "The redemption of mankind," this thought came to him over and over again. It was nagging him but he could not place it. "Where did that come from?" He asked himself. He could not place it but he could not shake it. Could it be that the main interest of the kingdom of God on earth was the redemption of mankind? If so, how could he participate in the redemption of mankind? What did He mean seek it first? Should his priority be the priority of the Teacher? Should he really be putting God above everything else, even his family? Should he really trust God to take care of all these things that make him worry himself to sickness, presently? Should he focus on serving God only? Would faith really satisfy his need while he pursues God's design for his life?

A passage from the book of Kings stuck in his mind. He had initially contemplated it when he began meditating on what the Teacher meant by first. He could hear Elijah telling the woman, "Bake me a cake first." It was as incredulous as what this Teacher was suggesting. It was however more real to this mystery than anything else he could imagine. What was asked of the woman seems to be what Jesus was asking of him.

He decided to take a closer look at this story. He was a very creative and practical person and he learned a lot more from illustration. He decided to illustrate as he meditated.

"The brook is dried!" Elijah said. The stick puppet this man had created looked at the lake of stones in front of him. There was absolutely no water there. All trace of water was gone. "How could a person who served the King with such vigor and excellence be experiencing such crisis in his life?" he thought. "The King controls all resources."

"Could it be that crisis, the absence of supplies, does not necessarily mean the absence of God? Could it be that crisis is an opportunity for another testimony; another triumph in God? Could it be that your crisis is an opportunity to bless others in crisis? Could it be that God uses crisis, to get us to shift location? The situation may change, but God still remains, He may have just moved on."

"What am I to do now?" The stick puppet asked. Well, no one else was there. The brook which responded in the past with a flow of water had ceased speaking. The man turned the head of the puppet upwards. The question was meant for God. "Ha!" the man said to himself, "When you are in crisis seek direction from God. In all your ways acknowledge Him. Seek a fresh word!" The stick continued his prayer, "I have only sought your interest my King. I have lived for You and nothing else. Everything I do is about Your kingdom. I have put it first and centre."

The man boomed to the puppet from his place of the creator of that puppet. He acknowledged himself as someone with greater knowledge than the puppet he created, greater wisdom, with the ability to do with the puppet anything he desired.

He said, "Go to Zarephath in Sidon. I have commanded a widow woman to supply your needs there." The puppet responded immediately. He gathered his things and began singing as he left the parched stone bed that once was a flowing brook. He sang:

*"When God speaks you listen, yeah, yeah, do what He
says, yeah, yeah. You do what He says!"*

The gates of the city loomed ahead. It was made of sticks
and decorated with grass. It was just a couple feet high, just inches
higher than the stick man he had created. The city was just over a
small hill at the back of the man's house but for the stick man, it
was a very long walk.

He came to the city hungry and exhausted. As he approached
the gate he saw the woman. She was also made of stick. She was
gathering wood for the fire. He knew she was a widow because she
had on her widow's clothes that identified her. He also knew from
within himself, this was the woman the Lord had selected to feed
him. The stick puppet called out to her in its own voice. It was the
falsetto voice of the actor. He said, "Please bring me a little water
in a cup that I may drink."

This woman was very kind of heart and hospitable. She left
her fire sticks and set out immediately to get the water. As she was
going to get it, he called to her in the same voice and said, "Please
bring me a small piece of bread also when you are coming."

The man, now an accomplished actor, responded to the other
stick puppet with a voice in high pitch tenor. This represented
the woman who stopped and responded, "As the Lord your God
lives..." Apparently not satisfied with the pitch he stopped and
took it higher. This time he was very pleased with the response.
The smile that lit his face for a brief moment told it all. She continued her response, "As the Lord your God lives, I do not have bread,
only a handful of flour in a bucket, and a little oil in a jar."He
could not help but pause to reflect as he continued the response
for the woman. "I am gathering a couple of sticks that I may go in
and prepare it for myself and my son, that we may eat it and die."

How could God have sent Elijah to a woman in such a desperate condition, both physical and mental? Then the response to his

question came into his heart like a flood, "Where kingdom sends, the king supplies." He was not there to draw on her resources, he was representing a kingdom and his kingdom would continue to supply him. "First with the ravens, now with this woman if she is obedient," he thought.

As he spoke the words of Elijah with the falsetto voice of the stick puppet the revelation he sought came. He said to her, "Do not fear; go and do as you have said, but make me a small cake from it first, and bring it to me. Afterward, make some for yourself and your son. For this is what the Lord God of Israel says, 'The bucket of flour shall not be used up, nor shall the jar of oil run dry, until the day the Lord sends rain on the earth.'"

If this woman was willing to put the kingdom of God first by sowing into the life of the king's representative, all her needs would be met. Everything that concerned her would be addressed. The woman listened and acted in nothing but faith. The man mimicked her movement, as she went about to do exactly what Elijah, the stick puppet, requested.

He thought, "This is exactly what I need to do, just as Jesus said." He brought the stick through the motions of how he believed the real woman acted. She and her son had food for a long time until the rain came again. The flour was not used up, nor did the jar of oil run dry, just as the Lord had spoken by the stick puppet representing Elijah.

It was clear to this man then that the needs of our heart are attended to as we attend to the heart of our God and the needs of His kingdom.

The man lamented the death of the woman's son which came about because of the woman's own confession. She had said, while she worried about her desperate situation, "We will eat this cake and drink and then we die."

Elijah had unwittingly endorsed it when he told her, "Go and do as you have said." Even this need for resurrection of the woman's son was taken care of. "Kingdom comes through all the time" the man concluded. Every area in which you are concerned or worried about, will indeed be added to you.

It would be centuries later that someone was sharing the story of this man's son with fellow Christians. He told of how this man's son became extremely wealthy. His father had walked with the apostles and had given himself to serving the church. God had blessed his son tremendously and used him to supply the needs of Christians in the early church movements. He was very influential and no one suspected him for some time. He saw himself as a riverhead supplied with water from an eternal source to supply an eternal purpose. He would eventually die for his faith.

It was modern time. A man was teaching the importance of putting the kingdom first. He was using an illustration. He looked around the room at all those who were gathered to hear his words of encouragement.

He had brought a jar with him and he filled it with big rocks until it was brimming over. He looked at his students and asked, "Is this jar full?" Everyone thought his question ridiculous. "Of course, it is!" they all said. He smiled. He then took a box with gravel and began pouring it in spaces until it was brimming. Everyone gasped. "You were tricking us," they all replied laughing. "Is this jar full?" he asked.

"Sure it is," they all replied. There were no real obvious spaces. He then pulled out a package of sand and began to pour it within the spaces and shake it down.

They saw they were tricked a second time. When he asked the question again everyone was very cautious. They did not want to be tricked again. One person was very bold and shouted, "It is!"

The teacher took the bottle of water he was drinking and began to pour it in the jar. This time the jar did not need shaking, the water found the spaces.

The teacher looked at the class and asked them, "What was the lesson I was trying to teach?" They all agreed.

"No matter how much you get into the jar, there is still room for more."

"That is how we tend to live our lives," he responded. "We make God an afterthought. We reserve the kingdom of God until we have achieved some predetermined personal targets, day to day worry and concerns, occupation. We then get so preoccupied and busy with these things that we find no place for God.

The lesson is: ***If you want to get the Big Rock in, you have to put it in first. If the King is really the Big Rock for you, the most important Person in your life, then put Him first. Build your life around Him. Let Him be the reason, source and centre of everything you do.*** He will have it no other way. If you do not do this, the kingdom will be displaced by everything you consider less important. Jesus assured us that everything we tend to worry about and give priority to will be added to us, by the Big Rock, the King. He will supply them and fit them in your life around Him."

The screen of the television clicked on. "I cannot tell anyone about this! Cannot tell anyone! What must I do?" A young man who looked fairly ordinary took center stage on the film the teacher turned on at that moment.

He was looking at an antique stash of gold plated coins he had just found in an open lot. He was digging for top soil for his garden when he made this exciting discovery. He jumped with excitement and began a wild celebration. His celebration was soon cut short as he began to think. "This is worth millions to me," he said. "This will be the prize of my collection." He was not very rich. He knew he could probably live luxuriously if he sold this treasure, but he was a collector. "I cannot just take it." He said softly. "It belongs to the owner of the field. How would I explain to the judges my new found treasure?"

He could see that this presented a difficult reality for him. He needed a plan and needed it quickly. If he was to steal this treasure he could not display it. His income could not support the purchase of this cache. He needed a story that would make this treasure valuable to him. He needed a way to legitimize it. He quickly looked around. He saw that no one was watching. He hid the treasure again in the field and left. He stopped for a few min-utes some distance away and watched. Nothing moved. No one had seen him. He had not awakened curiosity in anyone.

As he went home he contemplated, "What shall I do? I have no money. I would buy the field but I have no money." The evening passed and the young man paced the floor of his home, excited and confused. "I cannot borrow money, no one will lend me. If they were inclined to they would want to know the reason. They would question the price I am willing to pay for the field to ensure the owner cannot refuse my offer."

He could not sleep that night but it was settled. He would sell everything he had to buy the treasure. The young man could not wait for morning to execute his plan. He approached the owner of the land at first light. It was an old man who was not very well off himself but he had strong sentimental value to things.

"I would like to buy your field," he said.

"You know I am not selling," the old man said. "What do you need it for anyway?"

"It would be the perfect place to display my collection," he said. He could not tell the old man that he had found in his field what for the young man was the treasure of all treasures, the prince of all his collections.

"You are joking," the old man said. To prove his point the old man decided to tease him. "If you really want to buy my field you have to pay me…" He named a price that was fifty percent higher than the actual value of the land. He knew only a crazy person would pay that much for the land. He had no intention of selling. He was visibly surprised when the young man said, "Deal."

"Where will you get that money?" the old man asked.

"Just give me a week," the young man replied.

"Deals, deals and more deals. Everything must go!" The young man had put his house on the auction block. He was also selling his furniture, all his cloth-ing that he could sell, every household item he could sell and his flock. He was willing to accept ridiculous discounts to get a quick sale. Everyone thought he was mad. They could not understand his enthusiasm. They were happy for the deals however and they soon stripped him of everything he had at ridiculously discounted prices.

The young man counted up his money. It was still short. He had his collection of valuable antiquities but he would not sell these. Where would he get the rest of the money from? No one would lend him now; they already thought he was crazy. He had nothing left. Well, not exactly, he had the portion of his inheri-tance his father had left him. "You do not sell your family inheri-tance in my culture," he thought. "But I must!"

He immediately went to his brother and offered him a deal. He was willing to accept a price that was just enough to provide the balance of the money that he needed. His brother had the value of a lifetime for a fraction of its worth. He was concerned for his otherwise very rational sibling but he accepted.

The young man was back with the elderly owner of the land within two days. The old man could not escape. The judges would enforce the verbal agreement especially given the sacrifice that was made on the basis of the old man's word. They would never under-stand it but they would enforce it. The deal was completed. The field and the treasure belonged to the young man. "Now the world would begin to see real wisdom," he said aloud laughing as he retrieved the treasure. The film ended, then a man looking just like Jesus appeared and said, "This is just what the kingdom of God is like, the real treasure of life!"

The teacher spoke up just then. When you understand the value of the kingdom of God you will be willing to sell every-thing to obtain it. You will give up everything to make it your priority. You will place it at the centre of your future objectives.

If you understand the kingdom will sustain you, you will build your life upon it. The kingdom of God is the treasure above all treasures, it is worth your surrendering all your treasures for it.

The screen flashed on and everyone could see a man dressed like a merchant looking down at something.

His eyes popped open like a huge ball and he closed it. He could not give away his excitement. He was buying and selling pearls for a long time. He travelled far and wide looking for deals. He had never seen a pearl like this one. He was an expert and he knew, this pearl was very expensive but even then it was grossly undervalued. He made a deposit with the promise to return in two days with the balance. He went and did everything the young man in the previous story had just done. He sold everything. This was for him a deal of deals, a treasure above treasures. He returned in one day, such was his excitement and anticipation. He purchased the pearl. He could build a future on this purchase.

The film ended, then the man looking just like Jesus appeared again and said, ***"This is just what the kingdom of God is like, the real treasure of life!"***

The teacher spoke up just then. "When you understand the value of the kingdom of God you will be willing to sell everything to obtain it. You will give up everything to make it your priority. You will place it at the centre of your future objectives. If you understand the kingdom will sustain you, you will build your life upon it.

The kingdom of God is the treasure above all treasures, it is worth your surrendering all your treasures for it." It was the exact statement he had made at first, but it was well received. The class was quiet and meditative. They had just been delivered a treasure they had overlooked for so long. They had decisions to make. It was all about repositioning. Everyone left motivated that day. They had many things on which to meditate and many adjustments to make.

The Voices in heaven had spoken. ***Those who would respond to the call of the blessings of Abraham, the kingdom of God, would be supplied by the fruits of the blessings, the storehouses and treasuries of God.***

---

1. If you give priority to your vehicle it will take you to your destination; if you give priority to the kingdom it will supply your expectations.

2. GOD HAS GIVEN TO YOU EXTRAVAGANTLY AND YOU ARE BLESSED INDEED, BUT THERE ARE EVEN GREATER BLESSINGS in store than what God can give to you. By the righteousness of His laws it happens WHEN YOU yourself GIVE EXTRAVAGANTLY; FOR IT IS MORE BLESSED TO GIVE THAN TO RECEIVE.

3. The blessing that you create for yourself by giving is greater than any blessing that can be appropriated by God to you by a gift.

KINGDOM MINDSET

He sat on the royal horse. It was the royal horse of the great king Ahasuerus who ruled over twenty-seven nations from India to Ethiopia. The horse had on the royal crest of the king. He was dressed in the royal robe of the king himself. This was a very sweet moment for him. Sweet because it was simply sweet and savory. Sweet because the king was doing this to honor him for his service to the king. Sweet because his daughter whom he had raised up and nurtured from childhood was queen of this nation. He could still recall the events leading to her selection:

It is captured here uniquely in the CWDS Bible, Esther 2:

WHAT are the things that you consider,
When you are looking for a queen?
One with a godly heritage;
She can be found where God is seen.
One who is purified;
Do you desire to have the pure,
One who will leave the "put on's"
And come with the heart's beauty and no more,
One who will captivate with inner beauty
And will find favor in all men's sight?
How about this last thing?
Someone who will save your life.
Esther 2

@King Ahasuerus, *what are the things that you consider?*
1 Is your wrath, O king, now appeased?
Are you thinking of Queen Vashti
And the things you have decreed?
2 Will you listen to your servants?
"Consider a virgin young and fair;
3 "Let the king appoint offiicers in every province,
To gather all the beautiful women there.
To the city of Shushan,
Let the young virgins be brought;
In the custody of Hegai the eunuch, to the women's house.
Yes, and consider purity; let them be purifiied.
4 "And let the young woman who pleases you,
be your new queen and your new wife."
The king liked this advice, and he did so.
5 Now near the palace at Shushan,
There was a Jew named Mordecai,
He was the son of Jair, the son of Shimei,
the son of Kish, a Benjamite.
6 Kish was carried captive from Jerusalem
With the captives taken with Jeconiah, Judah's king,
Who Nebuchadnezzar the king of Babylon had carried away
with him.
7 And Mordecai had brought up Hadassah,
that is, Esther, his uncle's child;
He took her as his daughter,
When his aunt and uncle died.
She was a lovely and beautiful woman;
Is this the queen you like?
8 When the king's decree was heard,
She seemed to fit just right.

She was gathered to the palace
with many young women who were gathered then,
And placed under the care of Hegai
the custodian of the women,
@But there is class, out class and best!
Here is something to consider,
One whose deportment pleases the mind!
9 Hegai the custodian will tell you, That is why
he treated her so kind. He gave her the things of
purifiication without delay and with generosity.
@You would think he was the lucky man,
But he knew just what a king would need.
She got all that was assigned to her, and
seven favoured maidservants too, who were
provided for her from the king's palace.
But from the day they met he knew.
Hegai gave her and her maidservants preference
To the best place of the women's house.
10 Esther did not reveal her family or her people,
for Mordecai charged her not to let it out.
One more thing to consider,
Parental care was right.
11 Every day Mordecai came before the women's
quarters to ensure his little girl was all right.
12 Each young virgin would go in to the king
after twelve months of purifiication,
Six with myrrh, six with sweet perfumes,
and other things of beautification.
@When you consider your queen,
Never forget this part:
Not only a purified body, But indeed, a purified heart!
13 So after this preparation, each woman went in to the king,

and she was given anything she desired
to take with her at that time.
14 She went in the evening, and in the morning she was retired,
To the second house of women, in the custody of
Shaashgaz the eunuch, who kept the concubines,
She would never see the king again
Unless he delighted in her and called her by her name.
15 Now the turn came for Esther, the daughter of
Abihail, who was raised as Mordecai's own.
@Here is another for you seekers; In her request it was clearly
shown! She requested nothing (no add ons) But what Heagi the
eunuch thought necessary. "For if the king desired a queen;
Then what he will get is that, just me."
She said, "Give me and I will take it,
Just the necessities you appoint!"
And so to everyone who saw her, she attracted favor in their sight.
16 And Esther was taken to King Ahasuerus
In the seventh year of his reign.
@From the moment he saw her, he knew it;
would not let her go again.
17 The king loved Esther above all the women,
She found grace and favor in his sight.
You can stop the deliberations, there you have it!
He made her queen instead of Vashti!
He set the royal crown on her head.
18 Then the king made a great feast, Esther's Feast.
He proclaimed a holiday in the provinces, and
gave gifts according to his generosity.
19 The second time the virgins gathered,
Mordecai sat in the king's gate.
20 Esther had not yet shown her family or people,
for Mordecai had charged his girl to wait.

Queen Esther obeyed Mordecai's command,
just as when he was raising her;
@A bond of respect existed,
That her new status could not undo.
21 And at that time when Mordecai sat in
the king's gate, there he overheard,
Two of the palace eunuchs, doorkeepers, Bigthan and Teresh,
Sought to kill King Ahasuerus, for they were very furious.
@By now you may have stopped considering,
But you will know the choice was right
When you have in your palace
A queen who will save your life!
22 Mordecai informed Queen Esther of the matter,
And Esther informed the king in the name of Mordecai.
23 When the matter was investigated, it was confirmed,
and the two treacherous servants were hanged.
It was written in the Chronicles,
@But you have one chance in life,
And to know what to consider
Is to find your Queen Esther!

@CWDSBible

He smiled. These memories were indeed very sweet. The moment was also sweet because the person now leading him through the streets and proclaiming great things about him was second in command in this great nation. He was exceeded only by the king himself.

But the bitterness for him was as intense as the sweet. The moment was very bitter because the person now leading him through the streets of the capital was his sworn enemy. Mordecai had refused to bow at the command of this kingdom official because he chose to honor God first. He decided that even if it meant his own death, his Supreme King and His kingdom must be given priority over the command of man. It was very bitter because this did not go down well with this man who was leading him. He did not accept the excuse that he was a Jew. He was so proud and hateful that he tricked the king into giving him fiat to destroy all the Jews.

It was also very bitter for him because he was condemned to be hanged by this very man. This man, Haman, made a gallows on which to hang him on in his own backyard. Everyone knew about it. But the sweet was also intense; there was no doubt about it. It was sweet because his daughter Queen Esther had sought and received an audience with the king to seek to reverse this situation. She decided to take a risky stand for her kingdom, Israel, above her person and position. He smiled as he recalled the moment she decided to put God's priority first, above her own life and safety.

This too is appropriately captured in the CWDS Bible, Esther Chapter 4:

Such bitter times of grieving
Such heart-rending cries.
God will certainly deliver,
But I cannot escape His "Eye."
Such a hard assignment
In such a time of blitz;
But perhaps I am placed here,
For such a time as this.

ESTHER 4

1 It came from Mordecai, A loud and bitter cry. It came from all the Jews. When he learned all that had happened, warm tears filled his grieving eyes. He put on sackcloth and ashes and into the midst of the city he went.

2 He went as far as the king's gate, For no one could
enter the king's gate with sackcloth on them.
3 Meanwhile there was a great mourning among the Jews,
In every province where the king's decree was announced,
Weeping, wailing, fasting, and many lay in
sackcloth and in ashes on the ground.
4 When Esther's maids and eunuchs told her,
The queen was extremely distressed in grief.
@*Whatever touched her uncle reached her heart as if through a sieve.*
She sent garments to clothe Mordecai, and to take his
sackcloth away, But he would not accept them;
The depth and urgency was great.
5 So Esther sent Hathach, One of the eunuchs appointed
to serve her, and commanded him to go and see,
why Mordecai grieved and what all this was for.
6 So Hathach went to Mordecai in the city
square, in front of the king's gate,
7 And Mordecai told him all that had happened,
and the money Haman has committed to pay.
He would pay it into the king's treasuries to destroy all the Jews.
8 He gave him a copy of the decree to authenticate the news.
Hathach was to show this to Esther, and he would elaborate;
And he charged her to go in to the king to plead for
the Jews, that they may live; that they may escape.
9 So Hathach returned and reported to
Esther the words of Mordecai;
10 And as she sent Hathach with her response to Mordecai,
she could sense it, "God's Eye." She responded:
11 "All the servants of the king and the
people of his provinces know,
any person who enters the inner courts to
the king without being summoned,
there is only one law, man or woman must die.

Except the king should hold out his scepter made of gold,
Only then they would be spared alive.
I myself have not been called to go in to
the king the past thirty days."
But then again, that "Eye."
12 So they told Mordecai Esther's words
that she sent to him that day.
13 And Mordecai returned an answer,
"It is such a bitter fate,
Just because you are in the king's house,
Do not think in your heart, you will escape.
14 "If you fail to respond to this crisis, deliverance
for the Jews will come from another place,
Yet you and your father's house will perish,
there is absolutely no easy way.
But in such a bitter situation;
In such a time of blitz;
Who knows, perhaps you are positioned in the kingdom
For such a time as this."
15 So Esther returned an answer;
She had just one reply
The truth was so soul reaching,
And she could envision 'God's Eye.'
16 "Gather all the Jews in Sushan, and fast with me three days.
Do not eat or drink three days and nights;
I too will prepare my ways.
My maid servants and I will fast also,
And then I will go in to the king, as you wish.
It is against the law, but if I perish, then I perish."
17 So Mordecai departed and did
all that Esther commanded him to do.
@Will you risk your life for God's truth?
"God's Eye" is upon you.

@CWDSBible

The emotions of the moment were very intense for this man being led. He could not push away the bitter realities of the moment. But every time he looked at the face of the man leading him, something strange happened. He was awash with satisfaction. This man, Haman, could not hide his disappointment, his dismay, his defeat at leading his enemy publicly in the streets and proclaiming grace before him. It was open defeat and humiliation for Haman. Everyone knew how he felt about Mordecai and the Jews and what he was about to do. He had branded it publicly to assert his authority. It was so amusing to Mordecai.

A flood of sweet would mix with the bitter in that moment. It created a feeling, a mix of emotions that could not be described by any one word. He tried: bitter-sweet-surreal, painful-exhilaration, apprehensive-authentic awesomeness, rainy-sunshiny cameo. No, this man Mordecai could not describe it.

What he could identify in the midst of the exhilarating feeling was this certain sense of hope and assurance. It told him that His kingdom was in control and his King was attending to all his concerns.

Time had passed and so much had happened. If being led in the streets by his enemy was a taste of triumph, he was living now in complete victory. Haman was defeated. He and his ten sons were hanged on the gallows that he had prepared for Mordecai. Mordecai was now second in command in this great kingdom, next to the king himself. As he had taken Haman's place of honor in the streets, he had also taken his place of honor in the nation, literally.

Every time Mordecai remembered these things he would lift his hands and have a moment of praise with God. At times he would slip into a quiet place to have an extended time of praise and to weep uncontrollably in thanksgiving. Many times the turn of event for this Jewish captive living in this foreign land seemed so surreal.

He could still remember the moment of Haman's defeat. It began when his daughter Queen Esther heroically baited him.

This is how it is captured in the CWDS Bible. Esther Chapter 7:

TRAPPED, but not as bondmen;
Delivered to death is what.
"Even as we speak, my king,
Know that your queen is trapped."
He felt a trap was springing;
Haman be careful, cannot do that.
Your own gallows awaits you;
I guess the word is "trapped."

ESTHER 7

1 So it was that the king and Haman Came
to the banquet of the queen;
@There was still hope in bitterness,
Or, is it that she baited him?
2 On this second day at the banquet,
The king asked Esther one more time,
"What is your request? I will grant it Up
to half this kingdom of mine.
"What is your petition, Queen Esther?"
3 Esther started her reply,
"If in your eyes king I have found favor,
All I ask is for my life.
Give me my life, and that of my people;
4 We are sold and that is what.
Someone seeks to kill and destroy us;
Your queen, O king, is trapped.
If we were trapped and sold as slaves,
I would not feel so much pain,
I would hold my tongue although for the loss to the king,

The enemy could not compensate."
5 King Ahasuerus answered Queen Esther,
"Who could dare to presume this in his heart?"
@While there was a silent listener
Who wished for a passage through the earth.
6 "The enemy is wicked Haman."
These words were like a slap;
Haman was extremely afraid before the royals,
But there was no escape; he was trapped!
7 The king rose up from the banquet In great
wrath and walked away; He went into the palace
gardens While Haman got on his knees.
This was hard food for digesting;
He never knew she would serve that.
He begged Queen Esther for his life.
Quietly opening up this trap.
8 The king returned from the garden;
What he saw made him go red:
In desperation Haman had fallen, On his Queen Esther's…
BED! "Will you also assault my queen before me?" And as the
words left the king's mouth, They covered the face of Haman.
Now there was no way out.
9 Then Harbonah a palace servant said,
"O king, even this night There is a gallows prepared
by Haman; Fifty cubits, I know the height.
It was prepared for Mordecai, Who has
spoken good of you, oh king.
It is even standing in Haman's house."
The king said, "Hang him on that thing."
10 So Haman was hanged
On the gallows that for Mordecai he had made.
@A trap was prepared for him, But he prepared the blade.
Can you destroy the stars of heaven?

Oh, no, you cannot do that!
If you curse the seed of Abraham?
I guess the word is "trapped."

@CWDSBible

As Mordecai sat there, in the midst of his personal palace garden, he reminisced: When you take care of God's business, He certainly takes care of yours. And boy does He know how to!

When you put the kingdom of God and the heart of the King first, even with limited resources, the King certainly showers you with abundance. He remembered in that moment the midwives in Egypt who refused to kill the male babies of Israel at Pharaoh's command. They placed their lives at risk because they feared God and placed His desires first. They were blessed with abundance in their land of slavery.

Mordecai could see clearly. **When you have the heart of God for the things of God, He is very lavish.** He is so lavish that you see from His point of view that all your past worries and concerns were less than minuscule in His sight. **When you have a heart for the people of God, God empowers you to live your heart. He gives you the ability to effectively administer His blessings…the blessings of Abraham.**

Mordecai made a commitment then. "I certainly will not hold on to this blessing. I am blessed to be a blessing just like Abraham to be a blessing. As I sought the welfare of the Jews with limited resources and limited opportunity, I will use my position and resources to guarantee the welfare of the Jews in this foreign nation.

I will honor my daughter Esther who placed her life on the line for this. I will honor my King who loves me. I will honor His heart for I know His greater interest is His plans and His people. He has a greater responsibility for His kingdom and will remove me if I obstruct Him. It is just as any earthly king would do. King Ahasuerus loves me but if I am not functioning, he will remove me. ***Earthly wealth and promotion is just a functional positioning in God's kingdom, not a privilege or a perk.***"

Mordecai was faithful to his commitment or rather to his new office in the kingdom…of God.

The end of his story is captured in Esther 10, by the CWDS Bible, as follows:

DO you seek the wealth of God's people?
Do you speak peace to godly seeds?
Are you waiting at the king's gate?
Then God will make you enter in.
You will be accepted of all people;
You will stand before great men;
If your heart is fxed on service,
Doors will swing wide open.

ESTHER 10

1 King Ahasuerus laid a tribute,
"On all the land, a tribute be!"
The king also laid a tribute
on all the islands of the sea.
2 And all his acts of might and power,
And how Mordecai became great,
Are written in the chronicles of Media
and Persia, and spoken of in every place.
@But let me tell you of Mordecai,
How the king advanced this man;
He was seated in the king's gate;
One day it swung open.
He was there and knocking daily,
While his heart knocked on God's throne;
And God knew that if He blessed him,

It would not be for him alone.
So God swung the gates wide open.
Mordecai the Jew became second in command to the king,
and all his people received him well;
for he spoke peace to all his fellow Jews,
and he sought their good and sought their wealth.
@Are you waiting for a blessing?
There is one thing you should know,
God is waiting just to bless you
If you will not stop the blessing flow.
Yes, if He can pass the blessing through you.

"You do not have because you do not ask. Wow!" Roger thought as he read of the exploits of Mordecai. "The reason you do not have is because you do not ask; amazing! You desire but you are fruitless. You do every earthly and evil thing imaginable to have but 'you cannot obtain.' All you need to do is to ask. You do not have because you do not ask."

"Mordecai certainly knocked on God's door. He never stopped praying. He was always positioned for the blessings of God. He asked and he received. But why do others ask and not receive?" Roger asked himself. He went back to the Scripture in the fourth book of James to look for answers. ***"You ask and you do not receive because you ask without purpose to consume it on your own pleasure."***

"Interesting, that was the summation of James in the fourth book of James," Roger thought. "Does this not rightfully define the success of Mordecai? He positioned himself, but purpose was on his heart."

@But let me tell you of Mordecai,
How the king advanced this man;
He was seated in the king's gate;

> *One day it swung open.*
> *He was there and knocking daily,*
> *While his heart knocked on God's throne;*
> *And God knew that if He blessed him,*
> *It would not be for him alone.*
> *So God swung the gate wide open.*

Mordecai the Jew became second in command to the king, and all his people received him well; for he spoke peace to all his fellow Jews, and he sought their good and sought their wealth

"Amazing! This also defined the success of Solomon. God said, 'Ask and I will give.' Solomon asked for an understanding heart to be a good administrator of the kingdom he was charged to manage for God." Roger paused to express his heart. "If there is a take away in this for every person it must be: *Are you waiting for a blessing? There is one thing you should know, God is waiting just to bless you if you will not stop the blessing flow. Yes, if He can pass the blessing through you.*"

---

1. How easy is it for God to get money to you? Very easy; isn't it? Would you block Him?

2. How easy is it for God to pass money through you?

HEART FULL OF RICHES

"**N**abal refused to give provision to David, even though David was so good to him," said Victor to his class of students who came to him to study the Scriptures. He was a teacher of The Word, full of wisdom and discernment. Many listened to his wise teachings every week. "Nabal died feasting and celebrating his harvest," a student observed.

"Just as the rich man Jesus spoke about who built bigger barns," Victor concluded.

"His riches possessed him just as the rich young ruler," a student interjected.

Victor said, "I am about to illustrate a very important lesson from a real story that took place centuries ago in time. The lesson was lost to millions but it had remained timeless.

"In introduction: It was King Solomon who said, 'He who trusts in his riches will fall, but the righteous will flourish like a green plant beside the streams.' This is found in Proverbs 11.

We can view many things in life from a philosophical or practical sense. ***When it comes to the practice of trusting in riches, it is difficult to separate the philosophical and theoretical from the literal.*** People trust in money, others trust their money only, and others literally worship the money."

Victor dimmed the lights as the screen flashed and the actors took centre stage. The scenes were basic but Victor narrated: "This is amazing!" Jerush said to his brothers as they sat there in the cool of dusk. It had been a long hot day in the merciless sun and they were happy for the shade. "Who would have thought we would have acquired so much wealth in such a short period of time?"

"I have never seen wealth in such abundance in all my life," his brother Zareth responded. "Nor have I seen wealth transferred to anyone in such abundance in such a short period of time."

"And with such willingness also," Jerush laughed joyfully as he touched the ring in his ear.

Narrator: Everyone had rings on display. Gold rings with precious gems, some with very intricate designs. It is as if what they lacked for years- wealth, respect, honor, pleasure- they would compensate for in these moments. They all paraded their trophies to the brink of almost idolizing their new found treasure.

Well almost, and only because they had someone there who represented a kingdom, their homeland, and its God to them. As long as he was present he made their God so much bigger than anything else.

Narrator: Jerush could tell many tales of his hard labor. The scene shifted to a few years earlier. Jerush was slaving day and night at his regular job. "I can hardly provide a proper meal for myself," Jerush complained. "The pay is non-existent. My provision is barely enough to give me and my family a proper meal."

Narrator: This was his complaint everyday he labored, and it was the complaint of everybody else.

Scene: Jerush stepped away from that job. His face was set.

Narrator: The future was uncertain but he was determined. He was thin and starving and his leanness was because of the harshness of the work he had submitted to for so long. He had moved away. He decided to put distance between himself and his employer. His employer had a way of getting him back and he wanted to avoid this. He could not submit to this slavery any longer. He had packed everything and was going far away, to his own promised homeland.

Narrator: The departure of Jerush, Zareth and the others was nothing but miraculous. Everything was credited to the man who motivated them to leave and who represented the kingdom to them. Everything was credited to the government of his kingdom who lobbied for them.

This man entered the scene to the sound of a ram's horn. The people gathered around him as he instructed them.

Narrator: He was telling them about their journey, about the land to which they were going, and about their king. They were pilgrims now, travelling to resettle elsewhere. The promise was very good and enticing. The meeting ended, night came. Jerush counted and weighed his treasures about four times before carefully hiding it in his tent and going off to sleep.

Narrator: This change of fortune was greater than he could expect. His employers had a sudden change of heart and had repaid him for all the years he had worked underpaid. Indeed it was with much influence and forceful pressure from the government of his new kingdom, but it was exciting. He and his family were now returning to their own country, rich, very rich. He trusted his government and was happy they came through for him.

Jerush: I have a secret and I cannot tell anyone, because it is my secret. I believe though, that it is everybody's secret also. My real hope is not in this new kingdom, and its king. My real confidence is in the stash of gold I now carry. This will allow me to settle well, anywhere. I can live a comfortable life in the land of my retirement, my new homeland.

Narrator: This was very selfish and it was a betrayal of the king who pressured his employer to release him and pay him up. "That is why it is my secret," Jerush whispered.

Narrator: The journey back was long and arduous. They had to make it on foot. They never lacked anything in spite of the absence of real life and food on their journey. Their new government had sent provision for them directly from his kingdom to satisfy all their needs. It was always delivered on time and at the right time. This was also one of the wow factors of the journey. "Awesome and amazing!" Jerush thought aloud as he mulled this.

Narrator: Now they were all at a crossroad. The actors stood before four arrows pointed forward, backwards, upwards and downwards and they all looked puzzled.

Narrator: The representative of their new kingdom was gone for a very long time. His king wanted to ensure everyone knew the rules of his government. He wanted them to begin to practice them in advance as they approached the land of their inheritance. He knew the value of what he had in store for them. He wanted to test their hearts to see if they would place more value in what he was giving them than the wealth they carried. The scene changed. There was an uproar and commotion. Some leaders among them were becoming restless and were getting boisterous.

A short and sturdily built man among them spoke up: "Our kingdom representative has been gone for a long time. We do not know if he is ever coming back. Let us build a god to lead us back to where we are coming from." Everyone agreed. This was the solution they needed. Now they could move beyond the crossroad.

Narrator: Together they went to the high priest of the new kingdom. He was the priest the representative had appointed from among them to act on their behalf. The stout man spoke up as they all nodded in agreement: "Make us a god to take us back to where we are coming from. We have no idea where we are going. The representative has deserted us."

"But..." The priest started to respond. They all shouted, "No buts. Action!"

"Ok then, give me all your gold rings and earrings," he consented. They all happily agreed. Yet grudgingly they took them off and laid them at his feet.

Narrator: It was difficult to let go but this was a way of immortalizing their wealth. The high priest was busy. He built a fire, a very hot fire, hot enough to melt the gold. With the help of experts he melted the gold and with much effort and skill, he carved a calf of gold from it. The actors began to worship the gold. Jerush and the others joined in and the worship became more and more vociferous and lewd.

The narrator closed the illustration. He had become the teacher once again. He turned to his students and said, "I am sure you know this story well."

"Moses and the Israelites," they responded in chorus. "That is correct!" Victor responded.

God gave the Israelites gold to test their hearts. It was not long before they began to trust the gold more than they trusted God who gave it to them.

Their confidence in their wealth led them to build an idol with it to literally worship it. *They transferred the worship of money from their hearts to an image. This is what happens when we get distracted by the wealth that God gives to us.*

Just as the Israelites gave up their God to worship gold, so it is with many rich people today. The gods in their hearts are exposed in the way they treat riches, people and God's business. When a person sets their heart on riches, soon all they will see is the gold and not God. The gold becomes a god. The gold regulates their actions, not God.

It is our great Teacher who taught us, "No man can serve two masters. He will love one and hate the other. He will obey one and disrespect the other!" The second Voice in heaven acknowledged this. It was the words he had spoken centuries ago, "You cannot serve God and mammon!"

"Money is a poor master," the teacher said, *"but it makes an excellent servant."* The teacher turned off the lights after this statement. He had another practical illustration. He rolled a clip in 3D, and immediately money of the largest denominations began floating in the room. It was wads of money. Hands were reaching out but it was elusive. It was just a clip, an illusion.

The lights came back on and the teacher, Victor said. "The sight of all that money up close will have inspired many of you. It would have caused some of you to dream or at least to desire. Some of you would have been happy to take home some of what you saw and forget everything else you learn here. Money is innocent at first, it is all about needs. Then money gets insistent, it is all about future needs. It speaks. 'You must fear the future, secure yourself, put your trust in me.' This is the entrance of a very dangerous pathway. This is a path where you risk shifting confidence, shifting your trust, shifting where you put your faith.

It is the next bend on this path that money begins to say, 'Love me!' At this stage, she is hard to resist. She says, 'Am I not the most wonderful thing that has ever happened to you? Do whatever it takes to get more of me.'"

The lights switched off and many scenes began to flash in the room at a fast pace: murders, adulteries, betrayals, bribery, destruction of countries and economies, oppression, slavery, unhappiness, misery, divorces, dysfunctional families, wars and many more devastations and social ills. At the end of every scene there was a caption, "Inspired by the love of Money".

The lights came back on and the teacher said, "Solomon did not acquire so many wives because of his wisdom. He acquired them because of his wealth. His betrayal of God in the end was because of his wealth. He had his heart set on his wealth and it even frustrated him. The miseries he reflected on in the book of Ecclesiastes were all inspired by the love of money.

His father David, on the other hand, went to God in peace. His testimony is, 'Money is an excellent servant.' Everything King David did was inspired by the love of God. He recognized that money was a tool and he used it to bless his kingdom and to provide for the service of his God.

He was happy to the very end. His name is revered on earth and in heaven. The Son of God from heaven was happy to be named after the lineage of David in his human form. The redemption plan of God is in good hands if you will make money serve you instead of you serving money."

It is this King David who wrote. 'Those who trust in their wealth and boast in the multitude of their riches, none of them can by any means redeem his brother, nor give to God a ransom for him. That he should continue to live eternally, and not see the Pit. For the redemption of their souls is costly and it will cease forever.'

There are a number of very salient points here that King David highlighted:

> *Firstly: Wealth has no direct value in the redemption plan.*
> *Secondly: There is eternal life.*
> *Thirdly: There is the threat of a Pit.*
> *Fourthly: The redemption of the soul is very costly, more costly than money or any wealth can purchase.*
> *Fifthly: There is no amount of money that can be used to redeem the soul of any person.*
> *Sixthly: The time will come when redemption will cease forever.*

David's statement here is prophetic at least and very revelatory. This statement was inspired. It pointed to an event that took place in eternity but was yet to be unveiled on earth. It points to what happens now while the book of time is open. It points to an event to come when the book of time is closed. Redemption of man would come only from Jesus.

Money would be needed to get the message of redemption out to the people of the earth. Man was to trust Jesus and submit the money to Him, not trust the money and submit themselves to it.

THE MASTERY OF MONEY IS THE ACCUMULATION OF WEALTH FOR THE MASTER'S USE. Time is a factor: redemption will cease forever. The people of

God are being prepared as kingdom officials whom He can entrust with kingdom resources. He will not approve corrupt officials who will shortchange the kingdom to satisfy their own greed. He will not approve men like Judas, who was the first to sell Him and the redemption plan for corruption and personal greed. And I say, the first...!

But what if you should say, 'I have worked hard for my own money; it is mine, not God's'? Then the Apostle Paul would like to respond to you: 'Let him who stole steal no longer, but rather let him labor, working with his hands what is good, that he may have something to give to those who are in need.'

Paul wrote this in the fourth chapter of his letter to the Ephesians. We must argue that a thief is a thief whether he steals as a profession or he steals from God in presumption. Paul says the remedy for this is work. Not just work to satisfy the person's needs, but work to satisfy the needs of the kingdom. Work with selfless ambitions. Work with a proper perspective on the purpose of wealth.

The Apostle Paul had something else to say. It is a command he gave to Timothy for all those who are rich. The command is found in the sixth chapter of the first book of Timothy:

'Command those who are rich in this present world not to be proud nor to trust in uncertain riches but in the living God who gives us richly all things to enjoy. Let them do good, that they become rich in good works: ready to give, willing to share, storing up a good foundation for the time to come; that they may lay hold on eternal life.' The kingdom of Heaven gives us all things to enjoy but the King wants us to do:...action; to be:...lifestyle; and to position ourselves in a state of readiness. He wants us to be willing, and to use the resources we have in time to impact our eternity. **THE WEALTH THAT MATTERS IS THE WEALTH OF GOOD WORKS. THIS IS ALL A COMMAND.**

For the Apostle Paul, there is only one conclusion: wealth and kingdom are married. The present must respond to the future; time must respond to eternity. God's kingdom has indeed come and it supersedes every other kingdom. The government is now on His shoulder. This command is a command from the King. He has laid claim on every earthly wealth as His own. He has given this command as His template for the use and administration of this valuable kingdom resource. He fills our cup with all things to enjoy but He is interested in the running over.

If you are still not convinced and you still say: 'I have worked hard for my own money; it is mine, not God's', will you listen to the ten thousand times ten thousand and thousands upon thousands of angels around the throne of God? Let me translate the portion that can be translated from John's vision in Revelation.

Let us hear it from the one hundred million angels plus the thousands upon thousands more around the throne of God with the elders and living creatures:

"Worthy is the Lamb who was slain to receive power and riches and wisdom, and strength and honor and glory and blessing!"

I would like to ask the question. **ALL THE ANGELS IN HEAVEN ASSERT THAT THE LAMB IS WORTHY TO RECEIVE YOUR RICHES, BUT WHAT DO YOU SAY?** Is the Lamb worthy to receive your riches? Is His sacrifice, the redemption plan, a justifiable cause?

Victor stopped his session then to give his class a chance to meditate on what they had learnt. He would come back to close the session soon. Victor went into his office to spend some quiet time to meditate. He wanted to absorb all the Lord had taught him today in his lessons. He wanted the perfect close for his students who were already engrossed.

> *It is best to have your riches full of heart than to have your heart full of YOUR riches!*

GIVING AS AN ACT OF WORSHIP

s Victor sat there, lost in worship, he was transported in a dream to an individual doing something. He was writing a song. Victor could see him clearly, hear his words, read his writing, hear his thoughts…

Victor kept hearing this title: **GIVING IS AN ACT OF WORSHIP.**

These are the words of the song he saw:

> More important to me
> Than wealth, riches, and treasure
> More important to me
> Than things that I possess
> More important to me
> I know You don't take pleasure
> In sacrifices, but that
> You are more important to me
>
> A broken and a contrite heart
> Is more important to You
> I bring my sacrifices Lord
> From the overflow
> Of Your love within me
> From my righteousness I give
> So that I don't leave this undone; but You are

More important to me

The mint and rue and cumin
The silver and the gold
Yet the love that's overflowing
Is everything I know
The love that caused a King to die
And make that royal sacrifice
Is the only reason why
I give my Isaac and my lamb
I give my silver and my songs
I give everything that I am
And everything that I should own
For You are more important to me.

The author of this song was lost in his own meditation as he wrote. He was transported back in time where he could see an old man, over one hundred years old. Victor travelled with him. This old man was taking a trip up the mountain. His face was shiny with sweat. His name was… yes, one of his servants said it, Abraham.

Abraham stopped at a sheltered place on the mountain he was climbing. The overhang of a tall tree made the place very comfortable for resting. He turned to his servants who had accompanied him and said, "You stay here until I return. I and the boy will go to worship and come back."

Abraham had a statement to make to God. It was a statement many people would make in words and in songs. The author paused for a moment and prayed, "Lord let this song that I write not just be another collection of empty words, but a living portrayal of my life."

He could think of the many statements that people of his time make in worshipping God. He could hear in his imagination the beautiful songs and rhymes coming from the mouths of millions, with their faces reflecting the intensity of the moment. He knew that for most of these people, if their hearts were tested there would be no legitimacy or commitment. Not many would be willing to put their money where their mouth is.

The catchy phrases from some of these songs flooded the mind of the author in that moment:

- You are everything to me
- There is nothing I desire on earth besides You
- You captivate my heart
- I love You more than these
- You are Lord
- You are my treasure
- I would rather have Jesus than silver and gold
- Withholding nothing
- You are the love of my life
- I love You endlessly
- Whatever you tell me to do, I'll do, I'll go wherever you tell me to go
- I give You my heart, I give You my soul, I give You full control
- You mean more to me
- All to Jesus I surrender
- You are my all in all
- In Christ alone, I put my trust
- Lord I give You my heart, I give You my soul, I live for You alone
- I give myself away
- I need You more
- You mean more than this world to me
- I would not trade You for silver or gold
- I would not trade You for riches untold
- You are my everything

- You are the air I breathe
- Till the end of my days I give my all
- We don't want blessings we want You
- We don't want anything but You
- This is my desire to honor You
- All that I desire is You
- All that I am, all that I have, I lay them down before You O God.

These are just some of the commitments that millions make as they sing each week. The author shook his head unconsciously as he processed this thought, ***"It is sad that the majority of these worshipers do not actualize these commitments."***

Abraham was about to tell God He was more important to him than his greatest treasure, his son. ***He was about to make a statement in a manner that was more profound, more powerful, more believable than mere words. He would make a literal sacrifice.***

Abraham was about to go where most other human beings could not come or fathom nor follow; this most definitely included his servants. Many can understand the words of worship and the sacrifices of things that are dismissible. They can participate in these sessions, but how many can participate in a session of worship where you literally release everything to God? They can easily participate in the talk; they can sing the songs without a real consciousness of, or connection with the words, without a test of their commitment. ***It is the giving however which demonstrates the sincerity of worship.***

There are people who get flustered at making real sacrifices for God. The author of the song remembered the story Jesus told of the two sons who the father asked to work in his field. One responded, "I will go," and did not, the other responded, "I will not go," and went. Jesus then asked, "Which of the two did the will of the father? Which one pleased the father? The worshiper, or the giver? The one who worshipped with his lips or the one who worshipped with his action, his gift?"

The author smiled as he remembered the time he left his job to pursue fulltime ministry. He was young and being constantly promoted. "I was in a very good job headed for the top. I was almost there. I was passing my professional examination and aptly positioned for the ultimate in the corporate arena. When I resigned to go to Bible School, people close to me had a lot of charges against me. 'Idiot, stupid, no sense,' but the one that sticks to me more closely is, 'fanatic'. This is what my father called me. The most amazing thing is that he was a full-time pastor in ministry all the days of my life, ever since I was born. "The author smiled again, 'It is easy to talk. How many of us are prepared to walk?'

The author saw David the king bringing up the ark of God into the city of David. He had stripped down before God. It was obvious he did not want his majesty to be a distraction to the worship of His majesty. All his worship in the moment should go to God alone.

The presence of God was much more important to him than his dignity, his position, his pride and his treasures. When the Levites carrying the ark had gone six paces, David sacrificed oxen and sheep. When David had placed the ark in the tabernacle he made a large offering before the Lord. *For David, worship and sacrifice went hand in hand; worship was sacrifice and sacrifice was worship; worship goes with sacrifice and then there is the sacrifice of worship.*

The generosity in David's heart was very abundant and dignified in his place of undignified worship. He offered so much to God that he had enough meat to distribute to every person gathered there. He gave them a loaf of bread, a piece of meat and a cake of raisins. The many thousands of Israel, both men and women received from a heart overflowing with love and worship.

At the place where worship becomes extravagant, sacrifice and generosity become extravagant. Worship brings out the generosity in you, the generosity in you commands worship, the generosity in you is worship.

This command was captured by Moses and ratified by Jesus as the greatest of all commandments: Love the Lord your God with all your heart, and with all your mind, and with all your strength - this is worship - and love your brother as yourself - this is generosity and is worship.

The author sighed as he softly sung the song he had just written with fresh commitment:

More important to me
Than wealth, riches, and treasure
More important to me
Than things that I possess
More important to me
I know You don't take pleasure
In sacrifices, but that
You are more important to me

A broken and a contrite heart
Is more important to You
I bring my sacrifices Lord
From the overflow
Of Your love within me
From my righteousness I give
So that I don't leave this undone; but You are
More important to me

The mint and rue and cumin
The silver and the gold
Yet the love that's overflowing

Is everything I know
The love that caused a King to die
And make that royal sacrifice
Is the only reason why
I give my Isaac and my lamb
I give my silver and my songs
I give everything that I am
And everything that I should own
For You are more important to me.

The author laughed to himself at his thought of the moment and said softly, "O how delighted would I be if every time I enter to worship, I hear God say, 'This is indeed a sweet smelling savor in my nostrils,' just as He does for the offering."

"I will glory in You Lord," Victor shouted at the heavens. "I will glory in You alone." He had just returned from his vision. He saw and heard it all in just a few minutes.

He spent the next few minutes doing a study in the word. He contemplated the word "glory". To 'glory in' means: to be proud of, to boast in, to rejoice in, to celebrate. Victor looked up to heaven and shouted, "I will be proud of You, I will boast about You and in You alone, I will rejoice in knowing You, I will rejoice in Your works, I will celebrate You." "I will glory in You Lord," he said again, this time in a reverential whisper to the heavens above.

Victor then opened his Bible to a passage on which he had been meditating from the ninth book of Jeremiah, "'Do not let the rich man glory in his riches. Let him glory instead that he understands and knows Me, that I am the Lord, exercising loving-kindness, judgment, and righteousness in the earth. For in these, I delight,' says the Lord." Victor bowed down and whispered again as if searching his heart repentantly. He made his commitment once more, "Lord, I will certainly glory in You alone."

Victor returned to his class. The students were waiting, anticipating. He looked at his class and said, "The governments of earth are very particular about their taxes. There are various laws in place to take action against anyone who evades tax in different countries. The Government of Heaven is also very particular about what belongs to it, its wealth. It takes action against all those who withhold their wealth from the King.

Solomon, in the book of Proverbs, advises not to put excessive labor into trying to get rich. According to King Solomon, we must cease from our own understanding and selfish pursuits, for God will have the last say. The reality is that riches will make wings for themselves and fly like an eagle toward Heaven, to its real owner.

David, in Psalm 52, has some words for those who trust in the abundance of riches and do wickedness. According to David, 'God will destroy you forever! He will take you away, and pluck you out of your dwelling place and uproot you from the land of the living.' Solomon also picks this up, he says, 'Riches do not profit in the day of wrath, but righteousness delivers from death.'"

The lights switched off once again. It was very dark. This time there were no flashes, no 3D illustration. The lights came back after a few minutes and everyone wondered what they missed. The teacher said, "Look down." All around the room was money. The teacher said, "Walk around". They all began to walk around. Some stepped on the money, and some were careful not to. A few of them picked some up and placed it in their pockets. The teacher said, "If you took money that was not yours, you may have just made it your god. You placed money above righteousness. If you avoided stepping on the money you showed it too much respect. For those who stepped on the money, this illustrates my point. If you have full control of money, you should not let money control you. ***Money was created to serve you, not for you to serve it. If you can walk on money, how can you let money walk on you; how can you glorify it? In Heaven this is what we do, literally.***

We walk on gold. Money must be put to kingdom use. If you desire worship, look to the throne of God, not to the streets of glory."Victor closed his session with this strong call for his students to put wealth in its proper perspective.

1. GRACE AND RELATIONSHIP DETERMINE IF YOU WORSHIP IN SPIRIT, BUT MONEY ANSWERS ALL THINGS, IT WILL DETERMINE IF YOU WORSHIP IN TRUTH.

2. WHAT YOU TRUST IN CAN BE DETERMINED BY HOW EASY IT IS FOR YOU TO LET IT GO.

KINGDOM POSITIONING

t is not often that someone would see an angel standing in his backyard. It is very unusual and frightening to see the angel just standing there not moving. What is really bizarre and uncanny is to see the angel standing between Heaven and earth in midair. The real scare is to see the angel holding a drawn sword in his hand. If that was not scary enough, it was an absolute terror for this man, and petrifying because Israel was in tears. The news had filtered about the many thousands who had died by a plague after seeing this same angel. Israel was running scared and the sons of this man were no different; they ran and hid.

King David had sinned by numbering Israel, and people had died in troves from all around Israel. There was an air of disaster and the action had shifted to the threshing floor of this Jebusite, Ornan.

Ornan saw the angel. His sons saw the angel. The sons of Ornan ran and hid. Ornan did not move. He continued to thresh his wheat. His sons peeped out and wondered, "How could it be that father is still working there? Are we about to lose our father?"

In the meantime, Ornan was nervous, very nervous. The human mind could not explain his actions. People were dying all around him. Israel was in a crisis. There was nothing Ornan could do about it; this was an angel from Heaven. He had a drawn sword!

Ornan was working hard but he was achieving nothing. In fact, he had been on the same spot for some time. So lost he was in the moment that if he was smashing his fingers he would not have noticed. The wheat under his instrument had become dust but he was not taking note. His mind was not there. His heart was pumping blood at the pace of lightning and his head was swollen. He was watching the angel through the corner of his eye. He had already figured out that if the angel wanted to harm him he would be dead. If he ran and the angel desired to kill him, he would be dead. Perhaps the angel needed something from him. Just perhaps there may be something required of him.

His nation was in crisis and instead of running and hiding like his sons, he would stand his ground trembling but waiting to get involved. Trembling at the state of crisis that had gripped his nation. Trembling at the death that was all around. Trembling at the prospects of more people being condemned to death, but positioned to do something if the opportunity arose. In a time like this, he would not reserve anything. He would put all his resources at stake. He was prepared to put his livelihood at stake. He was prepared to put his land at stake. He was waiting and ready to be called. Waiting and ready for the Lord to instruct him what to do, how to get involved.

It was in this position that King David found him when he came hurriedly not long after. The angel was still suspended in the air with his drawn sword, and Ornan was in the middle of his field working away at the same spot he was one hour before.

The Lord had instructed David to make a sacrifice at Ornan's threshing floor to stop the plague. David came so hurriedly that he did not bring any sacrifice with him. He came empty handed.

When Ornan saw King David he was so relieved. Now was his opportunity to offer himself. Ornan ran to King David and bowed down. When he heard David's mission he said immediately. "Yes, yes! O King. Take everything! Take the land! Take the oxen to offer! Take the cart for wood!" This was a man who was ready.

David, however, would not sacrifice anything without a price. He paid the full price for the threshing floor and the oxen and the cart. It was after this that he took everything from Ornan the Jebusite, and sacrificed. This threshing-floor, previously owned by a Jebusite, would become the holiest site in Israel, the Temple Mount. It is the place on which the temple of Solomon was built.

Humanity is in a crisis, and this is the crisis positioning of people submitted to God, always ready, waiting for instructions from the Lord. The kingdom needs men and women who are ready and waiting with their wealth and all their resources. This is how we honor the Lord with our substance. ***There is a need for people positioned to get involved; waiting for instruction from the Lord as to what He desires, when, and how much.***

It is good for people to recognize the crisis, however, unlike the crisis in which Ornan was caught up, people are not just dying, but they are destined for eternal death! We cannot just run away and hide. We cannot just hide ourselves and our wealth away, hoping the situation will disappear. We must be positioned to participate; ready to let go at the request of the Master.

> *THE REDEMPTION PLAN OF GOD NEEDS KINGDOM PEOPLE WHO ARE STANDING IN POSITION WITH EVERYTHING THEY HAVE... READY, WAITING FOR THE KING'S INSTRUCTION.*

TWO OUTSTANDING MEN

They knew him as a prince. When he came, they bowed and gave him full honor. He lived in the palace of the most powerful and prosperous nation on earth at the time. A nation that not long before had been the economic capital of the world. Everyone brought their wealth to that nation to trade, or rather to buy food. This prince had everything he desired. He had access to the wealth of Egypt. He shared its power and its perks. This is a royal position that was attained only by birthright. It was unique, it was lavish, it was power. Many have murdered to protect much smaller treasures.

They were the least of the least of all people in that nation. They were not only poor farmers- they would have been happy to be but they were unpaid slaves who were counted as property and treated as common animals of burden. They worked in the heat of the desert sun and in the torrential rain. They rested only when their masters felt they should and they ate what they were given. The women were ravished at the will of their slave masters and the men had no power to even protest. The state of this people was deplorable. Their lives were very difficult.

The lives of these two people, the prince and the slaves, were so very distant, so very different. The slaves wished for freedom but would hardly dare to dream about the palace. The thought would have been treason. There was no prince ever known who desired to be a slave. This prince was very different, however. He lived in the palace but his heart was with the slaves. He had a big secret, his parents were slaves.

He was not content to be a prince and see his nation in slavery and do nothing. ***He was not content to be blessed and watch his nation struggle in their squalor.*** He itched to do something about it. One day he saw a slave being mistreated. As an Egyptian, he was supposed to do nothing. As a prince, he was supposed to find it entertaining. This was not the case from this prince. Not only did he find it disturbing, but he could not stand by and do nothing. His anger boiled over and he stepped in and killed the Egyptian.

This one act was an act of surrender of all the privileges he previously enjoyed. He was no longer an esteemed prince, he was a fugitive running for his life. He surrendered all his wealth to get involved with a people, his people in slavery. His willingness to act and to surrender would propel him to leadership one day. God would use him to free the people and to lead them. His name would be memorialized.

It was much later that an apostle named Paul said to this man's memory: He chose to suffer affliction with the people of God rather than to enjoy the pleasure of sin for a season. ***He esteemed the reproach of Christ to be worth greater riches than the treasures in Egypt.*** He looked beyond the present to the reward. This prince could easily be nominated for the most outstanding sacrifice award, but before it is decided we must now take a look at the second outstanding person.

This second person was no ordinary person. He was rich, very rich, but unlike the prince, he was entitled to it. His name is Jesus. Many people thought He was poor. They will tell you He walked around with little to eat and no place to sleep. Some argue, though, that this image of Jesus is very wrong. He had wealth and was a very rich man. They will tell you that there was nothing poor about Him; that He had everything a person could want and had no reason to lack.

They will tell you Christians walking around in poverty have a poor image of Christ. They will say that those who say being poor is acceptable for it is being just as their Master are misled; Jesus was rich.

I tend to agree with this position. The apostle Paul in the second book of Corinthians and the eighth chapter asserted that Jesus was rich, extravagantly rich. He said that although Jesus was rich, He became poor for our sake, that through His poverty we might become rich.

Paul considered this an amazing statement of the grace of our Lord Jesus. He gave up His expansive riches to become poor. This is why we connect Him with poverty. We see His sacrifice, not His glory. To understand the riches of Jesus we have to understand Heaven, where Jesus belongs, His home, where the streets are made of gold. Not just ordinary gold but gold purer than any on earth; so pure it is transparent. No glory can be compared with what Jesus gave up. In fact, millions of people sacrifice here on earth to live forever in Heaven. It is the dream paradise of earth.

This is not all, He was so rich that His breath created the world and all its treasures and wealth. He was rich because He owned everything He created. He owned the world He lived in and all its treasures. He notably told Pilate, "You could have no power at all against Me, unless it was given to you from above."

This is what He gave up but it was no ordinary sacrifice. He gave it up so that all mankind through His poverty may become rich. Just like the prince before Him, He saw a people, His creation, enslaved to sin and living a depraved life. Just like the prince before Him, He gave up everything and His rights to access His wealth to intervene. Just like the prince before Him, the people He sought to help did not appreciate his intervention and it got Him in serious trouble. Unlike the prince before Him who ran for His life, He was murdered. For both the prince and the Lord, their sacrifice brought freedom to the people they desired to help and secured their wealth and abundance.

These are indeed two very outstanding or rather extraordinary persons of history. They understood sacrifice. They both stepped away from money to pursue purpose. It is not much of a debate about who you will say is the most outstanding. It must be Jesus. He sacrificed the most in order to give the most.

If Jesus is prepared to sacrifice so much for our redemption, is it not a very small sacrifice if we surrender everything to take His redemption plan to the people for whom He sacrificed?

Will your name be on the list of most outstanding persons that lived? It is all about sacrifice, surrender, redemption, freedom, willing to be poor to make others rich, to help them obtain the riches and richness of Christ.

We have been given the DNA of Christ. We have been made to partake of His divine nature. In every Christian is the potential to be just like Jesus. He is the grain of wheat that died so He could spring up in us.

"He is a hard act to follow, but I am going to try," Paul said to himself. *"Who could have thought that wrapped up in that package of human flesh and baby giggles laying in that manger was generosity enough to reach the entire world?"* Who would have thought that the potency in the seed, wrapped in human flesh crying for hunger, was love enough to cover the earth...?" He was indeed a gift that kept on giving. Everywhere He went He was about doing good. He was determined to feed a large crowd even if He had to multiply a miserly meal. He healed people everywhere. He carried a money bag with Him for the poor. The amazing thing is that while He was battered and mutilated by the merciless whip, while He was being gored by the thorns pushed ruthlessly on His head; while the women looking on could not help but weep; He could turn His heart to them and to their reality instead of to His own. He said to them, "Weep not after me, but for yourselves, and for your children weep." He had the presence of mind to prophesy to them about the evil days to come. A time that will be so bad that they will say, "Those who do not have children are blessed." It will be a time when the people will beg the mountains to fall on them.

Again, while He was on the cross, His entire body numb and throbbing with pain, His heart was broken because of the state of the heart of the people. He had heard those who cried, 'Hosanna', scream, 'Crucify Him!' He was mocked and spat upon by the Gentiles while the Jews cheered. He had the sin of the world upon Him, His greatest and most excruciating pain of all, for He knew no sin, He was holy. He knew His Father would turn His back on Him for He could have nothing to do with sin. They had always been one, but now... the thought of this had turned His sweat into blood.

Even then, through all this pain, external and internal, through all this noise of His broken heart, He could hear the voice of a sinner calling out to Him. ***There is no way to explain it but that He had a 'generosity override'.*** His response was, "Today you shall be with Me in paradise!" He kept giving.

Through all the animosity of the people attacking Him and killing Him - literally, ***He could see their need above their actions. There is no way to explain it but that He had a 'blot out generosity'.*** He said, "Father, forgive them for they do not know what they do."

Paul was forced to correct himself at that point. "He is not just a gift that kept on giving," he thought to himself, ***"He is the gift that keeps on giving.*** Everyone who calls upon His name is being saved and shall be saved. He did say, 'If you ask the Father in My name, I will do it!' 'To this point you have asked nothing of Me...' Interesting! Everything that we have asked to this point is nothing in the context of His capacity to give. Every provision for life: health, wealth, wellbeing, and for godliness is made in Him. The Holy Spirit?... Is He not His most precious gift to us?"

Paul concluded that the Baby born in the manger was the most perfect gift to humanity. This gift was indeed that leaven that keeps spreading and revealing Himself perpetually in the most extravagant of ways. "He is the most outstanding person that ever lived and His seed is in us. He is a hard act to follow but it does not excuse us. He did say, 'Deny yourself, take up your cross, and follow Me!' I will certainly try!" Paul committed.

> *THERE IS A PRICE TO BE PAID FOR FREEDOM, COUNTED IN SACRIFICE, COUNTED IN BLOOD, COUNTED IN MONEY; ARE YOU WILLING TO PAY THE PRICE?*
>
> *THERE IS A PRICE TO BE PAID FOR FREEDOM, YOURS WAS PAID, THEIRS WAS PAID, SOMEONE PAID TO GET THE GOOD NEWS TO YOU, ARE YOU WILLING TO PAY TO GET IT TO OTHERS?*

CHAPTER

5

KINGDOM MOTIVATION - COMPASSION

"It touched Him," John said to his brother James.

"It always touched Him," James said with tears in his eyes. They were having a private memorial for this Man they had loved so much. Everyone was in confusion at the painful death of this Man, this hero. It helped very much to mull over His memory. "It was as if He could feel every pain we feel," John said.

"His heart was full of compassion," James said.

"That is it!" John said, "Love and compassion!"

"He felt what they were feeling and He acted. He acted because He felt, He felt and He acted. Compassion moved him to act." They sunk into their own private thoughts for a moment. James found himself on a hill-side in the desert. His memory injected some needed energy to his spirit as he was with his Master once again.

He could feel the buzz around him. He could see the atten-tiveness of the crowd. They were drinking in every word from the Master as He taught them important lessons from the kingdom. They were in the middle of a crisis and the Master could see it. It was clear He could feel the hunger pangs that ate away at the stom-achs of the crowd as they chewed away at His word.

He could hear the Master say, "I have compassion on these people for they have been with Me for three days. It is some distance to the nearest town. If I send them away without food, they would probably fall down faint on the way."

He could remember the sweet sensation he felt as he observed the Master in action. "Compassion," he thought, "sympathy, consideration, concern, kindness, care…, He would feed them… everyone of them even if He had to work a miracle to do it."

Compassion always moved Him to action. Sometimes to love children, at one time to weep over Jerusalem, but many times to heal sickness and disease among the people. At times he healed every one of them who came. James could remember the time Jesus touched a leper in his contagious state to heal him. So great was His compassion.

"It is an indictment on us," John thought. "It is an indictment on our religious institution. It is an indictment on our religious leaders." He was replaying a story the Master had told them in His mind. The story unfolded in picture colors: Reuben kissed his wife and his sons and set out for Jericho. "I love you," he said, as his wife Sara called after him, "Be safe, dear." As he left Jerusalem, he had no idea he would neither be safe nor see his wife and sons again. Well, that was if it was left up to the religious brethren of his nation and his religious leaders.

The day was humid and there was no cloud in the sky. He was thankful for the donkey he rode. It made the journey tolerable. He had heard stories of robbers in the region recently. He was hoping to meet other travelers to travel with for safety. He had a small cache of funds on him to do business in Jericho and he wanted to keep it safe. He had no such luck.

The barren pathway of the wilderness stretched before him like a forgotten painting. The rocks and hills that blocked his view were all parched dry. As he journeyed he entertained himself with this song:

Only rocks and sticks and barrenness
But I am going through
To trade and find my fruitfulness
Not far away, in Jericho
Lord I depend on You, no less
To bring me grace and fruitfulness.

Through these rocks and sticks and barrenness Reuben came to a small pathway in the road between two rocks. He was always very alert whenever he passed this area. There were so many places here for thieves to hide.

As he turned a bend, singing in his mind and very watchful, they struck. He saw flashes of men rising up from the rocks on either side of him. He felt something hard come crashing down on his back. He made a heavy thud as he fell to the ground. Reuben felt blows raining all over his body as he lost consciousness.

Reuben came back to consciousness sometime later. He could not determine the time. He was alone. The bandits were gone. He tried to move but it was too painful for him. He had no clothing on. His donkey and his money were gone. He was in an awful state, bleeding all over. He drifted in and out of consciousness. He was vaguely aware of the vultures circling above him. They sensed the inevitable.

Somewhere in his subconscious, he heard footsteps. He opened his eyes and he was sure of this, it was a priest. One of the religious leaders of his nation was coming. A flood of joy entered his heart. He was about to be helped. No better person could have come in his moment of need than a priest. They were, in his eyes, guardians of the laws of God. They were men who had the heart of God, who taught and diligently kept the commandments.

His excitement quickly died as the footsteps continued past him and faded in the distance. "No," he said to himself, "it could not have been a Priest. Not our Priest!" Through his blurred vision, he was sure that the man was clothed like a Priest.

He hesitated. "He did not act like a Priest though," he thought. "Why would a Priest walk on the other side of the road from the scene where a fellow Israelite wallowed in his own blood?" He was convinced this was a mirage of his desires. He was sure his mind, too, was affected by the assault. He slipped again into unconsciousness.

Sometime later, he was awakened by footsteps again. His parched lips cried out for a taste of water and his wounds throbbed for attention. He saw what appeared to be a Levite. The Levite came close and looked down at him. This time he was sure it was a Levite. His half blinded eye met the man's eye and relief flooded his heart. The Levite stooped down slightly and Reuben was sure he would assist.

This was a man appointed by God to serve in the temple. This man looked as if he was trying to assess the damage. "He can see that I am alive...can't he?" Reuben thought. The Levite then straightened up as if he had resigned himself to the thought that he could do nothing. It was as if he had accepted the death of this, his fellow countryman. Perhaps he was not willing to undertake the risk of staying in that place any longer. Whatever the reason, he too was gone.

Reuben was not so sure anymore that it was a real person. "How could a real person, a fellow brethren and leader, be so heartless, so compassionless?" he thought as he drifted back into unconsciousness.

Reuben woke up to the sound of voices around him. He realized he was in a room. He was on a bed. It was obvious time had passed, perhaps days, but he did not know how long. His wounds were bandaged. Yet still, they were very painful and they throbbed. He could not move but he was fully conscious. The face that smiled down at him was not that of his countryman. This man was a Samaritan.

He heard the innkeeper say to him, "You should be grateful to Josh, he rescued you." He was referring to this Samaritan. Reuben slightly nodded his head and managed a brief smile as he wondered, "How could this…this dog, this Samaritan be so caring, so compassionate? How could he sacrifice so much when my own countrymen were so unwilling?"

Reuben listened as the Samaritan told him how he saw him on the roadside, almost dead. The birds were on the ground nearby and he drove them away. He was amazed as he told him how he cleaned the wound and poured in his oil and wine. "He actually gave of his wealth to save a stranger," he thought, "amazing!"

Not only did he give of his oil and wine but he placed him on his own donkey. "He gave up his transportation and walked so that he could save my life," he thought, a tear entering his eye. He did not need to say anything more. He had purchased for him the best care and the best accommodation possible. He was leaving and he paid the inn-keeper in full. He then promised to pay any balance remaining when he returned.

John jumped, startled from his own thoughts. It was the voice of James that startled him. James had said aloud, voicing his own thoughts, "Compassion." John thought of this, "Compassion should make people willing to sacrific**E *their wealth, their resources and their comfort to meet the needs of others.*** This is what the Samaritan did."

John thought of the parable. "Jesus was simply answering the question, 'Who is my neighbor?'" The Samaritan was the only true neighbor to the wounded Israelite? A neighbor must be the person who acts neighborly. It must also be the person who willingly pours in the oil and wine and commits their resources to this wounded world. It has nothing to do with nationality and proximity, it has all to do with action. The word "neighbor" in the kingdom is a verb.

John paused, "But this is a command. In fact, Jesus tagged it as the second greatest command, 'Love your neighbor as yourself.' I have never seen anyone who is sick and wounded who will not give everything to be well, even if it makes them poor. This is what the woman with the flow of blood did."

A drop of tear fell from each of John's eyes. This confirmed the most important lesson he learned from his Master, the lesson of love. "We are commanded to be neighbors; to give everything, to commit everything to help this hurting world." He turned to James and said. ***"The greatest commandment indeed is love. We disobey God if we fail to actively love God and to actively love mankind.***

My brother James, I commit myself to giving to the very end. I want Heaven to know I understand who my neighbor is. ***Your neighbor indeed is your opportunities to impart and to impact; to be neighborly.*** This is what the Master did. This is what I will do for the rest of my life."

John then sank back into his private thoughts, "But why did the Master point his finger in such a way at the religious leaders and the brethren in such a way? Is it that He requires more from us? Is it that we do much less than Heaven expects and demands of us? Is it that we talk more than we act? Is it that we unreasonably hold on to Heaven's resources and withhold our love?"

James looked at his brother and said, vocalizing his own thoughts, "David says in the Psalms that the Lord is gracious and full of compassion."

"He really is!" John sighed. He would defi-nitely get back to his meditation on love later, in a quiet place.

Peter sat there by himself as he listened to the conversation, but this time he did not participate. He was busy. The conversa-tion sparked similar thoughts in him. He felt compelled to docu-ment it. He bent down and made a note on a scrap of bark. He made a mental note that he would definitely include this in the first book he wrote.

Later when he was writing his first book, in the third chapter he included his script. "Finally, I instruct all of you to be of one mind. Have compassion for each other; love as brothers, be tenderhearted."

145

> *1. Compassion is compulsion because you take it personal; the heart gets involved.*
>
> *2. Every human heart of flesh is full of compassion. Bid passion to come; acquire the heart of Jesus, where tenderness and ACTION meet naturally.*

THE COMPULSION OF LOVE

"For God so loved the world that He gave…" John was now alone. It was evening. He had gone back to that garden. It was that place where he resorted with Jesus many times. It was the place to which Jesus was taken.

He loved this place although it held such bitter memories. It was beautiful. It was quiet. It brought him closer to his Lord. John felt pressed in his spirit by the thought which he had mulled over earlier. "Who is my neighbor?" he kept hearing. "Love is the summation," he kept responding.

He did not tell anyone where he was going. He needed to do this in quiet. A cloud passed over the evening sun and it cast a sweet shadow over the surrounding decorated with blooming trees. He was not interested in the ambiance. His heart was full.

He could see her, beaming with joy as his father placed the gift he had brought her in her hand. She was old but her steps became like that of a young child. It had a certain spring and a dance. Her eyes lit up like the stars and sparkled at her husband. She reached up and kissed him. It was a deep, intense kiss. Realizing that their son John was watching, she would clear her throat, disengage, look at John and say, "I love this man so much."

This happened almost every time his father would come home from a successful fishing trip. He always stopped to buy her something special. His mother had come to anticipate this. Many times she would pull him away to the privacy of their room and they would be gone for what seemed to be a very long time. John remembered his father saying to him as a young man, "This is how you keep the fire going on. Love gives…"

"Love gives," John said to himself as he meditated. "For God so loved the world that He gave just like my father. Love really gives." John thought about the gift that God gave and he was moved to tears. "This is why I need to be alone," he thought. "This kind of love breaks me up. He did not give an angel. He gave His only begotten Son. He gave Himself. This gift was a sacrifice to replace the animals we offer. He had to be slaughtered." The passion and emotions that John felt at this thought were very intense. John had to pause in silence for some time to allow it to settle.

"What a demonstration of love!" John thought. "Now I understand why father did what he did for mother. I still cannot come to terms with this kind of love that God demonstrated, though. How could the Creator give Himself to die for His creation? How could someone so powerful, rather so all-powerful, omnipotent, submit Himself to such a death? Are we that valuable to Him?"

John spent some time trying to piece together the puzzle. The more he contemplated it, the more complex it became. He saw clearly that he was losing. There was no way he could fully come to terms with the love that confronted him.

He had to come away with something. He settled for, "Love gives…" John thought of his mother and father. They were always saying nice and kind things to each other. They were always praising and affirming each other. John could not imagine how it would have been if he had grown up without the same affirmation. Every little gift his father gave him, every thoughtful action, every day to day provision was a statement to John of love.

He understood that there is no love without giving. "No wonder, children who have never received anything from their father, even a touch or a kind word, conclude that they are not loved," he thought. "Love gives!" John remembered Joseph's coat of many colors. Joseph knew it was a statement of his father's love. His brothers knew it too, and they hated him.

"Yes!" John said, "That settles it. Love gives…" Then he began his meditation: "How can we know if love is really love?" he thought. "We can know love by this: Jesus laid down His life for us. If Jesus did this for us, we ought to also lay down our lives for each other. Love indeed gives." This deliberation would later be recorded in 1 John 3:16 which we call the reciprocal verse of John 3:16. John was not finished, he continued, "If anyone has wealth or any earthly possession and he sees a brother in need, he is compelled to help. If he should shut up the bowels of his compassion from his brother, if he should close his heart, how could he say that he has the love of God in him? Certainly, he has nothing of this type of love that brought Redemption? Love must be restorative, love must be redemptive. Love must lift up and propel." John would later sum this up in the third chapter of his Book of First John. He would admonish the brethren, saying, "Do not let us love in tongue, with empty words, but in action and truth." ***Action speaks the truth with the most commanding voice. Love gives!***

John was not satisfied. It is as if a highway into the heart of God was opened up with this revelation. He began to meditate on love, true love. He captured his meditation in the fourth chapter of the book of First John. John had come to the conclusion that God not only loves, but God is love. This was the only way he could settle the puzzle that confounded him: God giving His only Son; giving Himself to die.

"The church needs to know this, to be instructed," He said to himself softly. "We must love each other, for love is of God. This is how we can attest that we know God. Everyone who loves is born of God and knows God. Anyone who does not love does not know God, for God is love. This is it! God is love personified.

This is how He made His love plain to us: He sent His only begotten Son into the world, that we might live through Him.

This is real love! It is not because we loved Him; He loved us and sent His Son to pay for our sins.

Oh my God! If God so loved us, we also ought to love one another. Everyone needs to know it. We have to be prepared to give selflessly for each other. We have to be prepared to make the sacrifice for each other. This sacrifice has to be everything that we have, all our wealth and even our lives." John paused as tears streamed down his face.

There was a witness from inside that told him he was speaking the language of Heaven. He felt as if he was caught up in a heavenly conversation that took place in a world not limited by time. He felt as if his life was caught up in the fulfillment of that conversation. He felt as if he had to say this. Heaven needed the world to hear its heart.

John continued, "No one has seen God at any time. If we love one another, God abides in us, and His love has been perfected in us. Love God with all your heart and love your neighbor as yourself, indeed! By this we know that we are living in Him, and He in us, because He has given us of His Spirit. This is one big love story and we are a part of it. His love lives in us.

We have seen and we testify that the Father has sent the Son as Savior of the world. There is no question that God who is Love abides in us. There is no question that we have the capacity to express this big Love. Anyone who confesses that Jesus is the Son of God, God abides in him, and he in God. This big Love is in him. We have known and believed the love that God has for us. God is love. Anyone who abides in love abides in God, and God in him. If we live in God we live in love and love lives in us.

When love is perfect among us we can be bold on the Judgment Day. As He is, so are we in this world. We are the demonstration of His love on this earth. Therefore, we can stand before Him with confidence on the Day of Judgment. It is love coming to roost. It will be love standing before Love. We can be nothing else but bold and confident.

We love Him because He first loved us. We would not have had the opportunity if He did not love us first. What if someone says, 'I love God,' and hates his brother? He is lying. If he cannot love his brother whom he can see, how can he love God whom he has not seen? ***If he cannot demonstrate love to his neighbor in action, his words are empty. Love gives! If he cannot give God, who is Love, access to his wealth and resources to fuel the redemptive work, his love is false. Love demands full access to everything we own and to our very lives.***

Well, these are not my words. This is the commandment we have from Him: Everyone who loves God must, without reservation or conditions, love his brother and sister also. Love gives!"

---

1. A word of encouragement, a compliment, a gift, a sacrifice... love build monuments, love creates memorial; love leaves a cross in His memory... love gives.

2. All the love in your heart needs a platform to express itself... only you can build the right one.

CHAPTER

6

BIG MONEY SMALL GOD

Dan was fascinated at the promises in the Scriptures that are covenanted to those who will be generous. He had always been a giver himself. He had asked God to make him a riverhead that is constantly supplied, but which pours out its supply for the blessings of many, far down stream. He wanted to be a continual, continuous supplier. A cry to whosoever will come. He wanted to be a retailer of God's wholesale blessings. He wanted to tap in directly to the Manufacturer and distribute Him.

Dan could not imagine being like Cain. His thoughts took him back in history, close to the beginning:

Ah, I have to give to God today. God did not help me to plant this, why should I? Well, it is good to have Him bless me, so I will definitely bring something. In any case, I cannot give my brother an advantage over me. Abel has been careful to select his offering, let me select mine also. That is really nice, it looks good. God would love it! Ha, caught you! Think I am stupid? If He is God He does not need my best anyway. He already owns everything. How about this? No, I am sure I can find something not so good but acceptable.

Ah, this should do. Naw! If I package this well it could make a gift to my father, he may accept it. God, here I come to offer my offering. I know, it feels like burning my trash in Your presence, but it is my offering. If you do not accept it, I will not take it back. I would have thrown it away anyway. Offer it to your governor

and see! "Where did that come from?" Dan thought. Dan was a
student of the Scriptures and he quickly reached for the passage in
the first chapter of Malachi. He would certainly come back to his
reflection on Cain, but he had to find this passage.

This is the passage in Malachi 1:

"OFFER it to your governor,
Offer it to him and see

If he will accept the offering
That you think of giving Me!
Am I not a great King?" says the Lord,
"Where is the honor that is Mine?
I have loved you, oh, how I have loved you!
Why offer Me the sick, the lame and the defiled?"

MALACHI 1

..."A son honors his father,
And a servant his master.
If then I am a Father, where is My honor?
5 "And if I am a Master,
Then where is My reverence?"
Says the Lord of hosts,
To your priests who despise My name.
"Yet you say, 'In what way have we despised Your name?'
You offer polluted food on My altar,
But say, 'In what way have we defiled You?'
By saying, 'The table of the Lord is contemptible.'
6 "When you offer the blind as a sacrifiice,
Is it not evil?
And when you offer the lame and sick,
Is it not evil?
Offer it now to your governor;

Would he be pleased with you?
Would he accept you for this?"
Says the Lord of hosts.
7 "But now, please, entreat the favor of God That
He may be gracious to us. While this is being done
by your hands; Will He regard you favorably?"
Says the Lord God of hosts.
"Who is there among you who would shut the
doors, So that you would not kindle fiire on My
altar in vain? I have no pleasure in you at all,"
Says the Lord of hosts.
8 "Nor will I accept an offering from your hands.
For from the rising of the sun to the going down of the same,
My name shall be great among the Gentiles;
And there in every place incense shall be offered to My name,
And a pure offering;
9 "For My name shall be great among the nations,"
Says the Lord of hosts.
"But you profane it, in that you say,
'The table of the Lord is defiled;
And its fruit, its food, is contemptible.'
You also say,
'Oh, what a weariness!'
10 "And you have sniffed at it."
Says the Lord of hosts.
"And you bring the torn, the sick and lame;
This you bring as an offering!
Should I accept this from your hand?"
Says the Lord.
"But cursed be the deceiver,
Who has in his flock a male,
11"And takes a vow,
But sacrifices to the Lord what is corrupt;

For I am a great King,"
Says the Lord of hosts,
"And My name is feared among the nations."

@CWDSBible

Dan caught his breath in fear at the thought of God having these negative emotions towards him. ***"Generosity cannot just be a prayer for me, it must be a compulsion,"*** he said to himself. Dan remembered the words of the Lord to Cain, "If you do good you will be accepted. If not, sin is waiting at your door to possess you."

"I must be a flowing river, a riverhead," Dan said to himself again.

He remembered the words of Jesus about the rich man who built bigger barns to entertain himself with his success. "Tonight your life will be taken from you. Who will you have stored up all these provisions for?" It was the next statement that came home to him forcefully, "So shall it be, to everyone, no exclusion, everyone who stores up, or rather hoards, treasure for themselves and is not rich towards God!"

Dan whispered softly as a gentle drizzle burst from the clouds above and greeted him, "I must be a riverhead like Abraham, blessed to be a blessing." This drizzle could not so easily move him from the place of his meditation in the open field. He would stay there awhile and enjoy the drizzle as he reflected on these truths.

The tears that came into his eyes as he thought of murder-ous Cain, reinforced his passion. If we receive and do not give we self-destruct. The body teaches us if we eat and do not utilize, the body accumulates fat and is plagued with diseases. The heart that is stingy is plagued with sin. As God told Cain, sin is waiting at the door of that person desiring to consume them. It is like a pack of hungry hyenas, licking their lips desirously… waiting. ***A river that does not flow soon becomes stagnant and infested with all sorts of things.*** For Cain, it was murder and arrogance. Dan thought of the servant that Jesus spoke of who hid the one talent. He was infected, rather infested, with rancor and complaint. He was angry and resentful and bitter and it was all because he did not have a generous heart.

Dan drifted off in his thought to the most glorious kingdom that had ever been on earth. It was the kingdom of Solomon. To him it was the closest reflection of the kingdom of God that ever existed on earth. He could see the kings coming to Solomon. It was a steady stream every month. Each came with presents to Solomon. They brought the best from their kingdoms. He was mesmerized by the gift and entourage of the Queen of Sheba. "She really knows how to make a statement," he smiled.

These kings carefully selected, prepared and presented the gifts they brought with them to Solomon. They knew their offering would be received as a reflection of themselves and their kingdom. ***They knew it would be received as a reflection of how they viewed the king to whom they were bringing the present and the kingdom of that king.*** They were themselves kings so they understood very well. You give to a king of kings like Solomon the best. You give to a king you have little respect for a tributary, nothing worthwhile. You really don't need their respect, you command it.

They knew the gift would determine how they were received by the kingdom they were presenting it to. It would determine if they were received at all. If a king felt disrespected by the present offered he would certainly not receive the gift or the person offering the gift. Cain understood this very well.

They were kings but they would be denied audience with Solomon if they did not show him enough respect. A poor gift could even start a quarrel or escalate to war. ***Kings are known to give to kingdoms they were procuring help from, every valuable thing in their kingdom.***

Dan scratched his head, it was so obvious. There is never a day or a minute that we do not need the protection and the covering of the kingdom of Heaven. He looked up to God with tears in his eyes. "You are the greatest of all kings," he said, "the only true King of kings." *I must give to God as kings give to kings, as a king give to the King.* "I am a king and a priest," he said, "I have the power to not just present my offering to You but to come before You and to offer it to the King of kings in person."

Dan thought to himself, "A riverhead! Isn't this the promise of the word that Jesus Himself reaffirmed, 'Out of your bellies shall flow rivers of living water'?" Yes, He was talking about the Holy Spirit but take me to the Revelation of John.

John saw a river flowing from the throne of God. It was pure and clear as crystal. On every side was the tree of life. Its leaves were for the healing of the nations. *If our bodies are His temple and the Holy Spirit lives in us, are we not a type of His throne? Should we not be facilitators of the flow of God that heals the nations here?* As we accommodate the presence of God, should we not be facilitators of His redemptive work here on earth. Are we not required to be living to give? The rich man died because he lived but would not give. Jesus said, "So is everyone…who is not generous towards God, meaning towards His commission." Are we not included with 'the' everyone, who is dead as we live, if we refuse to give? "Lord make me a riverhead!" Dan shouted and ran for cover as the rain came down in torrents.

---

1. IF YOU CANNOT SEE GOD ABOVE YOUR MONEY AND YOUR NEEDS; IF HE CANNOT BE HEARD ABOVE YOUR MONEY DECISIONS YOUR MONEY IS BIGGER THAN YOUR GOD.

2. There is a Person inside every believer who is God and who has the fullness of the heart of God. He would like to express God from His throne in our spirits. We are commanded not to quench (restrain) Him.

KINGDOM SACRIFICES

"I want to write a song, daddy, will you help me?" The child asked.

"What do you want to write about Rhema?" His father responded.

"I want to write about seven," he said, "for I am seven years old."

"Let's do it!" daddy said, not sure what was on his heart.

> *If there is just seven in the earth of these*
> *Would it not be wise then if I should keep*
> *All seven until they increase*
> *And they become many?*
> *Should I take one from seven and decrease*
>
> *The seven; Why should I give*
> *The future of the species*
> *To prove that I believe?*

Rhema's father had caught on immediately where he was heading and had helped him to put his thoughts into words. He had told him the story of this righteous man who had made a real sacrifice. He remembered the look of awe on his face as he related: He came out and looked around. A feeling of exhilaration flooded his heart. It felt so good to put his foot on dry land again. He was on his boat for almost a year in a limited space. This felt so good for him. Like a normal boat ride he travelled on the water. Unlike a normal boat ride, these were flood waters with huge boulders and other debris floating around. The ground was soggy but it was land. This felt good. Everywhere around him was total devastation. All the trees were down. The few leaves that were intact had lost their pigmentation for being under water for so long. But this was dry land and it felt good.

Noah said to his son Shem as he disembarked, "The flood destroyed the civilization, but it saved humanity."

"Should we let the animals out?" Japheth shouted from the deck of the ark. He was waiting for the day he would get to release all these animals in his floating zoo to their normal habitats. Many of them had become his friends over the long journey. He anticipated their excitement at being released, "You may my son." Noah responded. "Leave a male of every clean animal."

"Why should I do this?" Japheth asked. They had a very long journey on the waters but they did not harm any of the animals for food. "We will sacrifice them to God." Noah said. Japheth had a problem with this. He could not imagine why his father would want to further diminish this limited edition of the earth species. Why not wait until they had reproduced sufficiently?

"God has indeed been faithful. He has proved Himself marvelously." Noah responded. "Without Him, we would have all been dead, every one of us. He has been and will always be the breath and hope of the species. It is best to have a little with God in it, than to have a lot without Him," he concluded.

Rhema's father remembered telling him. "This must have been one of the most precious offerings received in Heaven since creation. Noah did not just offer one of the seven he had, he offered one of the seven of all that existed in the earth. As the aroma of the sacrifice reached Heaven, God must have received it and added fertility to the few that remained on the earth of all the species. Look around today and see how many of each animal there is," he said to Rhema.

Rhema looked up at his father in admiration as he repeated the song, encouraging him. He then added a chorus to his delight.

If there are just seven in the earth of these
Would it not be wise then if I should keep
All seven until they increase
And they become many?
Should I take one from seven and decrease
The seven; Why should I give
The future of the species
To prove that I believe?

A little committed to God is better
That a lot in any factor
Commit everything to God
And let faith settle the matter!

Rhema's father, recognizing the impact the story had on his son, decided to tell him another story about sacrifice. He began: The widow looked into her cupboard and sighed. It was empty and clean, there was nothing there to eat. Her husband had died some time ago now and she had no children. She was grateful for the little her neighbors contributed from time to time. She made it serve as best as she could. She was lean and hungry but she survived. She looked in the old rag that she kept whatever coins she was fortunate to come by. She knew the outcome beforehand, she had only two mites, valued a fraction of one penny. She was saving it for some time now. It could buy her one meal and that meal must be purchased only in extreme necessity. She always carried it with her in the event of need. This was one such occasion, however, she would wait to see if anyone would come to her assistance first. This was the Sabbath and she was going to the temple of God to worship. On many occasions, she would not leave the temple empty. Her religious nation took pride in ministering to the needs of the fatherless and widows. There were some occasions, though, when she left empty handed.

There was one thing about this woman. She was diminished in stature because of her needs but she was distinguished by her love for God and her confidence in His provision. As she entered the temple, she was captured by the awesomeness of her God. This happened to her every time. He was so much bigger than every-thing and everyone, and this made life worth living.

She saw as everyone began to put their gifts into the offering. Some brought mint, some brought gold and other bits of treasure. Her only disappointment was that she had nothing to give. Well, she had only two mites but she wondered if God would really accept that. It was then that faith entered her heart. Something told her that God would certainly accept her sacrifice. She remem-bered the Teacher telling the people that with the same measure you give it will be given back to you. This was a full measure. Not a portion of her wealth but everything she had.

The joy filled her heart as she opened up her old rag and took the mites out. She heartily brought it to the altar to offer it to God. Her heart was so full of love and passion. She was so capti-vated she did not notice that the person standing there at the altar, paying careful attention to the offering was the Teacher Himself. She saw Him turn to some men nearby and say something but she paid no attention. This was a love moment for her and she felt elevated by her sacrifice. She certainly did not have another meal now but she remembered thinking, "If it is not enough in my hand, it is better off in the hand of God anyway." If she could have heard the Master in that moment, she would have realized that He actually affirmed her gift.

The men He had turned to were His disciples and He was saying: "This poor widow has given into the treasury more than everyone else. Everybody of their abundance brought a portion and gave. This woman of her lack gave everything she had. She gave a full measure."

"What happened to that woman?" Rhema asked.

"Well this is subject to your imagination," his father responded. "Let us imagine things changed for her from that moment on. Her brother who had gone away returned home. He had amassed a lot of wealth. He did not communicate with her for many years and was happy to have found her alive. He took care of her lavishly for the rest of her life."

Rhema silently pondered the story. He turned it over in his young but very sharp intuitive mind many times. He paused only to listen to the song his father started to sing in reflection. It was about sacrifice.

Go take your son, your only son
The one you love
Who is dear to your heart
And offer him, a sacrifice
Unto Me
That's the offering I want

Oh you could think
Of seven things
That you could offer
That you could give
If only just, your son could live
If only just your son could live

And heaven sings of sacrifice:

I'll take My Son
My only Son, the one I love
Who is dear to My heart
And offer Him an offering
For all mankind
For that is what the world requires
Sacrifice.

"Tell me about that story also," Rhema demanded.

"Enough for tonight," his father said. "I will tell you tomorrow." He knew Rhema was not likely to forget his promise. He sang the song to him once more as he fell asleep, still mulling the story of the widow.

> *I'll take My Son*
> *My only Son, the one I love*
> *Who is dear to My heart*
> *And offer Him an offering*
> *For all mankind*
> *For that is what the world requires*
> *Sacrifice.*

Sure enough, the following night, Rhema demanded his story. His father smiled at his son. He was enjoying his interest in God. He hoped one day Rhema himself would be among those willing to sacrifice everything for the faith. "God's redemption plan needs men like these," he thought as he said to his attentive son:

"Giving is an act of faith, son. The gift you present to God is a visible portrait of the image of God you carry." Now the song I was singing is two stories of sacrifice. Both stories are connected and together they make our story possible. It is about one promise that was made to one person, received by the other and passed on to us.

The first story begins:

The man of faith rose up early in the morning and saddled his donkey. He was a very small man but he was not short in faith. His faith was very big. With him was his son, Isaac, and two of his servants. God had spoken to him the day before and told him to take his son, his only son, Isaac. He instructed him to go to the land of Moriah and offer him there as a burnt offering on one of the mountains He Himself would point out.

This was the most painful sacrifice anyone could ask. Abraham was very old and having Isaac in his old age was itself a miracle. To lose him now would be a great tragedy. To lose this son by his own hand would be a double tragedy. Abraham did not wait to be obedient to God. He went and looked for the wood immediately. He prepared for his journey beforehand. He knew he would be away for about one week. He got up early the next morning and they journeyed out.

The journey was three days long, but when he arrived God said to him. "This is the mountain." Abraham did not hesitate. He told his two servants to wait while he and Isaac went to the top. Abraham was numb for the rest of his journey; it was as if he was sleepwalking. He was going through the motions as if he was dreaming. His picture of God was big, however. He loved his God more than anything he had, anything he owned. He loved his God more than his own son.

His son was undoubtedly the most precious thing to him in his life and this was not just an offering, it was a sacrifice. It was a sacrifice of his own heart. Did God deserve this, a complete measure, everything of meaning to him? He had already settled this question; God for him was life itself. Nothing in life could be compared to God, not even his son.

Abraham built an altar of stones. He then placed the wood on the altar. He tied up his son, Isaac and placed him on the wood. It was very tough and uncomfortable for Isaac. He was very afraid and sweating but he trusted his father. As Abraham lifted his knife and was bringing it down to his throat to kill his son tears fell down his face. It blurred his vision. A drop fell on Isaac's lip. He could taste the salt of his father's struggle amidst the bitterness of his own. Abraham wiped his eyes. His real pain was the pain in his son's eyes. The pain of love and betrayal. He could see the resignation that replaced it and recognized that his sacrifice was Isaac's also. He understood. He resolved to be quick and decisive.

As he was about to strike, an angel called out to him and told him to stop. He looked around and saw a ram caught in the bushes. He was very happy and relieved as he untied his son, his only son, the one he loved, and offered the ram instead. This time God would accept the ram instead of his son. God would continue to accept rams for offering until the end of the other story.

God said to Abraham then, "Because you have done this. You have not withheld your son from Me. You have not placed the gift I have given you above the Giver. You have not limited My access to what you possess, even to your only son. I will certainly bless you and multiply your children as the stars of heaven and the sand by the sea. Your descendants shall defeat and occupy the land of their enemies. In your seed shall all nations, all families, of the earth be blessed. Because you have obeyed Me."

Time passed and the promises God made to Abraham were fulfilled – well, mostly. His descendants had grown in numbers. They had defeated their enemies and possessed their land. They had continued to offer rams and bulls to God in sacrifice for their sins. This was not adequate however. God accepted this but it could not take away their sins. It was like bandage on a cut that would never heal. To take away the sins of mankind, to heal the wound forever, God had prepared a sacrifice. This sacrifice was His own Son, His only Son, the Son He loved, Jesus Christ. It was impossible for any natural seed of Abraham to become the blessings to all nations of the earth. They themselves were limited by sin. It is not possible for sin in any format or package to be a blessing.

The blessing was for someone who had never sinned against God, someone who had never ever disobeyed the Father, someone who was always in good favor with the Father. This blessing could only be obtained by someone who was, as you would say, one with the Father God. Can you imagine a father sacrificing someone like this? This must have pained God more than the sacrifice of Isaac pained Abraham. Isaac was a good son, but he could never have been this perfect. No relationship that earth can ever boast can be this perfect.

God was to send His Son, born into the family line of Abraham, to receive the blessing. ***The blessing He had issued by decree which*** *was already in the earth, allocated to a lineage...but waiting. Waiting to be received; waiting to be distributed to carriers.*

His Son would be sacrificed, not by a single blow from a knife. He would be sacrificed by the most excruciating death imaginable, the death on a cross. It would be painful torture that would last for an extended time before death. It would be public humiliation and death. This time the crowd would be brought along and they would not hinder the proceedings but spur it on. This time the sacrifice would be completed. God would no longer accept a ram for sins, and He would provide none.

In time, His Son Jesus came and He was sacrificed. Now everyone who believes in Jesus Christ has received the blessing of Abraham. The blessing is a blessing for every person of faith in Jesus Christ. It is a blessing, however, intended for all nations of the earth. It is a blessing that must be passed on by sacrifice. We must be prepared to give God full access to everything we own, just as Abraham did. We cannot love anything more than Him. ***Nothing can be too dear to us for us to submit it to His purpose.*** This includes property, time or wealth. If God was willing to give His Son, He will not accept any lesser commitment from us. ***His love for the world remains just as intense as the intensity that surrendered Christ from Heaven. The redemption plan of Heaven, the dissemination of the blessings of Abraham, requires sacrifice.***

Then daddy said to Rhema, "I have completed my song, son, would you like to hear it before you go to bed?"

"Please daddy," Rhema said, "please sing it for me!" His father sang the song he had written, just the night before:

> *Go take your son, your only son*
> *The one you love*
>> *Who is dear to your heart*
>> *And offer him, a sacrifice*
>> *Unto Me*
>> *That's the offering I want*

Oh you could think
Of seven things
That you could offer
You could give
Easy to part with aye, aye
But that your son would live

Blessed to be a blessing
The earth needs sacrifice
From one to the other Abraham to Christ
Blessed to be a blessing
Yours through Christ by faith
The families are waiting on
What sacrifice creates

And Heaven speaks:

I'll take My Son
My only Son, the one I love
Who is dear to My heart
And offer Him an offering
For all mankind
For that is what the earth requires

Isaac lived, but He must die
No ram can take His place
The redemption of all mankind
Will take sacrifice and faith

Blessed to be a blessing

The earth needs sacrifice
From one to the other

Abraham to Christ
Blessed to be a blessing
Yours through Christ by faith
The families are waiting on
What sacrifice creates

As Rhema drifted off to sleep his father resigned to his room also. He was lost in his own thoughts. "People do not give," he said to himself, "because they say, 'I do not have.'" His thought went back to the story he told Rhema the night before. "What if the poor widow had taken that approach," he thought, "she would have missed her moment of being singled out by Jesus." He remembered a story he had read. "Wait! I still have that book," he thought aloud. He began to search through his collection of books and sure enough, there it was. It was a story written about a certain doctor named Luke. He sank down on his bed and opened the book and began to read.

1. Noah's philosophy: six extinct species blessed
is better than seven not blessed.

2. As nothing in heaven or on earth was too precious for God to sacrifice to express His love for us; we cannot hold anything we possess too precious to sacrifice to express our love for God.

3. As love is measured to God in sacrifices it is measured back to us with the same measure. A sacrifice demands good measures.

HAVE AND HAVE NOT

R hema's father drank in the introduction of this book slowly: It was abstract but it was real. It was his story and yet it was their story. It spoke to their everyday lives. It read:

> Dr. Luke was mulling in his mind this parable of Jesus as he lay on his bed that night. He had just written some notes for his Gospel and his spirit was fluent. What he did not know then was that it was the second Voice of the Deity of Heaven to have spoken this. The person he knew as Jesus had spoken this with the authority of the Redemption plan drafted long ago, in a place where the first Voice says, 'Let Us…' He said to himself, "The Master has spoken in a way that you could walk with Him in your imagination. He painted a picture for the eye of the mind to look at." In the eye of Dr. Luke's mind, he found a character. His name was Sewag.

The story unfolds: He sat there at his table in his house. He was dressed as if he was about to travel. He also was packed as if he would be away for some time. Sewag had summoned three of his servants to him. He would not be around but he wanted to entrust some of his wealth to each of these servants to see what they would do with it. He wanted to determine how much they would gain by trading. He needed to determine if he could trust them. He wanted to test their character.

The servants listened to his instructions and accepted the money from their master, Master Sewag. The first one beamed as he was entrusted with five talents. The second servant was joyful as he accepted two. The third servant tried hard to hide his open disgust as he accepted the one talent his master gave to him. He was happy his master could not read his thoughts but he was sure he would be able to read his heart when he returned.

Sewag had them in training and had appropriated to them talents based on his assessment of their ability to manage. He knew that their character would greatly enhance their ability to be successful. He left that day to the cheers, celebration and good wishes of his household and his servants.

He had great plans for his servants but he had to test their faithfulness first. He had great plans for each of these servants but he could not give to them anything greater than their ability to manage and their attitudes.

The servants were busy at work in his absence. The first servant used all his ability and creativity to seek out and maximize opportunities to increase his five talents. He worked hard, he worked late, he worked smart and before long the money began to work on his behalf.

The five talents began to increase, slowly at first and then with more consistency. The servant with the one talent taunted him. "Why are you working so hard?" he said. "Whose money do you believe this is? Who will benefit from all the money you are making?"

"Master Sewag will," he responded, *"I love him. He is my master and he has all rights to determine how I spend my time. I belong to him. I also took his money and integrity demands that I maximize it."*

The servant with the one talent turned away, more discontented than ever before. He had buried his one talent and he complained. He complained about the master. He complained to justify his actions. He became more and more bitter with each of his complaints. He swore to himself that he would address his master with the truth when he returned. "Someone needed to tell him," he argued.

He was disgusted with the first servant. He was even more disgusted with the second servant. The second servant had only received two talents and yet he was as enthusiastic and as faithful as the first.

Time passed and both the first and the second servant had doubled their talents. The servant with the one talent had refined his onslaught of the master with time as the others increased his wealth. He wanted to tell the master everything that the other servants were denying, even dispelling, by their actions. They were ready to greet him with good news. He was ready to greet him with the truth.

"Master Sewag is coming," they heard a female servant cry from the window of a building. Everyone ran outside to greet him. They could see from a distance that he was even more affluent than before he left. He had a larger entourage and he seemed happier than ever before.

He spoke of the success of his mission and everyone was delighted. He was anxious to know what his servants had done with his money. It was not because it mattered that much, but because he had so much more to administer and he needed responsible managers.

When the first two reported, he was delighted at their success. He made them rulers over many things. They were willing to administer another person's money without any promise of personal benefit. Their promotion came with all the perks of the position. They were delighted and very thankful that they had remained faithful.

The last servant came into the room hesitantly. He was very angry with the anger he had built up by his own self-talk in his master's absence. He was angry because he had rehearsed the right attitude to let the master know he was very serious. It was a bad attitude and he had rehearsed it many times. He was jealous because of how the master treated the other servants. He was angry because he was jealous. He was angry because he had to hide the jealousy and reservation he always had and carried inside.

He had rancor in his face and fire in his eyes as he faced the master. This time there would be no hiding or holding back. "The master should be rebuked just by my presence," he said to himself. He spoke to the master like an angry father to a very naughty son. His words however, were not corrective, it was condemning.

"You are a wicked man who loves to reap what you do not sow!" he said to Sewag. "Here is your money. I hid it in the ground so you can have just this, what is yours." He had forgotten that he belonged to Sewag. He was a slave. Sewag could do anything he desired with him.

Sewag was very annoyed and he could not hide it. "You wicked and unprofitable servant," he said. "You know I am wicked and that I reap what I do not sow. You should have at least taken my money and given it to the bankers so I could receive what is mine with the standard interest."

Sewag then said to his other servants, "Take the one talent this man has and give it to my faithful servant with ten talents."

Everyone was surprised. They said to him, "But Master Sewag, he already has ten."

The final statement that the Teacher made resonated with everyone. He said, "To those who have, more will be given. From those who do not have, will be taken even what they have."

As Dr. Luke contemplated the story. As he analyzed and meditated, he was amazed. ***"Everything belongs to the Master,"*** ***he exclaimed. "The earth is the Lord's: everything in it and*** ***everyone in it. He owns us. Everything we own belongs to Him*** *and we must give an account of what we do with it. No wonder Solomon instructs us to honor God with our substance, everything we have. He also said to honor Him with the first fruits of all our increase, but then…the balance becomes our substance with which to honor Him. This is such a closed case.*

We must all be prepared to maximize our talents for the King, and for the kingdom, not for our own selfish purposes." Dr. Luke laughed as he continued, "We are all unprofitable slaves. When we are finished we should not even look or hope for reward. All we should say is, 'I have done what I have been instructed to do.'" *The master did not take the talents from the servants, so he allows us to keep what we are maximizing. He even gives us more.* The master rewards our faithfulness with the little, with promotion over many things. With promotion comes the perks and the benefits of the job for as long as we are in position.

How many people are willing to work hard, and with an excellent attitude, knowing all the benefits belong to someone else, to God? Should it change our approach to know that all the money we earn and everything we own belongs to the King? A true heart of love will work even harder. How many persons are willing to apply their full ener*gy, enthusiasm and creativity knowing their employers or rather Employer, Master and Owner, stands to be the one who benefits?* Joseph in Egypt could. His slavery did not diminish his initiative and excellence in securing his master's interest. Even in prison, this did not change. He did everything as unto God and it made him successful and limitless. He was rewarded with promotion.

This unprofitable servant could not accept this concept. He got angry and he complained at the thought. He hid the talent and cursed the master. The master felt he was robbed because he deserved his own with its natural interest.

Is it possible that the gifts of God committed to some individuals can reap negative returns for the kingdom? Everything belongs to God and it will all go back to Him. Is it possible that instead of gaining souls for the Master, what he commits to us can be used to block or thwart the redemption plan? "Certainly this is possible! But what about the gifts committed to me?" Dr. Luke thought.

"It is very clear that every talent that is hidden robs the kingdom. It is very clear that every talent not used with full account-ability to the Master in mind robs the kingdom. This includes my gift of writing and all my money," Dr. Luke concluded.

"Everybody has!" Dr. Luke jumped at the revelation. "If a person who does not have can lose even what they have, it is clear that even a person who does not have, has…something to lose."

If we have something to lose it simply means we have something to use…to offer, to give. 'Do not have' is therefore only an attitude of the heart. It is the same attitude of the complaining bitter servant. Perhaps if we would place ourselves on the Job deduction scale we would begin to count and appreciate our blessings. We could then commit ourselves and our talents to the Master's redemption plan.

We just need to ask ourselves as we take a mental picture of Job's decline: "Do I have money to lose? Do I have my children to lose? Do I have a spouse to lose? Do I have my health to lose? Do I have my honor to lose? Do I have my friends to lose? Do I have the influence to lose? Do I have a voice to lose?" We should then ask ourselves:

"Do I have money to use, to offer for the kingdom? Do I have the blessings of my children? Do I have my spouse? Do I have my health to use? Do I have my honor to use? Do I have my friends upon whom to call? Do I have the influence to use? Do I have a voice to use? Do I have time to give? Do I have connections to use? Do I have an ear to give? How valuable are my skills? Can I give a word of encouragement? Can I give comfort? Can I share the Scriptures? Can I give a prayer? Do I have breath?" This paints a better picture of what you have available to you.

Dr. Luke sighed and said to himself, ***"Nobody escapes! The Master will punish every servant with a 'do not have', 'do not need to give account' mentality.*** It is no wonder Solomon said we should not to put too much effort in accumulating personal wealth. Riches will take wings and fly back to heaven, to its rightful owner. And you, if you choose to be an unprofitable servant…?" Dr. Luke sighed again and it appropriately summed up his thoughts. Rhema's father fell asleep at this point. He dreamt that he was a part of a building that was a part of a construction team, building a tabernacle.

---

1. It is very difficult for people to accept that they have no rights to a personal vision; that they do not belong to themselves. Jesus said, "Take My yoke upon you." Our freedom makes us the Lord's slave; our money is His servant.

2. It is very difficult for people to accept that they should work and give without looking for a reward. Doing our best means simply doing our duty.

3. We do not have the rights to complain and to make excuses. Joseph could have; he had every reason and every rights but he would have died in his prison just as the unproductive servant.

4. Wake up complainers, your cover is blown; excuse not accepted…you have: the ability to create an impact; the blessing of Abraham to deposit to the redemption plan. You do not have, but what you have is enough!

CHAPTER

7

BUILDING A TABERNACLE

A very long time ago, close to the beginning of time, because time had a beginning, a deity, the only deity, was doing something amazing. This deity had just made a clay man. This deity had all power in His word. He spoke and everything that existed was created, the trees, the animals, the universe, everything. This would be recorded as the most productive six days in the history of time, but then time was also among His creation. This deity was so powerful yet He chose to get His hands dirty to make this clay man. Perhaps He knew He would have to get His hands dirty, even bloody, to retain this bit of His creation. *Perhaps because He intended this creation should be extra special, one with which He would interact, with which he could share Himself, and even live in. Perhaps He was building a tabernacle for Himself.*

Centuries later, a child on a picturesque Caribbean island, Jamaica, playing with clay did exactly what this deity had done centuries earlier, he made a clay man. It was the perfect image of man. He had made a replica of himself as the deity had done before. He was elated. The child tried to take it up, but it broke into pieces, he cried.

This deity was doing something else, He bent over and breathed His breath into man. He could have just spoken but He chose to get up close and personal. Perhaps He intended for His Spirit to live in man, not just the breath of life like the other animals. Perhaps He intended for man to live and breathe Him, not only to just exist. Perhaps He was building a tabernacle. When the deity breathed into man, into him went the spirit of life and the spirit of God. Man became a living person. Man could now move, and talk and interact, and create, like the little boy who made a replica of himself. ***Man was also an alive person and a life breathing person.***

Things continued for a while where man enjoyed the fullness of life and the fullness of God. "I am so happy, soul happy," this man said to himself. He had now become two. God had made him a woman and they did not have to dream, they were living the dream. This creature, the man Adam, was living in the most beautiful and fruitful place imaginable. He did not know anything else. This one creature among the many in that place had the ability to meet with God. He had the very life of God in him. Man was, as it were, the tabernacle for the presence of God.

Time passed. ***Man continually enjoyed eternity in time in a place where time and eternity danced together and that was simply normal.*** Unfortunately, this would not last forever. Man would surrender the life of God that was in him by his disobedience to God.

Man was no longer the tabernacle of God. He had now become just an empty worn out corrupt vessel. Man became frustrated and bitter, angry, and murderous, evil and sensual, as he searched for something, or rather things, to replace the glory he once carried.

Time passed and man began sending up sacrifices from one dimension to the other, just to reach God. Man was so aware of the absence of the Presence that he sought this Presence through offerings and sacrifices. Man was also very aware of his own corrupt state and he sought the grace of God with his offering.

And time passed. With time came murders, wickedness, plots, deception, ill-conceived developments that left men babbling, and a flood. Then God selected a person through whom He could restore His plan to tabernacle with man once again. He promised this person that He would bless all the nations of the earth through his seed. The intention was that people would once again have His life in them again. They would once more be His tabernacle.

And time passed. The descendants of this man found themselves in bitter slavery. After a very long time, many heartaches, many heart breaks, many deaths, God delivered this people. It was a great and memorable deliverance. On their journey from the nation of their bondage, God revealed a plan to tabernacle with them. He gave their leader the plans for a specially designed and consecrated box called an ark in which His presence would dwell in.

This was not His eventual desire. His real intention was His original idea, the tabernacle He had built Himself, with His own hands. This real tabernacle could not contain Him just yet. Man still carried the sin of the first man. The life of God cannot co-exist with sin. This was why God departed from man in the first place. Man literally died the only death that mattered, the death of his spiritual existence. Now God was prepared to tabernacle with man once again in a specially built box to be carried around on the shoulders of consecrated priests.

Moses stood up on a hill. He was slightly elevated above the thousands of people who had gathered to him. It was the full congregation of Israel. A gentle breeze cooled the air in the otherwise humid wilderness afternoon as he addressed the people.

"Hear O Israel," Moses said, as a hush fell upon the people gathered there. The respect for this man Moses went deep among the audience. Moses had been in the presence of the Lord and his face shone with the glory of the Lord. He always wore a veil so he did not become a distraction. They held him with such high regard that when he spoke it was as if God was talking to them. They did not question his word.

"Hear O Israel," Moses said, "the Lord has commanded you to give an offering to the Lord. Everyone who has a willing heart should bring an offering to the Lord. Bring your gold, silver and, bronze; bring threads of blue, purple and scarlet. You are commanded to bring ram's skin, badger's skin, and acacia wood. Bring oil for the light and spices for the anointing oil and for the sweet incense. Bring onyx stones and stones for the ephod and for the breastplate. Give your labor and your time. All who are skilled should come and do all that the Lord has commanded. Come and volunteer your skills to build the tabernacle, its tent, its altars, and all its components."

When Moses spoke, the hearts of the people were stirred. They knew Moses was about to build an ark in which the presence of the Lord would dwell. They had seen the cloud of the Lord descend upon the tent of meeting when Moses was inside and lift away when he stepped out. ***They knew the awe of having God with them. They wanted this Presence.***

The people gave. They went home and they prepared and they gave. They gave the gold, the silver and the precious stones. Moses brought the offering to the workmen and they built. As they built the people brought. It was overwhelming. ***They recognized how important it was to have God tabernacle among them and they brought more and more.*** They brought so much until they had to be restrained from giving, it was too much. ***When people understand the importance of having God tabernacle with men, their giving will be generous and unrestrained.*** They will give to establish the tabernacle of God among them.

"You have a son," the midwives said to Leah. She was very relieved and drained after her extended time of labor. Now it was over she could smile and embrace another son. She managed a weak smile as she responded: "Now I will praise the Lord!" She named her son Judah which means praise.

Time had passed and in the process of time the tribe of Judah settled in Bethlehem. It is there that history would find a young boy committed to his sheep yet absorbed in the praise and love for his God.

He brought the God of Israel very close in his worship and in the power of proximity he found boldness that empowered him to tackle a bear and a lion. On both occasions, he won. On both occasions, he killed his fearsome opponent. On both occasions he proved God. He would later take his exploits to the battle field and kill an oversized human being, calling upon the name of his God.

His passion for God had not only endeared God to him but had endeared him to God. He constantly knocked on the door of God's heart. When it was time for God to select a new king for Israel, God selected him.

David was sitting in his house, contented, but his heart was on the Lord his God. He wanted to build his God a house. David called for Nathan the prophet and said to him, "Look at me. I am living in a house of cedar, but the ark of the covenant of my God is in a tent with curtains."

David wanted to build God a tabernacle to house the ark. Previously, he had mixed experience in taking the ark up to the city of David. When it eventually came, he had danced before the ark unreservedly until naked, but for a loin cloth. He lost his dignity so he could transfer the glory to God only. He recognized the importance of having the tabernacle of God with him and he would give anything to establish this, even his dignity.

Now he wanted to build God a house of permanence. He wanted a tabernacle where God would establish His presence among Israel. The prophet Nathan said to the king, "Go and do whatever is in your heart." But that night the Lord spoke to Nathan and told him, "This is not a job for David but for his son." God then made David a promise to build him an everlasting house because his heart was on the house of God.

David blessed the Lord for His promise. "I cannot build the temple," he said to himself, "but I can certainly prepare." David knew he would not live to enjoy the tabernacle that was to be built but he could certainly prepare. He wanted to see the tabernacle of the Lord established among His people. He had pictures in his mind of the glory of the Lord filling the temple just like the tabernacle in the wilderness.

He could see his nation coming to the tabernacle to entreat the mercies, favor and forgiveness of God. This was worth to him everything he had and everything he could muster. He understood the importance of the tabernacle of God to Israel. *Above everything he had achieved as king, building a bridge to God for his people must be considered one of his greatest achievements.* It did not matter that it would be accomplished by his son. *He would set his wealth aside to ensure that the tabernacle got the priority it deserved. He would not leave it to the probation of his estate, he would build a trust for the tabernacle of God in his lifetime.*

He gathered the foreigners in Israel together and put them to work to cut the hewn stones to be used. He prepared iron in abundance and bronze beyond measure. He prepared cedars in abundance and had them imported. David said, "My son Solomon is young and the house he must build shall be exceedingly magnificent. It must be famous in every country."

David prepared one hundred thousand talents of gold for the house of the Lord and one million talents of silver. He had skilled workmen in place and ready in every capacity desired. He commanded Solomon to set his heart and soul to seek the Lord and to arise and build.

David was not finished. He wanted to do everything he could while he was alive. The Lord had given him the plans for the temple and he was determined to do everything he could in his lifetime. He organized the Levites and the priest and assigned them duties and responsibilities.

David understood that when a person knows the importance of having God tabernacle with men, he will give gener-

ously and unrestrainedly to see it happen. David also understood that once God revealed His plans, a person with the heart of God, or with a heart for God, will do everything he can in his lifetime to see it established.

Solomon, also, was lavish in his giving and unrestrained in his efforts as he gave himself to building the temple of the Lord. He understood the importance of the temple to Israel. He supervised the building himself. He took pleasure to see this vision his father gave him progress to perfection.

He could not wait until it was finished. He wanted to dedicate it to God himself and to decree its designated purpose with his own mouth. Finally, the day arrived and Solomon poured out his heart regarding this tabernacle. *It was clear that Solomon had dedicated his time and so many resources to this magnificent temple because he understood its purpose and significance.*

His prayer of dedication is captured 2 Chronicles 6 as follows:

"HEAR our cry, O Lord! To our prayers attend!"
Solomon prayed concerning the house,
every action and the end.
"When we sin, then, Lord, forgive us,
If tears of grief should fill our eyes; If we pray unto
Your house, Lord, Then, Lord, please hear our cry."
1 Then Solomon said, "The Lord said
He will dwell in thick darkness!

2 CHRONICLES 6

2 I have built You an exalted house,
A place for You to dwell in forever."
3 And the king blessed the whole congregation of Israel...
10 "...And I have built the house for the
name of the Lord God of Israel.

11 "And I have put in it the ark which contains the
covenant of the Lord which He made with Israel."
12 Then Solomon stood before the Lord's altar, and
spread his hands out in the sight of all Israel,
13 (for Solomon had made a bronze scaffold; five cubits
wide, five cubits long, and three cubits high.
He set it in the middle of the court, stood on it and knelt down
before all Israel and stretched his hands towards heaven);
14 and he said, "O Lord God of Israel, there is
no God like You in heaven or on earth,
who keeps covenant and mercy with Your servants
who walk with You with all their hearts.
15 "You kept with Your servant David all that
You promised him;
You have spoken with Your mouth,
and fulfilled it with Your hand as it is this day.
17 "...Now, O Lord God of Israel, let Your words
be verified which You have spoken to David my
father; for You are a God who cannot lie.
18 "But will God truly dwell with men on the earth? Behold,
the heaven and the heaven of heavens cannot contain
You; how much less this wooden house I have built!
19 "Now, regard the prayer and supplications of your servant,
and listen to the prayer that I am praying before You:
20 "that Your eyes may be open toward this house day and night,
toward this place of which You said You would put Your name,
and You will regard the prayer which Your
servant prays towards this place.
21 "Lord, please hear the supplications of Your servant and of
Your people Israel, when they pray toward this place.
Hear from Your dwelling place in heaven,
and forgive when You hear.

22 "If a man sins against his neighbour and is made to take an
oath, and takes the oath before Your altar here in this house,
23 "then hear from heaven, and act, and judge your
servants, by repaying the wicked, and bringing his
way on his own head, and justifying the righteous,
by giving him according to his righteousness.
24 "Or if Your people Israel be put to the worst before
their enemies because they sin against You, and
they return and confess Your name, and pray and
make supplication before You in this house,
25 "then hear from heaven and forgive the sin of
Your people Israel, and bring them again to the
land You gave to them and to their fathers.
26 "Hear our cry in times of drought, when
because of their sin there is no rain.
If they pray towards this place,
and they confess Your name,
and because You have afflicted them
from their sins they turn away,
27 "then from Your place in heaven hear, and
the sin of Your servants forgive,
that You may teach them the good way in which they
should walk and by which they should live;
and send rain on Your land which You
have given our people to inherit.
And when You have taught us the good way,
28 "hear their cries in time of famine, pestilence,
blight and mildew, locust and of caterpillars, when
their enemies besiege them in their cities in the
land; whatever plague, whatever sickness,
29 "any prayer or supplication anyone should make, or
all of Your people, when each knows his own sorrow and
his own grief and lifts his hands to this house, Lord:

30 "hear from heaven, Your dwelling place, and
forgive, and give to each according to their ways,
for You know their heart__
You alone know the hearts of the sons of men
31 "that they may fear You, to walk in Your ways, as long
as they live in this land which to our fathers You gave.
32 "And hear the cries of the strangers, those who
are not of your people Israel, but have come from
distant countries for Your great name's sake,
and for Your mighty hand and Your outstretched
arm, when in this house they come to pray,
33 "hear them from Your dwelling place in heaven, and
do according to what the stranger asks You for, so that
all the earth may know Your name and fear You, just as
Your people Israel, and that they may know that this
house that I have built is called by Your name,
34 "hear their prayer and supplication from
heaven and maintain their cause.
35 "When they sin against You,
(for there is no one who has not sinned),
and You get angry with them and deliver
them over to their enemy,
and they carry them away captives to a distant or near land,
36 "yet if they rethink in the land of their captivity,
and repent, and make supplication to You there,
saying, 'We have sinned, we have done
wrong and acted wickedly';
37 "and should they return to You with all their
heart and soul in the land of their captivity,
and pray towards this land which You gave to their
fathers, and towards the city You have chosen,
and the house I have built for Your name,
39 "then hear their prayer and supplications from

Your dwelling place in heaven, and forgive the sins
of Your people who have sinned against You,
and their cause maintain.
40 "Now, my God, let Your eyes be open, I pray, and let Your
ears be attentive to the prayer that I have made in this place.
41 "Now, therefore, arise, O Lord God, to Your resting place,
You and the ark of Your strength.
Let Your priests, O Lord God, be clothed with
salvation, And let Your saints rejoice in goodness.
42 "O Lord, do not turn away the face of Your Anointed;
remember the mercies of David Your servant."

@CWDSbible

Will God truly dwell with man on earth? This was the question of King Solomon. This question would be answered in the building of another tabernacle. This new tabernacle would be a tabernacle that hands could not build. It would be a tabernacle whose building would demand the greatest sacrifice of all. It would be a tabernacle that would demand the priority and resources of men with the hearts and vision of David and Solomon to make it glorious in the earth.

It would be a tabernacle that would contain and carry the glory of the Lord. It would demand wealth and sacrifice to reflect its true magnificence in the earth. Yet its magnificence would not be defined by the wealth assigned to its building. It would be a tabernacle of people and it would be called the church. Its true glory would be the building of lives. When you understand the value of the tabernacle, you give everything to establish the tabernacle.

God immediately responded to the prayer of Solomon and to the sacrifice of his father David. Fire fell from heaven and the glory of the Lord came down. It is what David foresaw.

This is captured in 2 Chronicles 7, excerpted from the CWDS Bible:

OH, the fire! Oh, the glory! God alone was doing this. But
His response to His people is conditioned with an, "if."

"I will hear My people, if they turn to Me and call; if they
defile the temple, the temple I will destroy." God needs
nobody to help Him; His name is "Awesomeness."
But His response to His people is conditioned with an "if."

2 CHRONICLES 7

1 Solomon had finished praying; and when he
was all done, a spark lighted in Heaven,
and fire came right down. It consumed the burnt
offering and the sacrifice; and the Lord's glory
filled the temple right before their eyes.
2 The priests could not enter the Lord's house,
because the glory had filled the place, they simply
stood in awe as the Lord had His glorious way.
3 When all the people of Israel saw the fire come down,
and the Lord's glory on the house, they bowed their faces
to the ground on the pavement, and lifted up their praise.
They worshipped and praised the Lord, saying,
"For He is good.
For He is good and His mercies endure forever!"
4 Then the king and all the people sacrificed before the Lord.
5 King Solomon offered in sacrifice twenty-two thousand
oxen, and one hundred and twenty thousand sheep.
So the king and all Israel dedicated the house of God.
There was no restraint in their sacrifices,
their attitude was generous.
They were sacrificing before to the Almighty,
whose name is "Glorious."

6 And the priests waited on their office,
and the Levites with musical instruments,
instruments David the king had made to praise the Lord, saying,
"Because His mercies endure forever,"
whenever David offered praise through their ministry.
The priests sounded the trumpets before them,
while all Israel stood.
They had an altar for burnt offering,
but the altar could not hold,
7 and Solomon sanctified the middle of the court
that was before the house of the Lord;
and there he offered burnt offerings,
and the fat of the peace offering, for the bronze altar
which Solomon had made was not able to receive the
burnt offering, the grain offering, and the fat.
8 At the same time Solomon kept the feast seven days,
together with all Israel, it was a very great congregation,
from the entrance of Hamath to where the River of Egypt ran.
9 On the eighth day they made a solemn assembly,
for they dedicated the altar for seven days,
and kept the feast for seven days.
10 And on the twenty-third day of the seventh
month, he sent the people to their tents,
happy and joyful at heart for the goodness of the Lord
to David, to Solomon and to His people Israel.
11 So Solomon finished the house of the Lord and the
king's house; and Solomon successfully completed
all that he conceived in his heart to make in the
house of the Lord and in his own house.
12 Then the Lord said to Solomon as
He appeared to him by night:
"I have heard your prayer, and have chosen this
place for Myself as a house of sacrifice.

13 "When I shut up heaven and there is no rain, or
if I command the locusts to devour the land, or send
pestilence among my people. Then know this,
when My people cry, I will respond;
should they understand My "ifs."
14 "If My people who are called by My name
will humble themselves and pray,
and if they seek My face, and if they turn from their
wicked ways, then I will hear from heaven, and
I will forgive their sin and heal their land.
15 "Now My eyes will be open and now I listen
attentively to every prayer that is made in this place.
16 "For now I have chosen and sanctified this house,
that My name may be there forever; and My eyes
and My heart will be there perpetually.
17 "But as for you, if- yes if - you will walk
before Me as your father David walked,
and do all that I have commanded you, and if you
keep all My statutes and My judgments,
18 "then I will establish the throne of your kingdom, as
with David your father I gave my covenant, saying,
'You shall not fail to have a man to be ruler in Israel.'
19 "But if you turn away and forsake My statutes and
commandments which I have set before you, and go
to serve and worship other gods__ if you turn away
and reject the 'ifs' that I have spoken, in that day you
shall know, when My 'if's' turn to 'then,'__
20 "for then I will root them up from My land which I
have given them, and this house which I have sanctified
for My name, I will cast out of My sight, and then I will
make it a proverb and a byword among all nations.
21 "And as then for this house which is high and lovely, shall be
an astonishment to everyone who passes by, and they shall say,

'Why has the Lord done this to this land and to this house?'
22 "Then they shall answer,
'Because they have forsaken the Lord God of their fathers,
who brought them out of the land of Egypt, and have
taken hold of other gods, and worshipped and served them;
therefore He has brought all this disaster on them.'"
You worshipped before God's fire, but you must remember this;
all the glory you have experienced is conditioned with an if.

@CWDSbible

---

*1. Tabernacles have always been built by generous giving
and willing sacrifices; this is no different for the church__a
building of people that continues to be built.*

*2. The glory of God first shone from a portable ark, then in
a temple built by Solomon on a mountain in Israel; now the
promise is that it will cover the earth in human tabernacles.*

3. Every person is a potential tabernacle; every gift extends the glory!

THE CHURCH

The two men talked with each other as they walked on the path beside the river bank. A solitary fisherman was sitting idly in a boat in the water. He was somewhat frustrated because he had taken time out from his busy schedule to fish but the fishes were not even biting. He was having a very bad day.

The two men smiled at him in a passing greeting and waved their hands and he managed a smile. "This is the true tabernacle," one man said to the other as the soft rays of the sun massaged their bodies. There was a mild wind blowing.

"God was not really interested in living in a box or in a build-ing. His plan is to live in the spirits of man."

"This is so true," the second person added. "This is not a new plan. It was what was obtained until that tabernacle was destroyed by sin."

"This is why it is a redemption plan," the first person interjected. The first per-son continued, "Jesus said 'I will build My church.' **We are truly His tabernacle, a building not made with hands.**"

They both fell silent for a short while as they walked. They did not notice the beautiful pair of doves calling to them from the tree top to the left. They had this discussion previously and the conclusion was the same: Israel was willing to sacrifice so much to build the ark because they understood the importance of having God tabernacle among them.

David and Solomon and all the people were willing to sacrifice so much to build the temple because they understood the

194

importance of having God tabernacle among them. What, then, should our own sacrifices be? ***Should men not be prepared to make even greater sacrifices to build the church, to build lives, since this is the ultimate plan of God?*** These two men were very wealthy Christians and leaders in their local churches.

"God has promised that His glory will cover the earth as the waters cover the sea," the first person said. "We carry His glory in our bodies. The Holy Spirit lives in men. Taking His redemption plan to the ends of the earth covers the earth with His glory. His glory is not just for a fixed tabernacle in some special location; it is designated for people all over the earth to possess. We know the plans of God for His tabernacle. Jesus laid the foundations but we must build."

The second person was silent, drinking it all in with the glow of the fading sunlight. ***"If these men of old were willing to sacrifice so much for what was never the true tabernacle..."*** he thought aloud. The other person knew what he meant. ***The church, the true tabernacle of God, the only one that will remain forever, demanded greater dedication and sacrifice.*** Man must see the plans of God, buy into the plans of God, and release God's resources to the plans of God. The resources we are charged to occupy until He comes and demands its allocation.

Man must be willing to sacrifice everything for His tabernacle. ***We must be willing to sacrifice everything to build people; to build lives.*** To build the Lord a glorious tabernacle called the church. Every person on earth is tabernacle potential. Our wealth can help to release that potential to its true purpose.

"Men committed to God must set their hearts and minds into building what is the only and true tabernacle, the lives of people," he muttered. The first person could not hide his excitement, "The church is the bride of Christ. If Jesus was willing to sacrifice so much for us, should we not sacrifice to prepare His bride?"

"We can use our wealth to give Jesus a wedding present,"

the second person laughed. "We know exactly what He wants, He already set the foundation."

They were silent as they placed it into the context of their own wealth. The first one managed a smile of relief as he came to the realization. *"I have nothing, but yet I have everything,"* he whispered. *"It is all God's but it is all mine. It is all God's because it is all mine. No one can block these resources from creating an impact. It is all mine because it is all God's."*

> *HAS THE OLD SAYING COME BACK TO HAUNT US: "BEAUTY IS IN THE EYE OF THE BEHOLDER"? HOW MUCH DO WE VALUE THE TABERNACLE OF GOD AMONG US? HOW MUCH ARE WE PREPARED TO SACRIFICE?*
>
> *THE ISRAELITES ANSWERED AND WERE RESTRAINED; DAVID AN-SWERED AND WAS RESTRICTED; SOLOMON ANSWERED AND WAS GLORIFIED; HOW DO YOU ANSWER?*

THE DUTY OF TABERNACLE CARE

The first person who had spoken in the conversation of the two travelers said in exclamation, "God help us!" He had broken a silence that had lasted about ten minutes. The second person was startled out of his own thoughts. "God help us!" the first person repeated. "Caring for God's tabernacle is not just a good decision, it is a command. We are compelled to care."

He then pulled a script from his back pack and began to quote from the book of Haggai. "The Lord said through Haggai, 'The people are saying, "It is not yet time for the Lord's house to be built."' But the Lord says, 'Is it time for you yourselves to dwell in your paneled houses, and this temple to lie in ruins?' Then the Lord said to them, 'Consider your ways!'"

"Bad things happen when we do not respond to the compulsion to sacrifice for God's tabernacle. These are some of the indicators that men oftentimes ignore: We sow a lot but it only yields a little. We make a lot of investments in business but we keep losing. We eat, but do not have enough. Our income is insufficient, we cannot make ends meet. An accumulation of loans and bills. We drink and we are never satisfied. Our clothes cannot keep us warm. Our salary is as if we put it in a bag full of holes.

God says *He is the one who blows it away. When all we do is care about ourselves, God blows away our resources so it does not satisfy.* These are the words of God: 'You looked for much, but it came to little; and when you brought it home, I blew it away. Why? Because of My house that is ignored, while every one of you runs to his own house.' Is this not applicable to His church, human tabernacles? Imagine, God also said, 'Therefore the heavens above you withhold the dew, and the earth withholds its fruit. For I called for a drought on the land and the mountains, on the grain and the new wine and the oil, on whatever the ground produces, on men and livestock, and on all the labor of your hands.' This one hits home hard, 'All the labor of your hands.'"

After quoting this, the first person lifted up a prayer for himself, "God help me if I neglect my duty of care for Your tabernacle, the church. I give myself, my time, my energy, my resources to building people, building the true tabernacle to carry Your glory. I give myself to identifying raw materials, every human being, and to release Your resources that I occupy to build them into glorious houses for You."

> *WHEN JONAH FLED FROM GOD A NORMAL BOAT RIDE BECAME TUMULTUOUS; THE SAILORS WERE FIGHTING A LOSING BATTLE AGAINST SHIP-BREAKING WIND BECAUSE SOMETHING THAT BELONGED TO GOD WAS IN THE BOAT. THIS IS WHAT LITERALLY HAPPENS WITH OUR FINANCES WHEN WE ARE NOT GENEROUS TOWARDS GOD WHO OWNS OUR CARGO AND OUR BOATS.*

CHAPTER

8

THE PRINCIPLE OF THE TITHE

braham was returning from battle. This lion-hearted man had armed his servants and had gone to battle against a confederate of kings. The leader of this Confederate, Chedorlaomer, had ruled many nations for over a decade. Among them were Sodom and Gomorrah. With him was Tidal who was known as the king of nations.

Abraham knew of the exploits of these kings. They had recently fought against the Rephaim, the Zuzim, the Emim, the Horites, the Amalekites and the Amorites and destroyed them all.

Sodom and Gomorrah had joined forces with the kings of Admah, the king of Zeboiim and the king of Zoar. They went out against these kings and were destroyed. The invading kings were interested in conquest and in wealth. They took all the wealth and provision that they found in the lands they conquered and all the people. They did similarly to Sodom. They also took Lot, the nephew of Abraham.

When Abraham heard that his nephew was taken captive, he armed his servants and went after the mighty kings to rescue his nephew. He had just a handful of men. They were less than a speck in comparison to the number of men they were pursuing. But Abraham had a secret. He knew that a little with God was bigger than all the earth without Him. His faith was justified. He defeated this mighty army. The sounds of celebration mixed with laughter could be heard amidst the boasting of exploits. Everyone had stories to tell and they were real. It was that kind of battle that made everyone a hero.

Abraham was carrying wealth beyond measure. It was the wealth of the many nations Chedorlaomer had conquered. Added to all this was the wealth these kings had brought into battle and of the men these kings had with them. Much of this wealth was in the forms of gods. These men had lavished their treasures on idols as they sought to create objects they could worship. For many, it was more than the gods, they got to worship their treasures, literally.

Abraham's most difficult task was to be able to carry home all of these treasures. As he slowly and laboriously made his way back with them, Melchizedek the high priest of God met him. Melchizedek was seen as a heavenly being, representing Jesus Christ. He had the reputation of not having father or mother. The Apostle Paul said much later in the seventh chapter of Hebrews that he had no genealogy, no relatives. He was also reputed to have no beginning of days or end of life.

In summary, Paul said he was much like the Son of God and remains a priest forever. Melchizedek blessed Abraham and his God who had given him the victory. Abraham then gave to Melchizedek tithes of all he had recovered from battle.

Abraham saw the king of Sodom coming to meet him. The king had escaped and had hidden in a solitary place contemplating the disaster that had happened to him. He was there when he heard about Abraham's victory. It was a delighted and relieved man that came to meet Abraham that day. He had a wonderful proposal for Abraham. No man could refuse this. He was once again taking control. The king of Sodom showed his respect for Abraham in greeting him. He then said to Abraham, "You take the goods, all the wealth, everything; just give me back the people."

Abraham responded to him with one of the most powerful and profound responses to money ever. Abraham looked at the king of Sodom and said, "I have raised my hand to the Lord, God

Most High, the Possessor of Heaven and earth, that I will not take anything, however small, from a thread to the strap of a sandal. I will take nothing that belongs to you lest you go boasting, 'I have made Abraham rich.'

I will only take what the young men have eaten, and what belongs to the men who went with me, Aner, Eshcol, and Mamre. Let them have what belongs to them." *Abraham was a man of strong ethics and he did not want his wealth associated with a corrupt and immoral nation like Sodom.* He trusted in the blessings more than the wealth to which he had access in the moment. He knew it was better to be blessed than to be rich. *He knew the blessings make one rich.* He knew the blessing was the greatest wealth possible. This was a faith position but he was a man of faith.

Abraham also made a very stunning revelation by his omission in his statement to the king of Sodom. He made absolutely no mention of the tithe he had paid to Melchizedek. From this omission and Abraham's assertion, it was clear that the tithe paid was never a part of the wealth of Sodom. It was taken but it was not reckoned. It was only handed to its true owner. *Abraham did not need to give account for the tithe.* Abraham would be wrong if he did accounting with the tithe. It was also clear that the king of Sodom had no jurisdiction over, or rights to, the tithe.

The tithe belonged to God and should not be included in any accounting, computing, or budgeting. Paying tithes is an obligation and is simply an act of giving to God what rightfully belongs to Him- one tenth of every spoil taken in battle, business or labor. We also know that the tithe Abraham paid is ten percent of everything he recovered. It was the Apostle Paul who would later write in the seventh chapter of Hebrews that Abraham paid to Melchizedek one tenth of all he recovered. The tithe is one tenth of all income taken in employment or business or received in any other way. It is taken out before any accounting, therefore, it is calculated from gross earnings. Man has no jurisdiction or control over the tithes, he should simply release it.

The tithe is consecrated once it is earned. It becomes holy to the Lord. Moses emphasized this in the twenty-seventh chapter of Leviticus. He said to Israel, "All the tithe of the land, whether of crop or fruit, is the Lord's. It is holy to the Lord. And concerning the tithe of the herd or the flock, of whatever passes under the rod, the tenth one shall be holy to the Lord." The principle of holiness and consecration is a very powerful one in the kingdom of God. It is worthy of separate examination.

The principle of tithe transcends time. The appearance of Melchizedek is very significant. He was not of the priesthood of Levi since he collected tithe even before Levi was born. He has no beginning of days or end of days and his priesthood is said to continue. Melchezidek is a heavenly being, a type of Christ. The priesthood that received tithe from Abraham is eternal. This priesthood is associated with the blessings of Abraham which were received by Jesus Christ. This priesthood was a reflection of the priesthood of Jesus Christ.

The principle of tithing would play an important role in the functioning and financing of the Kingdom of God among men and in the propagation of the redemption plan. ***The body of Christ would pay and receive tithes to fulfill the mission of the everlasting priesthood.***

Nehemiah sat there in disbelief. The house of God was forsaken. The Levites who performed their duties in the temple had returned to work in their fields. The offerings for the people could not be offered up and the temple ceremonies were abandoned.

The Levites were hungry, they had to go. They were performing the services in the temple of God but the people were not paying their tithes. They did not value the command of God and they did not value the services of the temple. The Levites and the singers had no option, they were starving.

Nehemiah was grieved in his spirit. He called the leaders together and reprimanded them. "Why have you forsaken the house of God?" he said. They had no answer. Nehemiah's urgency impelled them to repentance and to immediate action.

After this, all Judah brought the tithe of the grain and the new wine and the oil to the storehouse of the Lord. Nehemiah then appointed faithful men of the priests and Levites as treasurers over the storehouse, who would distribute food to their brethren.

The ministers of God returned to the service of the Lord and the work of the house of the Lord resumed. The cry of Nehemiah would continue to echo throughout the centuries to the many who would continue to place money above God's command to tithe. The cry is, "Why is the work of God forsaken?"

---

1. What is tithe doing in your budget?

2. IF YOUR NEIGHBOR GIVES YOU SOME MONEY FOR SAFEKEEPING AND YOU SAY, "I MUST BUDGET AND MAKE SURE THAT I HAVE IT WHEN SHE COMES." YOU ARE A THIEF! YOU CANNOT MAKE PLANS FOR WHAT DOES NOT BELONG TO YOU OR EVEN BORROW FROM IT TEMPORARILY WITHOUT PERMISSION! THIS IS THE CHARACTER OF YOUR TITHES!

KINGDOM TAXES

"We will not hide it from you my lord, we have nothing left but our bodies and our land. Buy us and our lands and we will be your servants." All the people came to Joseph and said this. Joseph listened to the people. He had previously taken all their money and their livestock in exchange for food. Now he would buy their lands and essentially also buy them.

"I will buy your lands," Joseph said. Joseph gave them food and grain to sow the land. "You shall pay twenty percent of your increase to the kingdom of Egypt," he said. This was the beginning of what would eventually be called taxes. This principle would be practiced in nearly every kingdom and nation on earth. The principle is that the nation owns its citizens and its land. The people pay taxes for the administration of the affairs of the nation.

This principle was started first in Heaven and is the principle of tithing. Melchizedek reported on behalf of his kingdom to collect the taxes from Abraham. Unlike the kingdom of men, the tithe of the kingdom of God has been constant throughout time, ten percent. ***Kingdom tax is an essential part of the redemption plan of God for the administration of kingdom infrastructure on earth.***

A CAR IS RUN ON GAS OR ELECTRICITY, NATIONS AND KINGDOMS ARE RUN ON TAXES, THE KINGDOM OF GOD IN THE EARTH IS RUN ON TITHES AND LIFE IS RUN ON PRINCIPLES.

ROBBERY IN PROGRESS

"**S**top thief!" the man screamed as he shouted in the direction of a man running away at a very fast pace. A few young men who were chatting by the roadside picked up what was happening and joined the race to catch the thief. They hoped to help bring the thief to justice and recover the stolen property.

Just then a blind man sitting by the road heard the foot-steps coming in his direction. He heard the angry cries, "Thief, thief."

He realized that one man was leading the pack and figured out it must be the thief. He listened carefully and timed the foot-steps. He had excellent hearing. As soon as the footsteps were close enough he put out his walking stick as if trying to adjust himself and the thief fell heavily to the pavement.

Everyone chasing him caught up with the man. They pulled him up. He rose, cursing his poor luck. They took the wallet he had stolen from his pocket and returned it. They then handed him over to the police. *Protocol observed, profile picture; charge pick-pocketing.*

She had a great time shopping. She was in the store for about forty-five minutes. She had put on an abnormal amount of weight during this time. She went to the cashier to check out the one item she was prepared to buy. Everything was going well and she felt vindicated. "They are stealing from us anyway," she said to herself to justify her actions. As she passed through the security scanner at the door it went off and the security guards descended upon her.

They searched her and found a number of items hidden on her person. The manager, wanting to send a strong signal, handed her over to the police. *Protocol observed, profile picture; charge shoplifting.*

He was the manager of a securities company. He had various strong connections with key persons in large companies. He had the privilege of getting the financial data on these companies long before they were made public.

He would trade this information in advance on the stock exchange and would make millions of dollars. The federal government finally caught up with him. *Protocol observed, profile picture: white collar crime, insider dealing, fraud.*

He was a popular movie star who starred in many action movies. He decided he would join a movement against paying taxes. He did not pay taxes on some of his income. He was arrested, charged and sentenced to spending time in prison. *Protocol observed, profile picture; tax evasion.*

He sat in his car opposite the market and drank an energy drink. His blood charged with excitement. He reached down and slowly caressed the shotgun he had on the floor below him. He could see Dexter entering the bank a short distance up the road. He had his hat held low over his eyes. Things were going according to plan and he was very pleased.

This was becoming routine for him. He had done this many times and to great effect. He enjoyed the notoriety that his escapades brought him. He also enjoyed creating the news, and he loved money. For him it was all about three P's: power, popularity and pleasure.

His phone rang twice and went dead. That was the signal. He was driving the getaway car and had two minutes to be in place. He saw a customer run from the bank then fall dead in the middle of the street. He then heard another three bangs. Something had gone wrong. His men were instructed not to shoot unless in an absolute emergency. They had murdered two persons by the way but it was necessary. He pressed on the gas to move off and then he saw them. Police were everywhere. They flooded the place so quickly as if they had been tipped off. He placed his car in reverse to turn around but something was blocking him. It was a police car. He looked around and saw the guns pointed at him. He had no option. He placed his hands in the air and surrendered. *Protocol observed, profile picture; aggravated bank robbery, murder.*

He borrowed and did not repay. He was taken to court and eventually sentenced. *Protocol observed, profile picture; thief.*

He slipped into the house through the open window. He had been looking for an opportunity to enter his best friend's house for a long time now. They had come home from college and would be back soon. There was some jewelry belonging to his friend's mother that he had to have. He had already found a market for it. Today he had tricked his friend to leave his window open. Now everything would be easy. The hardest part would be looking into Mrs. Simons' face after the theft. She loved him and really cared for him. She had been very generous to him and had done him nothing but good. He closed his eyes as if to shut out this memory. He took the jewelry and escaped without an incident. No one noticed.

He was at the home to greet them when they returned. He heard Mrs. Simons scream when she discovered her loss. He was there to offer sympathy and to grieve with the family. He saw her tears and wished he could undo what he had done, but he had his own expenses to meet first. This would have to be his priority. He knew she could afford it. He was happy he would be off to college in a few days.

His heart fell when he heard Mrs. Simons say, "It is such a good thing I installed the cameras last month. Now we will be able to tell who this dirty good for nothing thief is." He asked to be excused. He could not remember the reason he gave. His mind was a forest of confusion. He left before they could respond.

He hurried home to pack. All the time he was thinking of the best place he could lie low for a while. He needed somewhere that was reclusive. Some place where he could not be reached until the anger had died down. He never made it. He was picked up by the police before he arrived home. Mrs. Simons had no mercy on him. She hated the pretense. Protocol observed, profile picture; burglary. *For Mrs. Simons it was not just burglary but the betrayal. It was the theft and treachery of a son.*

Will a man rob God? There are many categories of theft at different levels, but these are all theft from fellow human beings. Nothing can be considered more despicable, or viler, than stealing from God. God is so loving, so tender-hearted and kind, and so thoughtful. Again, no theft can be considered more stupid than stealing from God. It is like an unarmed person stealing ammunition by force from an army, under the watchful eyes of the soldiers. God is so powerful and He sees everything. It is like stealing your own university savings from your parents. God holds your future in His hands and all your promises and hope are in Him.

But really can a man rob God? Is that really possible? For a man to rob God, they must steal something that belongs to God. How would you plan a robbery against God? "Hands in the air God, I have a gun. Give me everything you have!" God would probably respond, "If you have faith you can receive it, but can you contain it?!"

We have been poking fun at this topic but God wants to have a say. It appears this is not a joke for God. The man He has created, whom He died for, who lives and moves in Him, is actually stealing from Him. They have very good excuses as all the other thieves above probably do but with the same effect. They have brought the definition of theft and robbery to a new level, or rather, to a new low. *Protocol observed, profile picture… is it yours?*

The question is on the table. The proponent is no other than God Himself. He was sitting on His throne in His supreme awesomeness. The angels and the elders bowed down before this magnificent throne. It was a throne of power, the seat of authority. They were worshipping the Person sitting on the throne. They do this continuously. They sing of His glory and speak of His power and His holiness. They know that He has all power in His hands. They know that the highest mountain on earth could not withstand His power. Just a slight shift of His hand and it goes tumbling. Such was His awesome power! They know that just a twitch of His finger and the seas stand at attention or flee away.

They know that in comparison man is just another of His creation; that man is sustained by His breath. He withdraws it and they are dead. They are just as the angels and yet a little lower. They die. They know that the thoughts of God are higher than the thoughts of man and His ways more excellent than the ways of man. The vastness of the difference is as high as the heavens are above the earth.

The full ludicrousness of the thought expressed by this divine being was not lost to them as they worshipped. He had said, "Will a man rob God?" They could not imagine the comparison so they dismissed the thought, saying, "Holy, holy, holy." They refused to focus on anyone but this being alone. It would not be worth it. This question would pierce eternity and descend into time and echo throughout the ages. "Will a man rob God?" Author God.

God was not finished. His next words were the words of a judge stated with such precision, knowledge, and finality. It carried no question of error or inaccuracy. It indicted a nation, it indicted a people, it indicted His people, the people of God. He said, "You have robbed me!"

He then considered their defense as they pretended ignorance. Everyone was asking, "In what way have we robbed You?!" It is clear that some never considered God to be the owner of everything. It is clear that some have not considered His word to be the final authority regarding the tithes, kingdom taxes. It is clear some were living in denial. It was very clear however that God was not taking excuses. It was also clear that ignorance of the law was no defense. God made the accusation plain. He said, "You have robbed me in the tithes and the offerings!"

God accepted no more arguments after this. He pronounced the judgment. God said. "You are cursed with a curse for you have robbed Me." Who is it that is under this judgment of the curse pronounced by God?

Well, He said it Himself, "This entire nation." He was talking about the people of God, kingdom citizens. Protocol observed, profile picture or rather mug shot…is it yours?

The walls of Jericho had fallen. It was a demonstration of the divine power of the God of Israel. The Israelites went in to conquer an already defeated Jericho. One middle aged soldier named Achan, heard commander Joshua charging the people. Joshua had said, "All the silver and gold, and vessels of bronze and iron are consecrated to the Lord. They shall come into the treasury of the Lord." They were to destroy everything else, living and non-living, they were cursed. Joshua had commanded them not to take anything off them or they too would be cursed.

As Achan went throughout the households he stumbled upon a wedge of gold and a cache of silver. He looked around but no one was watching; he was alone. Achan understood the command of Joshua well, but… no one was watching. This treasure was irresistible. It would build a great future for him and his family in this new land and… no one was watching. He understood the gold and silver are consecrated, holy to the Lord, but… no one was watching. ***He knew it was blessed for God's treasury, but cursed if he held on to it, but…no one was watching!***

In every respect God gave the same command about the gold of Jericho as He gives for the tithe, but…no one was seeing! ***The tithe carries the same curse for anyone who holds on to it, but blessings if surrendered to the house of the Lord.*** The gold, silver and bronze of Jericho were only blessed in the treasury of the Lord, just as the tithes, but people take solace that no one is seeing. ***There is a general tendency to ignore the all-seeing eyes of God.*** There is also a tendency to be presumptuous regarding God. A battle not long after and Israel lost against a seemingly weak opposition. Something cursed was in the camp and Joshua had to sniff it out.

The curse did not need an administrator, it carried its own sensitivity brain. It had brought a curse and defeat to an entire nation that was pressing forward to possess a promise. Because one man held on to the holy thing that was blessed for the house of God, one hundred percent of a nation with the command of God was cursed. Joshua had to act swiftly. With the precision of Heaven who possesses all knowledge, and who keeps full account, Achan was pointed out. His account was opened before all Israel. Achan, his entire household, his livestock and animals, and all he had with the gold and silver he had stolen from God were covered in a heap of stones. Israel had stoned them and covered them up after burning them with fire. That same battle a few days later resulted in a resounding victory for Israel.

By His prophet Malachi, God made it clear. His tithes are consecrated to Him. If we withhold the tithes, we have robbed Him. The blessed tithe is now cursed and the persons who withhold it are under the curse.

We do not have to remain there, however. The Judge being just and merciful, opened a door of escape. God continued, saying, "Bring all the tithes into the storehouse, that there will be provision in My house."

This is a welcome reprieve, but it is still a test for those who love money. Are we willing to let go of God's property to escape His curse, or do we elevate the added security of the tangible above the fear of God? God recognized that the issues of everyday life are real. Some people would have real challenges meeting their obligation. God understood that for many persons, the tithes and the offering would require real sacrifices. He recognized that the world had genuine needs. *For many people, tithing would require real sacrifices. Even with this knowledge, God did not give people an excuse from paying tithes.* He did not relent on His law of tithing, even in the midst of real need, He did not remove the punishment of the curse for disobedience. God instead laced His command to tithe and to give with a very enticing promise for obedience.

It was a promise, not just to supply the needs, but a promise of abundance. God said, "Try Me now and see if I will not open for you the windows of heaven and pour out for you such blessing that there will not be room enough to receive it." For many, this promise would have been enough, but not for God. He recognizes that many people will be blessed with abundance, but are unable to retain it. Some will have their wealth stolen from them. Some will lose it because of waste. God completed His promise with wisdom to manage, blessings for perpetuity, and divine protection of the wealth.

God said, "And I will rebuke the devourer for your sake, so that he will not destroy the fruit of your ground, nor shall the vine fail to bear fruit for you in the field."

Man in no circumstances is excused from giving or paying tithes. However, just as in every other relationship of man with God, giving would require faith.

Anything received by grace must be appropriated through faith. It is by faith that it may be by grace. This means that even though God has given it freely, anything we receive from God, including salvation, must be received by faith.

Without faith, it is impossible to please God. To interact with God we have to understand who God is. When we give we must constantly remind ourselves that He is…God. We must be assured of His ability, His power, His love, His wealth and His omnipotence. If we have confidence that He is, then we will have no problem in accepting that He will reward. He will certainly keep His promises. With that confidence, we will give with the assurance that our obedience and generosity have brought us to the place of outpouring. Even before seeing it tangibly, we will accept God's divine outpouring in such measure that our rooms can never be enough to contain. We will begin to embrace His blessings to the extent that we cannot build enough rooms to catch up with God.

The question is, however, how many persons can see God in this manner? How many persons in the kingdom of God have the faith to engage the King in His fullness? This is why God said, "Try Me in this; bring everything to Me, all the tithes and all the offering, and try Me!"

By His challenge, God is saying, ***"My word is trying you, testing you, to see if you have the character to manage My abundance. By your obedience you get to try Me, to test Me, to see if I have the character to fulfill My word."***

It is after this that God said something that put it all into perspective. God said, "And all nations will call you blessed, for you will be a delightful land." This phrase sounds very familiar, and that is because it is.

Our giving and God's abundance is all about the blessing of Abraham. "In you, all nations, families, of the earth will be blessed." This blessing is very consistent with everything the Lord has done and said throughout the Scriptures.

It is very consistent with the heart of God and with the redemption plan that was drafted and executed before creation. If we can understand this then it is easy to believe for the abundance. Our God has not changed nor has shown any shadow of turning for new situations. The command to give is consistent with His original design. The blessing that comes with it is the same that was introduced through Abraham. The purpose remains, to bless all nations of the earth.

God is seeking riverheads into which He can pour. He wants to bless us if He can pass the blessing through us. The attitude of our hearts to the tithes and offering is the faith test that determines approval for God's lavish outpouring of His blessings. It is the same faith that Abraham fathered.

> *1. IT IS BEST TO HAVE 90% BLESSED THAN TO HAVE 100% CURSED. (author unknown)*
>
> *2. EVERY KINGDOM HAS ITS PENALTIES FOR STEALING, USUALLY JAIL TIME, THE KINGDOM OF GOD IMPOSES A CURSE.*
>
> *3. TITHING IN DIFFICULT SITUATIONS WILL REQUIRE FAITH; SHOULD GOD EXCUSE US FROM FAITH?*

THE CHARACTER OF TITHES

The tithe has its own character. It is holy and cannot be exchanged. When God consecrates anything as holy, He gives specifc instructions concerning it. There is normally severe penalty, usually death, if those instructions are violated.

"Must be carried by the consecrated priests upon their shoulders. Must be carried by consecrated priests upon their shoulders." David kept repeating to himself. He did not want to get it wrong this time. His heart still grieved for his servant Uzza. "If I had only taken the necessary precautions," David scolded himself. "Uzza is a good soldier but not a Levite. I sentenced him to death by entrusting him to carry the Holy Ark on a cart. He had all good intentions when he put his hand out to steady the Ark. Good intention is not good enough when it comes to holy things, just obey." David thought about the tithes and all the other things God had consecrated holy. He reminded himself not to touch the Lord's portion.

David reflected on the time the men of Beth Shemesh opened the ark to gaze inside and fifty thousand and seventy of them were struck dead. They were presumptuous. They perhaps thought that because the Ark was captured by the Philistines it had lost its holiness. They were curious to see what was inside. The most important thing present was the Presence and their hearts could not see this Presence. If they could see the Presence that made the Ark holy they would have stayed away. They would have observed the instructions strictly.

"If men could only see the Presence that is upon the tithe they will stay away and fearfully follow the instructions of God," he thought somberly. "The Presence that consecrates the Ark and makes it holy, is the Presence that makes the Ark a blessing. Amazingly, it is the same Presence that brings the curse if the Holy Ark is violated." Then David drew a profound parallel, ***"The Presence that consecrates the tithes and makes it holy, is the Presence that makes the tithe a blessing. Amazingly, it is the same Presence that brings the curse if the holy tithe is violated."***

David remembered in that moment, the passage from the Torah that was read in the temple last Sabbath. It was a passage that had stuck with him all week. He had meditated on it and made his own personal commitments to God.

The passage read: "All the tithe of the land, whether of the seed of the land or of the fruit of the tree is the Lord's. It is holy to the Lord. If a man wants at all to redeem any of his tithes, he shall add one-fifth to it. And concerning the tithe of the herd or the flock, of whatever passes under the rod, the tenth one shall be holy to the Lord. He shall not inquire whether it is good or bad, nor shall he exchange it; and if he exchanges it at all, then both it and the one exchanged for it shall be holy; it shall not be redeemed."

David came back to his recital. This was important for him to remember. "Must be carried by consecrated priests upon their shoulders," David said again. He would be taking the blessed Ark to himself at Jerusalem. He wanted the blessings for his kingdom. This time he would be very careful to follow all the instructions God had given for the transportation of the Holy Ark. This time there would be no omission or presumption.

1. To understand what holy means is to understand the fear of the Lord. When you approach or have in your possession anything that is holy you must find and follow God's instructions for it in minute details at the very first opportunity.

2. Your tithe is holy as soon as it is earned or accrued.

SHOULD MINISTRIES TITHE?

The bishop sat across from his board of directors and complained bitterly, "They tell me that I am supposed to tithe. Look at the amount of good this ministry is doing. Look at the number of lives we are touching daily. Ridiculous!"

His ministry had been hemorrhaging for many years and was suffering a serious financial crisis. The debt had piled up to the ceiling and the entire property that was given to that organization was at risk of being taken over by the government for unpaid statutory deduction; payroll taxes. The bishop would go home that night asking himself, "Where is my God in this crisis? Look at all the good we are doing!"

A young minister who was also the accountant on the board was awed by the expression of the bishop. How could someone so seasoned defy wisdom in this way? The institutions of government are not exempt from the salary related taxes of the government.

Later that day the young minister sought a counsel session with the bishop. He really wanted to counsel him on the matter but he diplomatically sought his advice. This bishop was happy to give his wise counsel to this young man. He gladly agreed to see him later that afternoon.

As they sat down, the young man began to discuss with the bishop some real issues of his ministry. The bishop was happy to offer wise counsel. He was on point in all the areas discussed and the young man thanked him. The young man then said to the bishop, "The book of Hebrews tells us that Levi paid tithes to Abraham. Levi was the ministers of their day, does it mean that ministers are expected to pay tithes?"

The bishop stalled in his response. It was obvious that this topic was very current on his mind. It was also very obvious that he had dismissed the prompting to give due consideration to tithing in the past. The young pastor took the short silence created by his pause to continue expressing his dilemma. "In the eighteenth chapter of the book of Numbers, God instructed Levi to pay tithes of everything they received. I have always wondered if we are excused from the obligation of tithing as ministers. They too were told they could profane the holy gifts and die. Is it that my ministry is excluded from the curse of not paying tithe but benefits from the associated blessings when I pay?"

"These are some serious issues my son," the bishop said in deep thought. It was apparent he was troubled.

The young minister continued, "I have always wondered about Abraham's tithe. Levi paid tithe to Abraham but it brings me back to the plain truth, Abraham tithed. When Abraham paid tithe he was not acting in the capacity of his own personal interest but as a ministry. He was in the ministry of deliverance and restoration. He was not handling his own money, in fact, he never claimed any of it. He used everything except for the tithe to minister. Should my ministry be excluded from tithing considering this example of Abraham?"

The bishop was silent. It was apparent he was convicted. He knew he could not advise this young minister not to pay tithes. While he could bear the weight of his own omission, he could not bear the weight of misleading this young man. His questions were deep and piercing, he could not ignore them. Was it possible that the finances of his great ministry were suffering the effects of the tithe curse?

"You must pay tithes," he said to the young man. "You must pay tithes!" He felt trapped and ashamed by his own declaration earlier that day. He excused himself then and went into his private study and cried before God. ***Tithing in this financial crisis of his ministry would take extreme faith, but he knew, without faith it is impossible to please God. He was no longer prepared to serve God, to represent God, and yet not to please God.*** "I would prefer to have ninety percent blessed than to have one hundred percent cursed," he said.

---

1. Qualification for leadership is servitude, leading by example. How can we receive tithe if we do not have the faith to pay tithes ourselves?

2. It is POSSIBLE TO BE A BLESSING AND STILL NOT BE BLESSED, TO HAVE SERIOUS FINANCIAL CONSTRAINTS. DO WE NEED TO CONSIDER OUR WAYS?

CHAPTER

9

THE PRINCIPLE OF OFFERING

He tried to stand up but he could not. He had a duty to minister but the presence of God in the temple was so awesome that his strength was totally sapped. The cloud of God had come down in the temple and it was overpowering. Solomon had earlier that day dedicated the temple and had offered a stunning sacrifice of twenty-two thousand bulls and one hundred and twenty thousand sheep.

What an offering! There were bulls and sheep as far as the eyes could see and beyond. It was almost endless. No one could imagine there was so much livestock in the entire kingdom. The king had them consecrate the courts of the Lord's house since the altar he built was to contain his offering. No wonder God had responded in such an amazing way. As he lay there soaking in the glory of his God, the priest could not control his tears. He let go of his responsibility and did something he would not normally do. He allowed himself to be ministered to by this holy Presence.

In his house that night, he could not let the moment go. He was still basking in the Presence until the wee hours of the morning. He was beside himself. For him, this was totally awesome.

He could recall the first time that temple mount, Mount Moriah, was used for making a sacrificial offering to God. It was the offering of Isaac by Abraham. His mind took him through the divine experience that Abraham had in that moment. He remembered the promise God reaffirmed to Abraham then.

"This temple mount has a solid history of offerings and divine encounters," he thought.

He remembered Jacob's promise to God as he experienced that vision of the ladder connecting Heaven to earth. Jacob saw angels ascending and descending from Heaven on the ladder and he saw God at the top of the ladder. He made the commitment to God then that he would pay Him one-tenth of everything he was blessed with if God covered his journey and gave him a safe return. "It all took place on this temple mount," he thought.

He recalled David's offering on this same spot of ground. David had just finished numbering the people of God. The angel of the Lord was destroying throughout Israel. The angel had stopped on the threshing floor of Ornan the Jebusite and King David was instructed to sacrifice there. This divine encounter was frightful. There was an urgency to save lives. David had bought back this holy spot from Ornan the Jebusite. An offering was commanded. This sacrifice was not just voluntary like Solomon's offering, it was compulsory. It was a sin offering. This sacrifice was redemptive.

The priest concluded that there was something about the offering that connected Heaven to earth, that connected man to God, that connected the natural to divine experiences, that connected the sinner to redemption, that connected the temple of God to God's redemptive plan.It had to do with Abraham and God's promise to him on this mount to bless all the nations of the earth through him. It had something to do with Jacob and his promise that connected this mount with tithing.

It has something to do with David and the offering he made to stop the curse of sin on this mount. It had something to do with the free and generous giving of Solomon on this mount in this temple. The priest was happy to be a part of this experience. None of the others experienced the presence of God as Solomon did. There must be something about his free and liberal giving. There must be something about this completed temple. Was this all about the temple all along? Did it have anything to do with the offering?

The priest drifted off to sleep just before daybreak, still wrestling with all these thoughts. It was not until centuries later that the Apostle Paul pieced the pieces together. The promise of Abraham was for Jesus Christ and for every believer by virtue of faith in Jesus Christ. Faith in Jesus Christ places us in His body, the church. The true temple is not just a building, even on a famous mountain, but is each believer and the corporate body of believers in Jesus. "Our bodies are the temples of Jesus," Paul said.

The sacrifice of Isaac by Abraham was a prototype of the sacrifice of Jesus by God. The promise to Abraham was really a promise to Jesus that He received through the completed sacrificial offering of Himself. The tithing commitment of Jacob was the template by which the church would operate.

David's sacrifice then, with death gripping the nation all over, highlights one key role of the temple: sacrifice and redemption. ***Man has a duty to give sacrificially in order to combat the curse caused by sin. Giving is wrapped up in the plan to reverse the sentence of death that is on every person.***

> *We are because somebody gave; we must see people by what they can be if we give!*

THE ATTITUDE OF THE OFFERING

"**B**reathe in, breathe out; breathe in, breathe out," the young student sat and watched the doctor of the law take what appeared to be breathing exercises. The doctor had become his mentor in spiritual things. The doctor was not aware he was in the room.

"Breathe in, breathe out..." he continued. Then he said, "Ooops!" becoming suddenly aware that he was being observed. He looked at the young student and laughed. *"Giving should be as natural as breathing,"* he said. The student knew that this was not just another breathing exercise, the doctor was analyzing some deep thoughts. He waited.

The doctor continued, "When you breathe, you give out carbon dioxide. If you refuse to give you die. It poisons you. The plant breathes in the carbon dioxide and returns to you oxygen. *When you give you are supplied with life in return by a process of nature set in motion by God.* God has made giving a way of life. You give, you live, you refuse to give, you die. Giving should be as natural as breathing!" The student paused for a moment suddenly caught up in the glorious world of the doctor. It was a world where physical laws synchronized with spiritual realities.

"Have the principles of the offering changed?" the young student asked the doctor of the law. "Moses commanded in Leviticus that if the offering is a burnt sacrifice of the herd, we should offer a male without any defect, it must be of our own free will, and it is to be brought and offered at the door of the tabernacle of meeting before the Lord. How does this relate to the mint and the gold we offer?"

The wise teacher looked into the eye of his student and said, "The principle son is this:
We offer the best
We give freely and generously, not because we are forced to
We present our offering
And we offer it."

The student knowing that this was the beginning of an analytical and wise discourse of the word that his soul craved, waited silently and patiently. He was correct, the doctor did not need any prompting, he began his discourse. He spoke in soft undertones as if talking to himself, yet just loud enough, as if acknowledging the presence of this student who was sitting there with him.

> *1. LIFE ITSELF DEPENDS ON AND IS SUSTAINED BY GIVING; anything that refuses to give dies.*
>
> *2. When you understand the tide it is best to row with it than to row against it; when you understand the wind it is best to let it carry you than to fly against it; when you understand the principle of giving you begin living with reduced human efforts.*

GIVING THE BEST

The doctor said to the student, "What we give to God is a reflection of how we view God. We tend to give the beggar on the street a coin. Sometimes what we give is not enough to buy us lunch. It is very sad when we treat God just as a common beggar. Cain could not envision God bigger than this."

The doctor then recited this poem.

The dilemma with which Adam's son Cain wrest
That he was not Able to give his best
For that would make his value so much less
Than he was after he was blessed

The young man knew he had composed it on the spot. He did it all the time. He was surprised however when the doctor looked at him and said, "Do you understand what this poem means?"

He would not respond immediately. He looked flustered as he mulled it in his mind. The doctor recognizing the young student was caught off guard, continued his discourse. "God not only rejects an offering that diminishes Him, but He also rejects the person who presents it.

The Torah tells us that God accepted Abel and his offering but rejected Cain and his offering. **When what we have becomes too big for God, we become too small for God to see.** Solomon, and also Abel before him, recognized that all they had could not properly define God. God would always be too much, too awesome. *They both allowed their offering to define their heart towards God* and their thoughts of Him. It does not matter what you give, the principle is the same. A person must not give to God reluctantly or because they are forced to. God loves a cheerful giver. This is why King David refused to offer to God anything that did not cost him.

It takes a big picture of someone for you to delight yourself in giving to them. It tells the person you love them more than you love what you give. When your gift is costly and sacrificial it tells the person exactly more than what you love them, and with what measure. It places a value on your love. *What you are happy about making the sacrifice, it tells the person your gift is genuine and your heart towards them is pure. God preoccupies Himself with everyone who has a big picture of Him.* His eyes roam the earth looking for all these persons. He will show Himself strong on their behalf."

The doctor paused, then looked at the young man again. "Do you remember the question I asked you?"

"Certainly," the young student replied. This time he was ready. He knew the doctor would come back to him. He always did. He was mulling it all along.

He responded, "You gave me a poem to interpret. I will respond to you with my interpretation in a similar manner. This is what I have come up with:

> *The dilemma with which Adam's son Cain wrest*
> *That he was not Able to give his best*
> *For that would make his value so much less*
> *Than he was after he was blessed.*
>
> *But he never opened up the door*
> *To see that it is still so much more*
> *Than he really had before God's blessing,*
> *and His pouring out.*

The doctor looked at the young man approvingly. He had always proved to be an exceptional student. He then said to him, "That is the principle of the offering to God. We must always give our best. We must give cheerfully and without restraint or compulsion. We must understand that everything we have comes from Him and belongs to Him.

"Now the offering must be presented and offered. To present an offering means you are present with it. Without debate, the offering should be selected beforehand. It should be put aside. It should be decided, or purposed in the giver's heart. *The thought that goes into the offering to God, is the heart that goes up to God from the giver.* It says, 'I am thinking of You. I have committed this because You are valuable to me. I am bringing You something very special and I cannot wait for the week to end to present and offer it to You.' Unlike an offering, a vow is presented once the vow is made. That is why the Bible compels us to pay our vows and pledges.

Once the offering is presented it is consecrated, holy. The giver has no freedom to change this offering, he must give it. *Unlike the tithe which is consecrated holy the moment it is earned, the offering is consecrated the moment it is presented.*"

The doctor drifted off in his own thoughts. He was silent as he was transported to another place, another conversation: "What do you think He meant by that?" Jonna said to James. "Leave your gift at the altar and go make it right, then come back and offer the gift."

"This is very interesting," James said, "He said 'If you are aware that anyone has anything against you.' It is not as if you are the one to have something against the person.

It is not as if they must have a justifiable cause. He said any-one and anything. And this is Jesus speaking. These words come with all the authority and knowledge of Heaven."

"So...what do you think?" Jonna asked.

James paused for a minute, then he spoke up, dragging his words slowly. "This is both a command and a word of advice.

There are some things here that are clear. Once we present our gift to God we are not free to do with it as we please, it is consecrated. We are not even free to leave with it and to return with it later. It is apparent presenting our gifts is very different from offering it. To present the gift is simply to dedicate it, to be present with it with the intent to give it.

It is also apparent that God is more interested in our relationships than in our offering. We could offer our offering in a cloud of broken relationships but it would not be accepted or abound to our blessing. God will receive the offering, the gift, but reject the giver. It is apparent that when God accepts our offering He also accepts the giver, just as it was with Abel. Jesus advises us to leave the gift at the altar and do what we can to mend the broken relationship. We should then come and offer the offering so we may be accepted by God and we may maximize the benefits of giving."

Jonna heard the heart of James and it made his own blood begin to race. "Could we say then that offering and people go together?" he said. "Can we say that we cannot really separate offering from relationships? Would it be fair to say that *the whole purpose of the offering is about people and relationships?"*

James marveled as he listened to Jonna. This was more advanced, a bit further, than he was thinking, but it had a certain ring too. "Do you remember the story in the book of Numbers? Dathan and Abiram and the two hundred and fifty elders?" James asked.

Jonna was quick to respond, he was a man of the Scriptures. "That would be Numbers sixteen," he said.

"Well they rebelled against Moses and Aaron and challenged their leadership," James continued. "When Moses heard it he fell on his face. He recognized that they were taking trouble onto themselves they could never be prepared for."

Jonna drifted into his own thoughts and the doctor followed him: He saw the two hundred and fifty elders standing before Moses and Aaron with their censers in hand. They were leaders of the congregation of Israel and very popular men among them. Their faces were set. They all held blank stares as they looked in the direction of Moses. Some refused to meet his eyes, they looked away. The sky was beautiful earlier in the day but it was slightly overcast now, eerily overcast. Today they would prove that they were not just leaders of the congregation, but equal with Moses and Aaron. Today they would show that the separation of Moses as leader and the sole communicator with God, and Aaron as the only priest was all a sham.

"We have prophesied too when God placed His Spirit on us. We have equal access to God with Moses. Today we will prove it; we will offer incense just as the priest."

The congregation watched. They too were very agitated with Moses and Aaron. Their leaders were rebelling against their authority and many of them felt this was the opportunity to get rid of the Moses administration. They responded to the campaign promise of Dathan and Abiram that they were about to have better days, the wilderness austerity would be over. They were motivated to believe that the promise was just a vote away, or rather a test away.

The two hundred and fifty elders placed incense on their censers. They stood with Moses and Aaron at the door of the tabernacle. Some of them felt justified. They had finally taken their rightful place at the helm of spiritual leadership of their people. They were standing together with the elites before God. It was just a handful of them who felt this way though. The emotions of the others ranged between anxiety and fear. There were some among them who were even trembling; they could hardly hold their censers. These were the ones who were influenced to join the rebellion but who retained the awe for Moses and who had some fear of God in them.

In that moment Moses looked at the congregation, and with urgency told them to get away from the tents of Dathan and Abiram! The two hundred and fifty felt their foundation rock as

Moses said, "This will be the first test of my leadership. If Dathan and Abiram die a normal death God has not sent me. But if the earth opens up and swallows them and everything that belongs to them, then you know God has rejected them."

The strangest phenomenon occurred just then. The earth opened up its mouth like a huge whale and swallowed the tents of Dathan and Abiram, their wives, their children and everything that concerned them. The elders, still holding their censers, could hear the screams of Dathan and Abiram and their household. It quickly got further and further away, or should we say deeper and deeper, with fading intensity. The hands of the elders went numb. They knew they were in big trouble. Israel was running away scared. They were afraid they would be swallowed up also.

The elders felt very conspicuous and out of place and wished they could have reversed the moment. It was as if they were the next target with no place to hide. They could not depend on the support of the people, and even then…time was immediate; it had run completely out on them. Fire came out from God in that split second and burnt up the elders who held the censers before Him. The heat of the fire was so intense in the moment that they all died immediately from severe burns.

"What did God tell Moses to do with the censers Jonna?" James asked. "Jonna!" James said again sharply as there was no response from his friend. Jonna jumped. He was brought back to the moment from his trip to the Moses era drama. The question James was asking popped up from his subconscious. This was easy for him, he was just there.

"God told Moses to tell Eleazar the priest, the son of Aaron, to retrieve the censers from the blaze for they were ho-o-o-ly," he said. He found himself stretching the last word, holy, as the realization of what James was getting at dawned on him. God had rejected the elders offering the censers. They were out of a relationship with their leadership, they were not aligned with authority, and they were not authorized to offer incense. God had however consecrated the censers as holy for they were presented before Him. God said so Himself.

God had said, "The censers of these men who sinned against their own lives are to be made into hammered plates to cover the holy altar. They were presented before Me and therefore they are holy."

"Wow!" Jonna thought, "This is very consistent with the teaching of Jesus on the subject."

James observed the reaction of Jonna and saw that he had gotten it. James then presented him with the script from the last chapter of the book of Leviticus in the Torah. As Jonna read the passage he knew very well, he was amazed.

Everything that anyone gives to the Lord shall be holy. They cannot substitute it or exchange it. They cannot change a good one for bad one or bad offering for a good. If the person attempts to exchange animal for animal, then both of the animals including the one exchanged are holy.

"No wonder Jesus instructed us to leave the offering at the altar and come back to offer it," he thought. We are not free to do what we desire with anything God consecrates. "That includes our bodies," he thought secretly. "Our bodies are His temple. We must glorify God in our bodies which belong to Christ."

Jonna continued reading. As he read he gasped, "The first-born of the animals, which should be the Lord's firstborn, no man shall dedicate; whether it is an ox or sheep, it is the Lord's."

For Jonna, it was so on point. "How can someone dedicate what belongs to the Lord? This is the true character of the tithe." He thought. ***The only thing to do with God's holy tithe is to give it into your local gathering at the first opportunity.*** It is blessed as long as it is not kept. If it is kept too long, the blessing becomes a curse. The tithe is as the manna that was gathered in the wilder-ness. The manna was pure, beautiful, and tasty. It was food from heaven itself, but if it was kept overnight against God's instructions it stank and bred worms. Yet God's instructions for the Sabbath changed the character of the manna for just that one night. They could now gather two days' worth without it becoming corrupt. God's instruction for the tithe is to bring it into His storehouse."

As Jonna read the conclusion of the chapter, it confirmed his analysis. "All the tithe of the land, whether of the seed of the land or of the fruit of the tree, is the Lord's. It is holy unto the Lord. And the tithe of the herd or the flock, of whatever passes under the rod, the tenth one shall be holy unto the Lord.

You shall not inquire whether it is good or bad or exchange it..." Jonna muttered to himself as he drifted again into his thoughtful analysis, ***It is certainly not our place to rationalize the tithes, just give it!*** We have no rights to even consider the size, how much it is, what it will be used for, is the minister honest? Just give it! If we hang on to our tithes it stinks in the sight of God. If we exchange it, then both the tithes and whatever we exchange it for is consecrated holy."

"Awesome!" Jonna said, as he read the final verse. It read, "These are the Lord's commandments." "We know the tithe, but how do we determine what is an acceptable offering?" Jonna asked himself aloud.

---

1. THE ATTITUDE WITH WHICH THE GIFT IS OFFERED, WILL DETERMINE THE ATTITUDE WITH WHICH THE GIFT IS MEASURED, WILL DETERMINE THE ATTITUDE OF THE RECIPIENT TOWARDS THE GIVER. GOD LOVES A CHEERFUL GIVER!

2. DO NOT PRESENT YOUR OFFERING UNLESS YOU RELEASE IT FIRST, FOR IT BECOMES HOLY WHEN PRESENTED AND RELEASES YOU.

ROBBERY FOR A BURNT OFFERING

"**P**astor, I have a very significant offering towards the mission building, here it is, fifteen thousand United States dollars."

Pastor Nyke mopped his brow as the punishing African sun challenged his energy and stamina in the moment. He could not keep pace with the local workers constructing this permanent mission facility.

He was of Jamaican heritage but was born in Canada. Destiny had placed him in a remote Cameroonian village where he had been ministering for eighteen months.

God had moved mightily in his ministry. People were coming to him for deliverance and healing and God had been faithful. His heart was on the upliftment of the locals. It had been somewhat difficult but he had great hope. The church was growing and the area was beginning to attract business residents and businesses.

This gift from Oganga made him very excited. The church needed it. It was growing and expanding. They took care of many widows and the poor. At that time no amount of contribution could have been too much.

"I am happy the way He has blessed you Oganga," he responded. "May God always honor your giving and your heart to give."

"Well Pastor, He really has. With the help of this kind God my business has grown, I was able to evade a significant amount of taxes this year also. This is working Papa. Also, now that I am a

Christian, my colleges are placing so much confidence in me and I have many opportunities. Sometimes I think God may not be completely happy with my business practices but I compensate with a good offering."

Pastor paused. He loved Oganga but he was not sure he was hearing correctly.

"Did you say evade taxes?"

"Well yes," Oganga said hesitantly, hearing the excitement drain from Pastor Nyke's voice. "But I give good offering; see fifteen thousand United States dollars."

He sounded somewhat unsure of himself.

"Did I also hear you say your business practices may not have been completely wholesome?"

"Well, it is the jungle out there, Papa. The fittest and wisest survive."

The sun has suddenly shifted in intensity and become torturous. It was aided by a feeling of failure that deflated the spirit and offered no resistance to its unforgiving strength and intensity.

For that moment the joy of serving had given way to the burden; the burden of the people. Yes, he needed this gift but not at the expense of his precious brother.

"How do I communicate this to him," Pastor Nyke contemplated.

"My son, do you remember when David sinned with Beersheba and Nathan came to him?"

Oganga nodded his head, no longer enthusiastic.

"This rich man had everything but he stole the one kid from the poor man for a meal for his friends.

David was burning with anger when he heard the story. Who would not burn at this wickedness? Tell me, if you were one of the rich man's friends who visited, would you have eaten the mutton if you knew where the lamb came from?"

"Certainly not Pastor."

"Well what if you found out after you ate the mutton?"

"I would vomit it out Pastor."

"Oganga, how do you believe God feels about someone who steals from their government to give to Him?"

Oganga was silent and contemplative. Pastor continued. "Lying is an abomination to God. It means you lied on your tax returns. It also means you are asking God to overlook the thing that He detest because you brought an offering from it."

Oganga was very sincere as he said, "The audacity of asking God to bless something He hates because He gets a tip from the benefit. It's like bribing God." His voice trailed off and faded into quiet contemplation.

"This is true for every form of robbery that is brought to God as an offering." Pastor Nyke's voice was low and deliberate to accentuate the solemnity of the moment. "If you rob employees to increase wealth, it applies; if you accept or pay bribes, it applies; if you are unfair to customer or suppliers, it applies. In fact, my son, though I can speak for God, I will let Him speak for Himself. Here is my Bible, read Isaiah 61:8."

Oganga reached for the Bible and opened it to Isaiah. The passage screamed at him immediately:

I THE LORD LOVE JUSTICE. I HATE ROBBERY FOR A BURNT OFFERING.

"Forgive me Pastor. I will make this right. I refuse to compromise my salvation and much more to compromise my God by the way I represent, or should I say misrepresent Him in my professional life.

"Could I tell the government I stole from them because God needed it?" Oganga chuckled, a bit of humor returning to his voice. "Would I not be misrepresenting God, making Him a thief and my accomplice, guilty of possession of stolen property? I would also make Him a pauper, needing stolen property to survive." He was joking now, having decided he would no more compromise his faith and eternity for mammon.

"Pastor, this is yours. It is for the church. I refuse to take back what I have dedicated. What I will take back is the heart I gave it with and return with a blameless heart so God may receive this gift."

"I will gladly accept this gift my son. Today, as it was with Zacchaeus, salvation has come to your house."

The sun had risen in its merciless midday heat and was even more piercing and punishing than before. It penetrated the sweat glands of Pastor Nyke but it could not get beyond the inner shield of joy, satisfaction and hope that he felt. He joined the men at work with renewed vigor.

"This justifies my mission to Africa, souls. This makes it worthwhile to be alive," he sang to himself as he labored.

> 1. *You cannot rob God and give to man or mammon (yourself), nor rob man and give to God. He curses both.*
> 2. *When you steal from God you make God a victim, when you steal and give to God you make God an accomplice.*
> 3. *You negate the laws of God, the heart of God, the word of God, the gift of God, the wealth of God, the Lordship of God, when you claim to be His child and steal for any reason.*

THE MEASURING POT

The measuring pot was very large
It lavishly disbursed abroad
One measure, just one measure please
One measure, much more than one could need
The measuring spoon was very small
He grudgingly surrendered half
Was not enough for one small bite
Though drawn from an abundant supply

My heart is large for I am God
You give to Me and I give back
You use a spoon and that is sad
I love to use a measuring pot.
To give exceedingly abundantly more
To make your cup overflow
Pressed down, shaken together and running… Splash!
I love to use a measuring pot

The inspiration of the moment amazed Jonna as he sat there and wrote this poem. It was packed with the revelation of the truth about the heart of God. James had left him. Time passed. Night had set in and the buzz of daytime activity was dying down. Jonna sat alone listening to the splash of the sea as his mind drifted to the words of the Teacher. As usual, he began to visualize.

"Boy, this is hard work!" the lazy young man, Jeb, complained, as he used a spoon to fill his cart with sand. "I have been here for three hours now and the cart is not full!"

An elderly man came by with a bucket and began loading his own cart. He filled up his bucket and poured it in his cart. Jeb sat there, amazed. This one bucket was more than everything he had done so far today. They were getting paid by the cart load of sand, and this man had already made three trips. Jeb was still trying to fill his first cart with the spoon. At this rate, he would starve.

The elderly man filled up his cart within ten minutes and drove it away. As he was leaving he looked over at Jeb and said, "Did you not hear what Jesus said, 'With the same measure you use, it will be measured to you again?'"

Jonna came back from his visualization to reflect on the Scriptures. That final chord hit a note that needed examination. These are the words of Jesus. He was giving an instruction to the people. The instruction was to give. He had said, "Give, and it shall be given to you in return, good measure, pressed down, shaken together and running over. Men will give this into your storehouses." But then there was a trick.

Everything was regulated by measures. He had said, "With the same measure you give, it will be measured back to you." If you measure out your giving with a spoon you get back your return with a spoon. If you use the bucket of a tractor, you will get bucket loads in return. *If you give unreservedly, God will lavish you without reservation, with His extravagance. This is the ultimate promise, open heavens.* "If we desire to maximize the blessing that comes with our giving, which is the open heavens, we must give with a generous heart," Jonna said aloud. "We must be prepared to release everything to God. This is the only acceptable offering for me," Jonna concluded.

The Doctor looked over at his student who was engaged in his own thoughts of reflection. Their eyes met and the gentle nod of the student's head showed he understood the doctor's absence. Time was gone. As they rose up to leave, the doctor repeated the words of Jonna in closing, "If we desire to maximize the blessing that comes with our giving, that is: open heavens, we must give with a generous heart; we must be prepared to release everything to God. This is the only acceptable offering for me."

"Everything," the student thought as he left the company of the doctor of the law. He remembered the story the doctor had related to him: "Our lives are totally finished," one leper said to the other nine lepers sitting there together in isolation. Nine of these lepers were Jews and one was a Samaritan.

The Jews knew they were separate from this Samaritan by culture and consecration, but now they were joined by this vexing disease. "This is a life sentence," they all agreed. It was very bad for them. They were destined to suffer hunger and scorn. They would be isolated from those who were once close to them, their children, their wives, their families. If they were in prison they could be visited. They would have hope of release. "Our lives are really finished," they lamented.

A very tall and athletic looking one said to the others, "I have heard about this Jesus. He has been doing many great miracles." He knew that although he was athletic looking with a toned body, he was a leper. All his physical glory was lost in this reality.

Another leper responded to him, "He has done many notable healings also." He was short and stocky and he had a large paunch. "Are you thinking what I'm thinking?" The first one spoke. They all nodded their heads as hope entered their hearts. "But how will we get to Jesus?" One asked. "I hear there is always a crowd around him. We are not allowed to go near people."

The athletic leper responded as a gleam of cunning entered his eyes, "That will be very easy. We just show up and say, 'Leper.' See how fast everyone will scatter and give us immediate and unhindered access."

"Surely," another leper said. "You may even get unwanted attention and 'decked' by a pile of stones."

"What if Jesus runs away, too?" One asked.

"If He does," the Samaritan responded, "He cannot help us."

"You are a Samaritan," the man with the paunch replied to him, now making the distinction, "He may not help you anyway."

Together they all set out. They found Jesus in a small village at the heart of a crowd, teaching them. The lepers watched from a distance and they could see rejoicing and excitement as something notable happened. They decided to get close enough to be heard.

"Leper!" they shouted. The crowd began to trip over themselves as they scampered to get out of the way. They did not get close, however, they stood at a distance and shouted, "Jesus, have mercy on us."

When Jesus saw them, He said to them, "Go and show yourselves to the priest." This was a command in the Torah concerning leprosy. The inspection only took place where healing is determined or believed.

As they went, sure enough they were all healed. Each of them began to laugh, to dance, to jump, and to rejoice. This was the happiest day of their lives, ever. The nine Jews took off running to get back to normal life and to show themselves to their families. They could not wait to be together with their wives and children again. There were things they wanted to do for a long time but they could not do because of their conditions. Now they would not delay another minute.

The Samaritan also took off, heading for home. It was then that he remembered Jesus. "Everything else must wait," he said to himself. "Let me go and tell Jesus thanks first." He ran to Jesus and pressed through the crowd. He fell down on his face before Jesus and shouted, "Glory to God!" At the top of his voice. "Glory to God!"

Everyone heard the voice of Jesus then. He said, "Did I not cleanse ten lepers? Where are the nine? Is it that no one else had the heart to come back to give thanks but this stranger?"

The young student could still hear the voice of the doctor as he concluded. It was a very deep thought provoking analysis. He always had interesting and abstract ways of delivering a point. He said, *"One out of ten, ten percent, the tithes, came back to glorify God. Sometimes for many Christians, even the tithe does not return or, rather, is not returned. Jesus is still asking, 'Where are the nine? Where is the ninety percent?' He wants to be honored with everything, all our substance. He wants access to everything with which He has blessed us with."*

The young student said to himself then, "Point taken." He then repeated the parting sentence of the doctor after personalizing it: "If I desire to maximize the blessing that comes with my giving, which is the open heavens, I must give with a generous heart. I must be prepared to release everything to God. This is the only acceptable offering for me!"

---

1. *The laws of nature revolt when someone who has been very mean to you in your time of difficulty requires massive favor in their own need. How do you measure your giving to God?*

2. *If God is everything that matters then release to God everything in full measures.*

SOWING AND REAPING

The doctor, too, had an interesting encounter after leaving the young student. He was in his carriage and heading home. He saw this interesting looking stranger who seemed to be heading in his direction. He was dressed a little differently. He looked tired as if he had been on the road for sometime, yet he looked fresh, jovial, in high spirits, as if he had a fountain of life inside that renewed him.

He stopped and offered the stranger a ride and he thanked the doctor generously and got in. They greeted each other and continued in silence for a few minutes as the doctor continued his meditation of the day. As they passed a field, freshly planted with corn, springing up, the stranger said. "That field is so beautiful." The doctor could not help but agree. It was just four weeks ago that the farmer and his team were tilling the soil and planting seeds. He watched them water it every day. The doctor remembered saying to himself, "As long as the earth remains, seedtime and harvest, cold and heat, winter and summer, and day and night will never cease.

There is a covenant that God made with every seed and it is as powerful as the covenant He made with the day and night." The doctor unconsciously repeated this passage from the eighth chapter of the book of Genesis under his breath. He realized he was thinking aloud when the stranger said, "The law of sowing and reaping. It is an eternal law, just as gravity.

Do you know that this law existed from creation?" The doctor felt as if he was in a class. He was once again becoming a student. He would be happy to hear this stranger and to draw out his thoughts. "Certainly," he said, "God placed the seed of all species of living things in themselves at creation."

The stranger said, "How many human beings were created?" The doctor responded, "One... well two."

"And how many families were saved from the flood?"

"Only one," the doctor responded. The wheels of the carriage groaned as it entered a rough patch in the road. He fully understood what the stranger was getting at, "Look at us now!" he said to himself under his breath, "millions; the power of the seed!"

The stranger could see that the doctor was getting what he was saying. He said again, "How many Christs were sent to die for sins?"

"One," the doctor answered, as he repeated to himself, "Look at us now!" His thoughts immediately went to a passage in the ninth book of Romans, "Unless the Lord of Sabbath had left us a seed, we would have been like Sodom and Gomorrah." These nations were totally destroyed from the face of the earth. Yet the passage did not say seeds or even a remnant, it said a seed.

Imagine the potency and the power that is in just one seed. His thought immediately switched to a passage in the book of Isaiah, the fifty-third chapter. "It pleased the Lord to bruise Him. He put Him to grief. When you make His soul an offering for sin, He shall see His seed. He shall prolong His days. The pleasure of the Lord shall prosper in His hands."

"Look at us now!" He said to himself. The doctor recognized that the stranger was silent, studying him. He said "Paul said in the second book of Corinthians, the ninth chapter, 'May He who supplies seed to the sower to sow the ground, and bread for food, supply and multiply the seed we sow and increase the fruits of our righteousness.'"

The stranger interjected, "This passage is a blessing for us to have an abundance of everything, for all liberal giving. It is a blessing of extravagance. Those with a giving heart will have everything they need to give and all the food they need to live and to share liberally. Both the seed and the fruit are to bless others. This will cause them to give thanks to God."

The doctor was enjoying this conversation immensely. He did not want it to end. He had almost reached home and it was already late. He had determined that the stranger was going to the next town, an hour away. He decided to take him.

The stranger was grateful. He said as if to himself, "Cast your bread..." The doctor picked up immediately. It was a passage from Ecclesiastes 11.

"You will find it after many days," the doctor said in reflection. This was a passage he knew very well and meditated on often. Solomon immediately followed by saying, "Give a por-tion to seven and also to eight, for you do not know what evil will be upon the earth."

It is obvious he is instructing us to sow now as a provision against the future. If we enact the seed time, then according to the laws of God, harvest must follow. "Just as day follows night," the stranger said, as if eerily reading his thoughts. "If that farmer who planted the corn was to have made the corn into a meal instead because he was hungry...?"

"He would be hungry again after the meal," the doctor interjected, "with no hope or expectation for the future. He would have no provision against the evil days to come."

"People do not sow because they say, 'I am waiting for the right conditions or preconditions. There is not enough money; must do this first; must have some measure of guarantee,'" the stranger said.

"They are observing the wind according to Solomon," the doctor added, enthused.

"Sowing is all faith," the stranger said.

The doctor began to think, "Every farmer sows with an expectation of a harvest. The principle of sowing and reaping is proven to them. They know that after process and time they will have a crop. Giving is also all faith. We have proven God and we know that after process and time every seed will produce."

"One of the main barriers to giving is that we don't know," the stranger said, interrupting the doctor's thoughts.

"Just as the mother does not know how her child's bones grow in her womb. She still talks to the baby knowing life is inside her," the doctor said.

"Is not this what Solomon was preaching when he said, 'You do not know the works of God who makes everything.'? Sowing is all faith!" the stranger said.

"Solomon commands us to sow in the morning and not to stop sowing in the evening," the doctor said, reflecting on his own seed of time and of his carriage into this stranger life. He had also spent a long day sowing into the destiny of his students.

"His ways are not our ways, nor His thoughts ours. The distance between His awesomeness and us is as far as the heavens above," the stranger said. "Yet it is He who sends the rain down to water our seed to ensure it produces. He does this to ensure His covenant with the harvest is fully realized."

"Whatever a man sows," the stranger said again. He was quiet, as if knowing the doctor would process it. He was right. "Galatians six," the doctor thought. "God is never mocked; the laws of seedtime and harvest cannot be mocked or skirted. A man will reap whatever he sows, good or bad. We sow to the flesh we reap corruption; we sow to the Spirit we reap life."

"Interesting," the stranger said, "whatever... love, money, time, shelter, the encouragement... whatever... hurt, pain, gossip, heartbreak, rebellion, malice, hatred... whatever; if there is seed-time, there must be..."

"Harvest," the doctor said.

This caused him to think seriously about his own life. "Is there any bad seed I have sown in my past that I need to uproot? Jesus Christ has erased my history, but how about this week? Have I become a victim of my flesh this week?"

He thought about the field of corn knowing the farmer does not just leave the corn there. He waters and fertilizes the good seed and he removes the weeds (bad seed) that find its way among them. "I have to manage my life for maximum returns," he said, "just as the farmer. I must employ prayer, the word, confessing, forgiving, and uprooting."

"Never get tired of doing good," the stranger interjected. "Paul was referring to the seed called, 'doing good'."

"You shall reap in due season if you don't give up," the doctor said, thinking, "if there is seed time, there will be harvest. God controls the sea-sons. Faith is the bridge between the seasons."

"What is certain," the stranger said, "is that everyone who sows through pain and sacrifice, going forth weeping, as Psalms 126 puts it, will certainly come again, with joy and celebration bringing in the harvest."

"Paul, in the fourth chapter of his letter to the Philippians, lauded them on their giving to him and their support of his ministry," the stranger said. The doctor was very quiet now, just listen-ing. This was a beautiful discourse that engaged his spirit and his soul, and he wanted the stranger to continue.

The stranger continued. "He told them how joyful he was to see how much they cared for him. That they did well to share in his distress. That no other church communicated with him in this manner concerning giving and receiving... seedtime and harvest. Though they only communicated the giving, the seed ensured the expectation. Paul could not leave it out. He mentioned the other side of the process they had initiated, the receiving, the harvest. Paul knew how to receive a gift. He told them the gift he had received, all the things they sent, was a sweet-smelling aroma in God's nostrils, an acceptable sacrifice that pleased God well.

He was careful to tell them that he encouraged their giving, not because he desired a gift. He had learnt how to be content in any state of abundance or lack he found himself. His source is Christ and through Christ, He could do all things. He knew how to endure severe hardship and how to manage God's blessings.

He did not desire gift but fruits that abound to the giver's account. He was happy they were a sowing church, not because of him, but because of them. They were enacting the principles of seedtime and harvest. In his absence he was assured that this church would remain blessed and prosperous. They had harvests coming.

It was easy for him to bless them because it would just be agreeing with the covenanted principle of God: the law of giving and receiving. This is the same law of seed time and harvest. He blessed them with a blessing many Christians often claim without first enacting the giving, thus without recognizing the seed time. He said, 'My God shall supply all your needs according to His glorious, unlimited riches...His riches in glory.' Note he did not say, 'May God supply;' he said, 'My God shall...' In other words God must respond to His own covenant. Paul was just stating the obvious." The doctor listened. This was a mouthful. He was happy he would have adequate time to digest it all while driving back along the quiet country road.

As the stranger disembarked he said, "Do you remember the passage in Hosea ten, 'Sow in righteousness, reap in mercy...'?" "Break up your untended ground," the doctor said.

"Yes, identify all your opportunities to sow and actively pursue them," the stranger said. "It is time to seek the Lord, in prayer, in the word, in worship, in giving, in righteousness, in understanding and por-traying His heart... how best to seek the Lord than to seek His kingdom and all its righteousness as the top priority? He will come and rain righteousness upon you. He will bring you a harvest of righteousness which will satisfy all your daily concerns and place you in His overflow."

The doctor was full. He could not have paid for this time of meditation. No wonder Paul said: you should not neglect to minister to strangers, as you may minister to angels not knowing. The doctor was certain he had just served an angel. If not in the literal sense, his contribution was nothing less than angelic.

The stranger turned to him and said in parting, "How many seeds do you get when you plant one papaya tree?"

The doctor could not answer, "Innumerable?" he thought.

The stranger, accepting the silence as acknowledgement, continued, "And how many fruits and seeds do you get if you should plant all of those seeds?"

He left knowing the doctor would put it together. "You never reap in the same amount as you sow," the doctor thought. ***Imagine that papaya seed ten generations down the line. Every seed in the life of a person is generational and impactful.*** I can-not get tired of sowing into the lives of my students. Wow! Imagine the impact I will have if any of my students become a papaya tree."

"Not be weary... in due season I shall reap... one family saved from the flood... the promise was to only one seed - Christ... that God may multiply my seeds and increase the fruit of my righteousness..." the doctor thought reflecting on the entire conversation at once.

"Father," the doctor said, lifting up his prayer, "in the name of Your Son, Jesus, please increase the impact I have on my stu-dents, increase the fruits of my labor, but also multiply my seeds. Let them reach generations and raise up others to reach generations after them. ***Give me a ministry tree that spans many nations, families, cultures, languages, and generations from the seeds I sow.*** He then made this commitment, "I will give a portion to seven and also to eight, I must sow my time and resources now, for I do not know what evil and degeneration will be on the earth. ***The earth needs crops of righteousness to combat the perilous times to come as Paul declared. The earth needs sowers who under-stand the true potential of every seed they sow.***"

> *1. YOUR SEED HAS THE POWER TO OUT-LIVE YOU, TO OUT-LAST YOU, TO OUT-PERFORM YOU, TO OUT-GIVE YOU; BUT ONLY IF YOU LET IT OUT; RELEASE IT.*
>
> *2. HEAVEN GIVES YOU THE CREDIT FOR EVERYTHNG YOUR SEED DOES.*
>
> *3. FAITH IS REQUIRED WHEN YOU HAVE NO CONTROL OVER THE OUTCOME; FAITH IS EXERCISED WHEN YOU FULLY RELEASE THE SEED TO THE AUTHOR OF THE OUTCOME.*
>
> *4. THE POWER TO INCREASE IS PLACED IN THE SEED; YOU RESTRICT THE SEED AND RESTRAIN ITS POWER, WHEN YOU WITHHOLD THE SEED AND RETAIN IT.*

GENEROSITY

We love Him because He first loved us. If love inspired in Him generosity and selfless unreserved giving, then His love should inspire in us…

"He who has a generous eye will be blessed, for he gives his bread to the poor." Dan was fascinated by this passage in Proverbs twenty-two. "A person with a generous eye, gives of his resources. *Is it that a generous eye sees the opportunity to be generous, and seizes the opportunity to be generous?*"

He went back and mulled the passage in Proverbs eleven: "The generous person will be made rich. He who waters will himself be watered." To be blessed, to be made rich, these are covenants to those who will be generous. Generous, hmm… to give lavishly, to be bountiful, to give without restraint, to give from the heart, to love to give, to give to love, not to love the gift more than the recipient, hmm…"

"The generous person plans generous things and by generosity he will stand. Isaiah thirty-two. To be blessed, to be made rich, to stand… to not just see opportunities to be generous, but to plan occasions to be generous… amazing."

"The hidden treasures of secret places and the riches of sinners are waiting for people with the heart to administrate it for God." Dan was reflecting on a passage in Isaiah 45.

Dan thought on his encounter with the children in his community earlier that morning. He laughed out loud and his entire body shook. "How old is that girl?" He asked himself, laughing even harder as he pictured her standing there, feet together, face set, full of a confident attitude, but missing her front teeth. "Must be five, perhaps six," he answered himself in his mind.

The boys had fled and left her standing alone, and did she stand! They were picking the big mangoes hanging from the limbs into the pathway outside of his home. She looked up at him as he came through the gate and said, "We did not steal from you, Mr. Dan. We picked from the branches hanging over the wall." He remembered how he replied in the most disarming voice he could muster coupled with a warm smile. "It is ok, my dear. That is the reason I left it there, for anyone who desires. I have more than enough inside. See!" he said as he handed her a bag full of juicy ripe mangoes. That was the reason he had come outside in the first place.

Many of his neighbors had cut the branches of their fruit trees that hung over the walls, and others had protected them fiercely and refused to have anyone pick from them. Dan was very intentional. He remembered Israel's blessing for Joseph. "Joseph shall be a fruitful vine whose branches hang over the wall." He knew Israel loved Joseph and had blessed him with nothing but the blessing of the first-born son. It was the blessings of Abraham, himself. Judah prevailed in the end, but Israel had blessed Joseph to be the blessing. The purpose of the overflow was never for Joseph. *It cannot be for you if it spills over your place of dominion and out of your control. The overflow is for others.*

If he could name the branches that grew over his wall he would call them, "Whosoever will may come!" Dan laughed again as he thought on the Scriptures on generosity. "What does David mean when he says 'my cup'? Was he referring to everything that he needed in life? Could it be interchanged for my portion?" Dan sat down looking out at the mountains. He could see a goat's kid frolicking in the distance. It could not be more than a couple weeks old. It was so happy and disengaged. All it needed was travelling right there beside it all the time. That heavy bag of milk with which its mother labored. The farmer was gracious enough to relieve her of some of the milk in the mornings.

If that goat kid had a message for the world it would be, "My cup runs over! My God has supplied all my needs according to His abundant supply." Could it be what David meant when he said, "My cup runs over?" Was he saying, "I have more than I could possibly consume myself. I am blessed to be a blessing?"

The chapter was all about God taking care of him; leading him as a good Shepherd into an abundant supply of food and drink. It was all about the Lord feeding him in banquet fashion in the most hostile situations, in the presence of his enemy. It was all about the anointing on his life that made his joy impregnable. Then the dam burst! His cup was running over. With this in mind, in the center of the overflow, he made a proclamation, "Surely! Goodness and mercy shall follow me all the days of my life."

Did this have anything to do with the overflow lifestyle? If you are generous you are assured of blessings. When you water, you yourself will be watered. God will continue to bring it to you if He can get it through you. If he can make you a riverhead to pour out from you He will be the river of supply to pour into you… all the days of your life. Did David understand this when he said, "My cup runs over"?

Was this statement an acknowledgment mixed with a commitment? Did he claim the blessing of his commitment when he made the statement, "I have this assurance that goodness and mercy shall follow me all the days of my life"? Why did he connect this with dwelling in the house of the Lord forever? Certainly, he knows that God is a generous God. He is the God of the over-flow; The God who gives exceedingly abundantly more. The God whose eye searches the earth to look for those He may pour His blessings into…for those who are as generous as He is. He selects those who will manage His blessings for Him and for His kingdom.

Dan laughed when he reflected on those who believe that the overflow of their cups means they should drink from their saucer. They are like those who build bigger barns. Their vision of life and God stops with themselves.

Could the Master have made it any plainer? Give and it will be given to you: 'Good measure', not spoon full but bucket load; 'pressed down', just as we do for wheat to maximize the space; shaken together as we do for grain to fill every crevice… Dan paused. Why would the Master go to such great length to ensure we are thoroughly satisfied? Why would He ensure all our needs are met and our storehouses are filled? Is it not to eliminate all our excuses before He pours in the overflowing blessing?

Can anyone justify hanging on to the overflow blessings after all this? The rich man tried. He built bigger barns. Jesus ensured He outlined Heaven's response to this behavior. "You will die tonight and leave it all. So shall it be to everyone who is rich towards themselves, who hangs on to the overflow, and is not generous towards God."

A generous God wants us to live in the overflow
To pour in to us exceedingly abundantly more
To run like rivers with His resource
If we will let His blessing run her course
A generous God wants sons, not just slaves
To give us the Kingdom, not just a wage
But we must position ourselves like Christ
To live the overflow lifestyle.

"Bring all the tithes and offering into My storehouses and prove Me…" Dan reflected. This is the only invitation God has given to man to test Him… interesting! And the result is that He will open the windows of heaven and pour out a blessing that will be much greater than our storehouses. Interesting! God is saying, "Be obedient and generous and experience the generosity of God.

Perform for my eyes and watch Me outperform your eyes. Play to My generosity and I will play to your awe and disbelief. Speak extravagance and I will speak overflow."

Dan's heart was singing as he rose up from his place in the open field that night. As he walked home beneath the glittering stars he was committed. All his branches would hang over the walls of his life. ***My fruits will hang low.*** It will be an open invitation to the world to come, enjoy my blessings.

The many testimonies for the faithful believers that decorate the centuries after Dan's time confirm everything he concluded that day. The generous God remains generous to generous hearts. This has been the case from the beginning of time.

This was the case with King Solomon. He offered one thousand burnt offerings on his inauguration day when he was obligated to offer just one. God said to him that very night, "Ask anything of Me and I will give it to you." Solomon stepped into the overflow blessings and his next notable offering on the day he dedicated the temple was twenty-two thousand burnt offerings. The presence of the Lord came down in that temple that day as the generous God basked in this outpouring of Solomon's love and extravagant giving.

Dan would have loved to take a peek into modern times, two thousand years after the death of Christ. In the next chapter we will hear and listen to a couple of the Dans of today share their experiences of God's generosity:

---

1. GENEROSITY IS LIVING not just a lifestyle.

2. GOD wants absolute freedom in all of His creation; generosity is the place where He is fully released; WHERE He is totally FREE in His human tabernacle.

CHAPTER

10

ARIEL THE 90% TITHER

A riel sat on her bed reading. She had in her hand a book on tithing and it was having a significant impact on her pre-adolescent mind. She had determined that she would live a life to honor God. It was very clear to her that tithing was an obligation. She was just a child in preparatory school ready to move on to high school, but she made a decision that day. "I am going to honor God," she said triumphantly to herself. "I am really going to honor God."

"Daddy, daddy," Ariel called to her father, a pastor and a leader among ministers in Montego Bay, Jamaica, studied his daughter as she revealed her heart.

"Daddy," she said, ***"God requires us to pay 10% back to Him as tithes. I want to pay 90% and keep 10%.*** I want to be the only person in the world to give God 90% tithes." Her father looked on proudly as he listened to the heart and innocent sincerity of his young daughter.

Ariel was talking about her lunch money. It was the only income she had. For normal parents, it would be devastating to hear their young child say she would be sacrificing her lunch money every day. Although Ariel's father had the normal parental concern, he understood the significance of generosity to God. He knew this would be one of the greatest investments his daughter could make in her entire life. He was not about to stop her. He would step aside but he would monitor her to ensure she was safe.

Ariel moved into high school. For the next year and the entire five years of her high school education, Ariel gave God 90% of her lunch money as tithes. Father watched as his little daughter packed lunch every day for the entire duration of her high school years. He would have loved to see her eat the best at school but he was not about to intervene. Ariel would search the refrigerator for whatever leftovers she could find each day, and she would put it in her lunch kit. The girls mocked her at her school, Montego Bay High. It was an all-girls school. To her, it did not matter - she was doing this for God. Ariel remained faithful to her decision to be generous to her God. She was very conscious that she was the only child to pack lunch for the entire duration of their high school years. She was proud of it.

God looked down and saw Ariel, sacrificing to honor Him, measuring to Him with a big bucket, being very generous towards Him. God was not about to be outdone. He had said "Prove Me," now He would show His magnificence. Ariel did her SAT for US colleges and got a score of 2250. She applied to a number of universities but was turned down. The only acceptance she received was to Stephen's Institute of Technology which required her to pay US$1000 per week after the scholarship. God miraculously engineered a transfer to another university on a full Presidential scholarship. Ariel graduated from university with a perfect 4.0 grade physics degree in 2010. She was then granted a smart scholarship by a prominent American university where she studied astrophysics to get into the space program.

God miraculously waived thousands of dollars in educational fees that confounded the family while getting Ariel into the best and enviable programs available. This was all because a little child decided to be sacrificially extravagant to God. Ariel's story is still being written…

Ariel has successfully turned the tables on the saying, "It is best to have 90% blessed than to have 100% cursed." In her commitment, in her sacrifice, and in God's response to her, she has proven, *"It is even better to retain 10% blessed than to retain 100% cursed."*

1. God cannot resist a sacrifice.

2. God will never allow a human creation to out-give Him.

3. IT IS BETTER TO RETAIN 10% blessed than to retain 100% cursed.

ROBERT MORRIS –
THE EXTRAVAGANT GIVER

Robert Morris sat with his hand around his wife Debbie, staring into the evening sky from the green van that had become to him like a second home. He was a travelling evangelist and he spent a lot of time on the road. His passion for her had intensified since he surrendered his life fully to the Lord. His passion for God was also propelling him to heights beyond his dreams. His experience was, as the saying goes, joy unspeakable and full of glory.

As he held Debbie, he also held a fear; it was the fear of losing her. He had been unfaithful to her after marriage, before he met Jesus, and he was afraid of what would happen when she discovered it. After meeting Jesus, he had desired nothing more than full surrender to God. He had immediately gone to bible school, and now, here he was, a travelling evangelist.

Robert understood what it meant to live by faith, but at least he could dictate his financial requirements before each engagement. His requirements were very similar to that of travelling preachers, pay my cost plus an offering. He would sometimes receive an honorarium from the church which would be a fixed amount.

He remembered as he was spending time before the Lord one day, the Lord spoke to him. It was not an audible voice, just an impression, but he knew it was the Lord. The Lord said, "Get your finances in order so I can bless you."

Robert knew what he had to do. For Robert, it meant getting out of debt. This did not include his mortgage. It was an appreciating asset and therefore a good debt. Robert and Debbie, however, sold their car and bought a much cheaper one that they could afford.

The Lord then spoke to him again and said, "Do not manipulate." Robert knew what he had to do, He would remove all financial requirements from his speaking engagements. This would be challenging given the fact that this was his only source of income, but Robert was prepared to obey and to honor God.

When someone called him to speak in the future, and they ask, "What is your financial requirement for coming?" Robert would respond, "I have no financial requirement." The Lord then said to Robert, ***I want to teach you who your provider is.***

Robert smiled as he remembered what happened on his very next assignment. The first person who called had asked him of his financial requirements. He responded, "I have none." The person had responded, "That is good! I do not even think we can pay your gas!"

"My gas!" Robert thought, "That is not even the full expenses." Robert was obedient to the Lord, however, and he got into his car on his journey to his engagement in Oklahoma.

He stopped at a gas station to fill his tank with gas. He then went inside to pay. The lady who was cashing said to him, "It is ok, your bill is already paid."

"What do you mean it is already paid?" Robert said to her. "It is already paid," she insisted. "When you pulled in, the Lord told me to fill up your car with gas."

Robert smiled again and repeated what he had said to himself that day, "Lord I prefer to do it Your way."

The third instruction the Lord had given Robert was, "Give." Robert was somewhat taken aback by this. He was a consistent giver. "I always give my tithes," he reminded God. The Lord then woke him up with this revelation. "You do not give your tithes Robert, you return it. The tithe is already Mine. If you do not return it, you have stolen from Me. ***You can only give what belongs to you. What you give is the amount over and above the 10%.*** "Robert stood there corrected. He asked God in submission, "How do I know what to give, when to give and how much to give?"

The Lord responded, again by a small impression "I will tell you." Not long after this, Robert went to a small church on a speaking engagement. There were about sixty persons in the audience. This was his only speaking engagement for the month and he had his monthly obligations. Robert knew this but he was consistent with his commitment to God. He told the pastor he had no financial requirement. The pastor conveyed to the church that Robert had no financial requirement for coming but he wanted them to give him a special love offering.

As the pastor handed Robert the check that day, the pastor expressed surprise at the amount that was on the check. It was the first time his congregation had given that much. Robert was even more surprised, the check was the exact amount he and his wife Debbie needed to meet his monthly obligation, cents included.

As the pastor handed him the check, Robert looked up and saw a man sitting at the back of the church. The Lord immediately told Robert he was a travelling missionary and he should give the check to him. This was a moment Robert questioned God. This was all he had for the month. He had no more engagements. "Lord, are You really saying what You are saying? Is it really You speaking?"

Even as he struggled, Robert knew the answer. This was God and it was what He required. Robert endorsed the check then, went over and discreetly handed it over to the missionary. He instructed him not to look at it until he had gone outside.

When Robert stepped out of the church a couple invited him and Debbie for pizza. Robert gladly accepted, they had no money. In total there were six couples eating together. The men sat together and the women together. As they ate the pizza, the gentleman sitting across from Robert leaned over and asked him, "How much was on that check you received today?" Robert thought it strange he should ask that personal question. He had only seen him one time before. They did not know each other. Without thinking he told him the figure including the pennies. The gentleman then went even more personal. He asked, "Where is the check?" Robert, not wanting to blow a trumpet about his generosity and his needs, told him a lie inadvertently. "Why! My wife Debbie has it," he said.

"I would love to see it," the gentleman said. "Go and get it." Robert knew Debbie did not have the check but he still went. He leaned over to her and said, "Are you enjoying your pizza?" Robert then returned to the inquisitor and said, "She does not have it."

"Where is it then?" he asked.

"It is in the car," Robert said, again responding with an unintentional lie. The gentleman did not ask him to go to the car this time. Instead, he said, "It is not in the car, is it?"

Robert felt that since this man knew so much, he should tell him where the check was. "Where is it then?" Robert asked.

"You have given it away, haven't you?" the gentleman responded. Robert was surprised. "How did you know?" he asked. The gentleman said, "God told me."

He then reached into his pocket and pulled out a check and handed it to Robert. He had written this check before he came to the meeting that day. He was not a member of the church but came for the occasion. Robert looked at the check and saw that it was exactly ten times the amount he had given away to the last penny.

This was stupendous. Robert held the check to take it but the gentleman did not release it just then. He was a giver and he wanted to impart the spirit of giving. He looked directly at Robert and said, "God is about to teach you about giving so you can teach the body of Christ."

Robert took the check and made a commitment to God then. He said, ***"This is God's money; all of it from now on is God's money." This was when Robert began giving extrava-***

gantly. Robert bought a car for a single mother and *he started paying salaries to persons who were out of a job. Robert began also to give 70% of all his income to the Lord.*

Money kept coming in from everywhere and he kept funneling it. He was a riverhead. A few years later Robert had a van. This same green van that he used to traverse between engagements. He was there sitting in his van with his hand around Debbie, and thinking back. This van was very important to him. He savored this moment's break with his wife. It was not long after this that the Lord told him to sell the van. As usual, Robert obeyed. He sold his van for twelve thousand dollars.

Not long after, Robert went on the mission field. He took the money with him. When he arrived, a missionary picked him up in an old rickety van with holes in this flooring.

Robert was inquisitive so he asked the missionary, "Why don't you get a new van?" The missionary responded.

"The Lord showed me the van we are going to buy."

"How much is it?" Robert asked. "It will cost twelve thousand dollars" the missionary replied. This was the exact amount Robert had sold his van for. He had the proceeds with him that day. Robert knew what he had to do. He bought the van for the missionary with the proceeds from his van. Giving generously to God became Robert's lifestyle.

A few years passed. Robert was worshipping and having his quiet time. He was reading in Philippians how Jesus gave up everything. It was then the Lord spoke to him, *"Would you give Me everything?"* Robert knew immediately what the Lord meant. He was being asked to give up his personal checking account, his savings account, his wife's savings account, the ministry accounts, his retirement, both cars, and his house. *Robert gave everything away. He had stepped into a place of extravagance towards God.* He gave his house to a pastor who had five children.

The following day, Robert was adding it all up. Everything he had given away. He really had nothing left to add up. He heard the Lord say to him, "What are you doing?" Robert quickly responded, "Nothing Lord!"

The Lord said to him again, "What are you doing?" To this, Robert responded, "I really don't want to tell you." The Lord said, "Tell Me." Robert responded to God then,

"Well Lord, You know that old saying, 'You cannot out-give God?' Well I think I just did. When You add up all that I have given, this time I think I have got You."

He heard the Lord respond, "So do you think you've got Me?" In that instant, the phone rang and Robert picked it up. There was a man on the phone. He said to Robert, "The Lord told me to help you with your transportation."

Robert thought, "God is giving me a car. I have just given away two cars. I am still way ahead." In fact, at that time Robert had given away a total of nine cars. He would give a lot after then. He asked the man on the phone, "So what did the Lord tell you to do?"

The man responded, "He told me to buy you an airplane, and to pay for the maintenance, the insurance, the hanger, the fuel and the pilot. Here is his name and number of the pilot. You just need to tell him where you want to go and when." Robert was stunned. He heard the Lord saying then, "I've got you!"

Extravagant giving to God became Robert and Debbie's lifestyle. They had never been able to out-give the extra-extravagant God. One day, Robert heard God saying to him, "Ask anything and I will give it to you." It was just as He had said to Solomon after he extravagantly gave one thousand burnt offerings. He heard God say, "I would not say this to a stingy person, I cannot trust them."

There was one thing Robert wanted more than anything else. He remembered his immorality in the early stages of his marriage. He said to God, "Lord, I ask that my wife and I be passionately in love all the days of our lives."

After thirty-five years of marriage and many great experiences of God, Robert would not trade his life of extravagance towards God and his constant sacrifices for anything else. He currently pastors Gateway church which has over thirty-five thousand members. The spirit of extravagance has been contagious. In one year alone, the church members gave away over one hundred cars.

> *This is an open invitation from God to everyone: will you meet Me at the place of extravagance? I am already here waiting!*

JESSE DUPLANTIS – THE GIVING PREACHER

"I give away one hundred percent of the income that comes into my ministry." The voice of Jesse Duplantis boomed from the PA system of the convention hall. "I do not give anything to God that costs me nothing. I pay one hundred percent of the cost of my ministry, travel, hotels and related cost.

When a speaker comes to my ministry I give him one hundred percent of the love offering, and in addition, I add something to it. Give me one dollar I give to you a soul; give me a thousand dollars I give you a thousand souls."

It is clear from this assertion of Jesse that there are some people who will give and some people who will go. But even those who will go are required to be extravagant in their giving. It maximizes the effect of their ministry. The heavens are open to those who will be free in their spirits.

> *1. Jesse lives his life in answer to the call to the place of extravagance; what will your story be?*
>
> *2. Will you meet God at the place of extravagance? He is already there waiting!*

JOHNSON SULEMAN
— NOT JUST A GIVER; A GIFT

A leaf in the wind of the Holy Spirit

A giver is a giver where he gives
Of his substance; of his things
Of himself; of everything
But when a giver gives himself to giving
and regards nothing else
And holds himself to account
That nothing he has he really owns
And anytime kingdom desires
Kingdom instructs and it's required
Where giving has no cap or cover
A competition between two passionate lovers
Where angels central in the game
To make his giving look like change
Where he gives for he brought nothing here
And its certain he'll take none away
Where the giver looks for ways to please
For living means to love and give
Then humanity sees what eyes may miss
Not just a giver but heaven's gift

The rise of the prophetic move in Africa and specifically in Nigeria is no joke. Fueled by prayer that raises the bar: twenty-four, thirty-six, forty-eight hours and more continuously in tongues; also encounters and manifestation that rival, or should we say, ratify the scriptures; extreme extravagant generosity on display daily and accurate and specific detailed prophesies. Individuals not satisfied to read and share the scriptures but to live them.

In this book we focus on one such prophet, Apostle Johnson Suleman, a person I have followed because of his obsessive love for God and his passion for the Holy Spirit; his addiction to the scriptures, committing most of the Bible to memory; his affectionate love for prayer and the contagion it has on his congregation and followers, most of whom have been impregnated with this passion; and his profound teachings fueled by his knowledge of and passionate pursuit of the scriptures, and the depth of his revelations.

Testimonies are a normal everyday occurrence in the life and ministry of Apostle Suleman. In his ministry many dead persons have been raised, some dead for days. You will see this live on his YouTube channel. When a blind person is brought to him, it is more surprising to see them leave blind than to see their sight restored. You will see these live on his Youtube channel also. One person born without eyeballs received eyeballs before the cameras. His prophecies are very accurate. He is one of those fireballs whose words does not fall to the ground. In addition, Apostle Suleman leads a church that passionately prays in tongues during services. Everyone prays when a prayer point is raised during services or in response to his sermons. They pray passionately also during Fine Night, his all-night prayer service every last Friday of each month. Prayer is the focus of his ministry. If the mission of the apostle is summarized, he will tell you it is to teach people to love God and to pray.

His testimonies of personal acts and preservation are astounding and mouthwatering. As a prelude to sharing the story of this giver, or should I say gift, we look at just a couple of these testimonies.

This first one is from his YouTube video entitled: Cook Yourself In Prayer.

Many years ago I went into a town in Abguta. While there with the bishop I saw a big tree, very massive tree. I saw cars, house, matriculation gowns, wedding gowns…. I say, "Lord what is this?"

He said, "The destinies of the people are in the tree."

I said, "What do I do Lord?"

He said, "Bring it down."

I turned to the man of God, I said, "God just spoke that this tree must go down."

The man of God turned to me and said, "I invited you to preach; preach and go, leave the tree alone."

I said, "If I want to do something with this tree, who do I speak to?"

"He said you speak to the Bale."

The Bale is like the king of the land. We went there. Fortunately for me the Bale was lying down. He had stroke. I was very happy. I knew if God allowed me to heal that man he would permit me to do anything.

While I was talking he spoke in his native language. I did not know he understood English.

I said tell him, "We will go around that tree and uproot it."

The tree was like the god of the village; they worshipped it.

He said, "The tree is not my problem; let me stand up. If I can stand and walk."

I prayed for him, the Lord healed him. He stood and walked. He then drew me to a corner. That's when I knew he understood English.

He said, "What are you going to use?"

I said, "Nothing."

He said, "What are you going to use to cut the tree?"

I said, "Just permit me."

He said, "Many years ago, some missionaries came to cut the tree. While they were using the motor saw the tree began to bring out fresh blood and people were crying from the tree. You don't have anything to cut it with?"

I said, "Just permit me."

He permitted.

I told the pastor to get some members from his church. He brought them and we moved around the tree and began singing warfare songs.

I said, "Father, I was told that motor saw could not bring down this tree. I knock on the door of thunder. Let thunder blast from the top to the bottom! Let lightning divide. Let the sun dry up the tree!"

Thunder struck. Divided the tree from the bottom and the sun began to dry it up. Where the tree was, is now a main road. The good news is this, young men and women began to get married; people began to go to school.

Apostle Suleman has other astounding testimonies that can be found in the sermons on his YouTube channel. In one such testimony, he was invited to dedicate a church in a particular place. Himself and a couple pastors checked into the place where they would be staying. Not long after the place was surrounded with gunmen. He tried calling the pastor who invited him but to no avail. He held the hands of the pastors with him and began praying in tongues. After sometime they found themselves outside the building and away from the gunmen. They looked back and saw the gunmen still guarding the house. They just kept walking. How they got out they have no knowledge, just a reference: Phillip in the book of Acts.

It is without doubt that Apostle Suleman is a gift to this and successive generations, but in this book I want to talk about his giving. He is a giving machine.

Places almost 100 widows on salary every month

Places university students on salary

Has a dream to put every struggling pastor on salary.

The apostle who comes from a wealthy family, knew poverty by choice. He speaks of hunger of such magnitude that his body protested. He recalls pushing a wheelbarrow in the market to earn money from the supplies he would carry. His family was Muslim. They rejected him when he became a Christian, totally committed and unashamed. His family name was Sule. They barred him from using that name so he changed his to Suleman.

They refused any form of support. His experience allows him to fully associate with the poor and hungry. He knows what they are experiencing and it is added motivation for his giving lifestyle.

His family is saved now, and many have changed their names to Suleman. He is extremely rich because of the blessings of God. In fact, he asserts that if you still know how much money you have in the bank you are poor.

<u>THE GIFT IN ACTION</u>

In an earlier recording of Apostle Suleman entitled Walking out of Poverty on YouTube, he testifies:

I had one car; I was worshipping God. He said, "Son, do you love Me? Give Me your car now."

I said, "Lord, is that You?" I brought the hand down. "You foul spirit of taking my car; I rebuke you!"

God said, "Your passbook also; every dime in your account."

I wept. I cried.

When Omega Fire Ministry just started we had one car, a Mercedes Benz 190. That car was an internal ministry car. One day we were worshipping God. I heard the voice of the Lord, "I want that car now."

I told Pastor John. He said, "Can we talk about it after service?"

I said, "I won't let you discourage me." Because after service they would deliberate it and give me reasons why I should not release the car.

I turned to Mama (wife) and told her God said this car must go. She said, "Ok" and continued dancing.

I said, "God said this car should go!"

She asked me, "Is there anything you have that He didn't give you?"

I said, "No."

She said, "Well, give Him."

The young man that washed the car every morning started crying.

I gave that car. It was Tuesday. On Thursday I went to Benin City for a program. While we were sitting in the hotel, a man came to the reception with a brand new car and a file with the documents and said God said I should give you.

We were happy. We were going to the morning session of the program and our host came to pick us up with their cars so we left the car.

When we were coming back from the program we noticed a BMW convertible, the latest series, chasing after us. We had a pastor with us. He told us to all go in. He stood by the door and asked the man what he wanted. The man said please it is important I see the apostle.

He said, "No the apostle is busy."

He said, "Please for the past three days I can't sleep, God said I should give him my car."

The pastor responded, "The apostle is not busy, come."

The cars came. It was two cars. Sunday we drove the cars to church. Members were happy. I told a man of God to come and dedicate the cars. The man of God came.

He preached. When I was sitting down God said, "Son, those cars are not your own. When he is going let him carry them."

I stood up on the altar and I said, weeping, "You see now; you see now; God said these cars shall be for the man of God."

Three ladies stood up in church and went home. At the end of the service I asked someone to ask them why they left like that. They said they have changed church. This man has mental case. One day he will gather all of us and sow us. This guy is not normal. They left drinking Panadol for another man's headache.

I knew where I was going. You can't be reached until you become an outreach. Can I tell you what changed my mindset? They call me Father Christmas. I'm not. I'm wise. Something changed my mindset. When Job said, "We came to this world with nothing and it is certain… certain we will take nothing out."

I do crusades around the world which I have sponsored with my own pocket; millions of naira at a time. I give cars to over a hundred and sixty people. (That has increased to over one thousand now). Many of them are pastors. You can't kill me. Imagine you try and I send a message to these pastors. Imagine all these pastors praying about you. I don't worry about flying because if I die now the kingdom will lose. I enter a plane, I sleep. I say God You know; a kingdom investor, sponsor of crusades. The reason you have problem with death is because you are not relevant to the kingdom. I have preached in people's churches and brought cars for them. Before I came to this crusade I wrote a check with what I am going to sow. Most people come expecting honorarium. What is honorarium without honor?

I preached in a church, I saw a widow. I looked at her and God said, "Buy her a car."

I bought her a car, three million naira. She said, "I am confused."

God said, "Before her husband died he owed rent of three million, pay the rent."

This was me building at that time. I counted another three million and gave to her. God said, "She has four children, pay their fees."

I counted money and paid their fees. When I was going I said to myself, "Was I charmed?"

After this, a man called me in Abuja. I said, "I am busy." I disconnected the call.

The guy called me again and abused the hell out of me. Don't you want God to bless me, send your account number. I sent my account number. It was significant.

Again, I was abroad and I had some money with me. God said, "Give it out."

I gave it out. I'm at a level now where nothing phases me. I gave it out and I sat down.

I was going to the airport. A lady stopped me and said, "Are you Apostle Suleman?"

I said, "I am."

She said, "Praise God. There is this money I have been carrying. God said I should not remove it from my car. I'm coming." She went to the car, came back and brought the money.

I said, "Kneel down." She did.

"I said, lady God bless your marriage."

She said, "I am not married."

I said, "Your children shall prosper."

She said, "I don't have."

I said, "They are coming."

One time we were building the conference hall. I stood up in church and said, "God said we should build the conference hall."
God said, "I didn't tell them, I told you."
I said, "I don't have money."
God said, "Your sacrifice is there."
We built that 600 seater in 29 days from my pocket.
You can't kill me, O. I have been shot many times at close range; bullets dropping. You can't kill me for this guy is a kingdom hooligan. What is a car?

One time I said to my wife, "The prayer of the husband preserves the wife, but the sacrifice of the husband must be different from the sacrifice of the wife." My wife started crying. I was preaching in church, she came out and dropped her car key. I kept quiet. I was still preaching, she loosened another car key and dropped. She called her PA and said, "Go home."
There was a land somebody had given her. She sent home, brought the documents and gave it. She cleared her account and wrote a check and gave it, same service.
I said, "When you are giving you must use wisdom. After giving, then you disturb your husband, is that necessary?"
The only thing I didn't do was to call her name, but she was the one I was talking to. She ignored me but I could see her crying. She said, "God I want my own financial strength."
We had a program in a Redeemed church (regional province). A man of God stopped me and said, "Sir we have a brand new car and God said I should give it to you."
The wife interjected, "Sir, it's not for you, it's for your wife."
A guy came and said, "Sir the last time you were here you prophesied my financial turnaround and said I should come back and marry this girl. Sir, everything I have I want to sow it as a seed."
It was several, several thousands of dollars. While I was still talking the wife said, "Sir, the Lord just spoke to me that we should give all this money to mummy (my wife)."

A guy who was outside came and said, "Sir, I have a massive land and God said I should give it to you. While I was upstairs praying God said this land is for your wife."

I called her and said, "Take the next flight and come. While I preach you preach. I can't be preaching and you are the one collecting all the rewards." (Laugh).

When I got home she was dancing. She drew out a massive bag full of money and four property documents. She said people came and said, "God said they should give it to me."

I said, "Sometimes ask me before you give. If I allow you to do this, very soon you will be the bread winner." (Joke). That's an error that must be deleted. Sacrifice is a lifter.

You cannot truly be a giver until you get to the point where this world means nothing to you. That's why you are stranded to pay rent. You are walking in your capacity. You have not handed to the Lord to take over from you.

We started our Ministry in Auchi. There was nothing there to reckon with but God told me, "God is not in a place but in a man." Anywhere a king stays is a throne. There is no dry ground, only dry men.

You can pray for the anointing, pray for gifts, pray for manifestation but there is a level of unction you can't enjoy until you are a terrible giver. God will not release that anointing on you if you are still materialistic. God knows you will commercialize the anointing. He must take you to a realm where nothing means anything to you.

Indeed, that place is where you become a gift to your and succeeding generations, just as this apostle is.

A MATURE GIFT

The manifestation of the gift is the testimonial experience of the many who have encountered Apostle Suleman, those who are graced to feed from his wisdom and drink of his goodness. As the queen of Sheba said to Solomon, those who are graced to serve him and to be members of his ministry; the many pastors associated with him who have received tangible blessings; the scores of widows he has on a monthly salary, the many others to includeuniversity graduates in in transition whom he also has on salary, the many students he has sent to school and university many of which are on monthly stipend; the many he has supported in business and ministry, the over one thousand recipients of cars he has given; the many whose rent he has paid; the many others he has given houses.

If this is not enough the testimonials are everywhere. In one video a woman came to him telling him she was wrongly accused by her landlord and given notice. He listened to her, then stopped and said, "Within two months…"

He paused, receiving another divine instruction. "The Lord told me to buy you a car and to give you a paid driver for the rest of your life." Then he returned to his original thought, "Within two months I will build you a house."

The woman fainted. This is the feature of his ministry. A heart of complete generosity.

He tells the story of his first private jet. It came from two stranded young men he helped through school. They went to Dubai. Became very successful. Called one day and said, "Papa, we have bought you a jet."

As if his lifestyle of giving was not enough, Apostle Suleman has a plan for money that is very extensive. He has no value for money apart from its value to the kingdom. He sponsors many crusades with a schedule extending for months at a time. His passion is to one day put every pastor in Nigeria on a salary. He encourages us to have a plan for money and to write down what we would do if God blesses us with wealth. He has such a vast plan that his wealth will play hard to catch up. And the joy of everyone is to see his ambitious plans realized day by day before our eyes.

Just recently the apostle realized one of his dreams to start a free food restaurant to feed the poor of all religions. This restaurant was launched and now feeds over 2500 persons weekly. This project is so extensive that it currently employs sixty-six full time staff. He is currently building a structure to exclusively house the restaurant.

Apostle Suleman says his intention is to fulfil the scripture that says, "I was hungry and you fed me, in prison and you visited me." In fact, prison has been one of his primary focuses. The apostle has bought a transformer for the local prison to assure it of light; he sends money to feed the prisoners with proper meals every month and he spends most Christmases with the prisoners at the prison facility.

He has also recently received a massive donation of lands with which he intends to build 200 housing structures over time to house the destitute. His intention is to fulfil the entire scripture.

<u>For indeed:</u>

A giver is a giver where he gives
Of his substance; of his things
Of himself; of everything
But when a giver gives himself to giving
and regards nothing else
And holds himself to account
That nothing he has he really owns
And anytime kingdom desires
Kingdom instructs and it's required
Where giving has no cap or cover
A competition between two passionate lovers
Where angels central in the game
To make his giving look like change
Where he gives for he brought nothing here
And its certain he'll take none away
Where the giver looks for ways to please
For living means to love and give
Then humanity sees what eyes may miss
Not just a giver but heaven's gift

YOUR STORY

illiam Colgate founded the Colgate Palmolive Company about two hundred years ago. He increased his giving from ten percent, to twenty percent, to thirty percent, then to forty percent, then fifty percent, until finally he devoted one hundred percent of his earnings to the Lord.

Henry Crowell founded the Quaker Oats Company. After forty years of giving sixty percent of his income to God, he testifies, ***"I have never gotten ahead of God. He has always been ahead of me in giving."***

J. L. Kraft, head of Kraft Cheese, for many years, gave twenty-five percent of his income to Christian causes.

John D. Rockefeller Sr. said, "I have tithed every dollar God has entrusted to me, and I want to say, ***had I not tithed the first dollar, I would not have tithed the millions I made."***

The next chapter of this book is about your story. You may begin to write it in living ink today.

EVERY GIFT PERPETUATES

"**I** do not want to die! I do not want to die!" Wheat shouted, terrified. "Hide me, please, hide me!"

Corn sat on the shelf beside Wheat. She, too, was in the same predicament as Wheat, and Wheat's fear was contagious. Corn trembled as she considered her fate. She would be put to death shortly, also.

They could hear footsteps as Farmer came into the room. Wheat and Corn knew they had no say in the matter. Whatever happened to them would be the decision of Farmer. Farmer owned them. They were his slaves. Farmer reached up and grabbed Corn off the shelf with some others. Corn was carried to the field outside where her sentence of death was executed. Corn was buried alive.

Corn felt the soil enclosing her and knew it was just a matter of time before she died. She could feel water seeping through her grave, and touching the outer layer of her skin. The warm soil, filled with moisture, was stifling her. Time was running out on Corn. She pushed out roots to resist this slow death. The root was sucking up the moisture and Corn could feel the effect of her system shutting down from the inside. The amazing effects of the soil had taken its toll. Something else was stirring inside Corn. The struggle intensified, but she was losing. Corn died, as green foliage pushed up from inside her dead cells and burst through the ground.

Meanwhile, Farmer returned for Wheat. As he picked Wheat off the shelf with the others, Wheat fell from his hand into a crack in the concrete. Wheat was safe. She would not die now. Where she was, she would live for many years. Time passed and Wheat sat there lonely and alone.

She could see Farmer bringing in the offspring of Corn, and she could not help but admire them. "How lovely they are! How many they are!" she exclaimed. She could see the careful attention Farmer gave to them. After some time, some Corns were returned to the ground and their offspring were even more numerous. She could see Farmer selling some to other Farmers just like himself. Wheat could see they were being transferred to many other places and she could imagine how plentiful they would become everywhere.

Time passed, and Wheat had seen many generations of Corn. She occupied herself in her lonely cell__ for she came to the realization that this was her reality, counting Corns. Before long, Corn had become too numerous for her to count. ***Wheat's only desire was that Corn could have been there to see her offspring. It was wishful thinking. Corn would not have had offspring if she was there.*** "Just as myself," Wheat agonized, "lonely and alone."

"Unless a grain of wheat falls to the ground and dies, it remains alone." Phillip could hear the words of his Master, Jesus. Jesus had now ascended into Heaven, but his voice was as clear in his mind as the moment He looked into their eyes and said it to them. He could hear Him say, also, "But if it dies, it produces much grain."

He was talking about His death because He has said, immediately before this, "The hour has come that the Son of Man should be glorified." He was not willing to abide alone, like Wheat. The occasion was that some Greeks had come desiring to see Him. Is it that Jesus was not willing to abide alone as a son of God? Did He want to create many Christs or, should we say, Christians? Is it also that He was including the Greeks in His vision of reproduction?

Andrew reverted to his own thoughts as something deep stirred inside him. "God had promised to multiply the seed of Abraham like the stars of Heaven. This is a literal analogy that had a spiritual reality. We know now that this promise was meant for Christ, the only Seed. We know the stars of God refer to the angels. We know a third of them fell from heaven with Satan. Is there a spiritual reality to this analogy? *Are stars being multiplied on earth to replace the fallen stars?* Is the natural process of reproduction of Jesus Christ the method?"

"Andrew," Phillip said excitedly, breaking the silence. "Do you remember what Jesus said, 'Unless a grain of wheat…'?"

"Falls to the ground and dies…" Andrew interjected. He had many fond memories of Jesus and this was certainly one. "I have been think-ing," Andrew said, "see how we are many now? Every gift we give is like a seed: A gift perpetuates. *Every seed continues to give until purpose is accomplished.*"

"Do you remember when God saved Noah and his family to save the world? With Noah, he saved only two of every unclean animal and seven of the clean ones. Noah even sacrificed one of each clean animal. Now see how the world is filled with people and animals today? I agree Christ was a gift to mankind. For God so loved the world, He gave… A gift perpetuates just as a seed. A gift continues to give until purpose is accomplished."

These men were both silent for a while, each lost in his own thoughts. It was Andrew who broke the silence. He said to Phillip in a low undertone, as if talking to himself in reflection, "Do you know that when we dedicate our lives it is like a seed?"

Phillip responded immediately, "Or when we give anything to the work of Christ: our time, our goods, or our money."

"Yes," Andrew said. "We die to what we give, it is no longer ours. It is God's."

"What we know is that every gift perpetuates," Phillip said. "You can never tell who you are reaching. Those little children we are investing in could become the next evangelists.

Your own children whom you spend time loving, reading the Bible with, setting a template of prayer and generosity are seeds. They could reach many, and raise up others to reach many.

288

*Every time we give, it places us at the top of a multilevel market-
ing tree that expands and keeps expanding until Christ returns."*

"That drives home!" Andrew exclaimed excitedly. "Do you
remember what Jesus said about the kingdom of God? Just like
the grain of a mustard seed, very small and microscopic when it is
sown. When it dies, it grows and becomes bigger than the
other trees. It is full of life itself and it sustains life."

"Indeed," Phillip added, "Leaven has a way of expanding."

Andrew responded, "What did God say to Noah? While
the earth remains, seedtime and harvest will never stop. *Our seed
will never stop producing seeds and bringing forth harvests."*
"Solomon said, 'The person who observes the wind will not sow,
and he who regards the clouds will not reap.'" Andrew chipped in.
"It is not for us to determine what happens to our seed - we must
sow. I have seen many who resist the word initially who are some
of the most dedicated Christians today. There is no excuse for not
giving or paying tithes. If the priest is dishonest, God will judge
him. If we are dishonest or disobedient, God will judge us."

"And there is no excuse for not sharing the word," Phillip
said, fully engaged. "Jesus spoke about the sower. He sowed and
some fell on various soils that were unproductive for various reasons. But some fell on good soil. Can you imagine the ones that
fell on the good soil? Can you imagine their generations? They
make the ones who do not respond minute. Can you imagine one
minister, or one evangelist rising up from our efforts… the many
they will reach? We must sow!"

"This is Solomon's conclusion also," Andrew interjected.
"He said, 'Just as we don't know the way of the wind, or how the
bones of a child grow in the mother's womb, so you do not know
the works of God who makes everything. In the morning, sow
your seed, and do not withhold your hand in the evening, for you
do not know which will prosper. It could be this one or that one

or both.' You do not know upon whose life you are making an impact, it could be the next national leader."

Phillip tried to steady his thoughts. This was a lot to consider. He knew this applied to the missionary or pastor who will reach millions generationally, just as the mother or father who raises a godly child. It applied to the school teacher who uses her influence to make a positive impact on the children for Jesus, or the Christian who spreads the love and displays the character of Christ at the workplace. ***Their gift will continue to give and their network will keep expanding. An adult saved could save a family. The impact is local, community, it is national, it is international, it is intergenerational.***

Did not God command Adam before he fell to be fruitful and multiply? Is it not the same command the second Adam, who did not fall, carries? If we make sacrifices now, to distribute our precious seeds, we will one day come rejoicing bringing in the sheaves, or should we say sheep, for our Master.

The two men parted company without any significant parting. They were both occupied by their own meditation. It was not long after this that the Apostle Paul would write the doxology to their discourse: ***May He who supplies seed to the sower, and bread for food, supply and multiply the seed you have sown and increase the fruits of your righteousness.***

In the ninth chapter of his second book to them, Paul was charging the Corinthians about giving. He had just exhorted them by saying that God is able to make all grace abound towards them. That they would have a sufficient amount of everything they needed. He, however, outlined the purpose of this. It was so that they would abound in every good work. He quoted the Scriptures to support this. "He has dispersed abroad. He has given to the poor. His righteousness endures forever."

The Scripture supported the conclusion that every gift perpetuates unto eternity. It was after this that Paul pronounced the famous verse used as the doxology above. It was a blessing of supply: the supply of seeds. It was also a blessing of increase: an increase of seed and an increase in fruits of acts of righteousness. ***All the blessing, both seed and fruit, is for sowing and is linked to sowing.*** Paul was not finished. He was so interested in the portion to be sown that he felt he needed to elaborate.

He continued, ***"You are enriched in all things, both food and seeds, for liberality which causes men to give thanks to God." According to Paul, even the food is seed potential.*** The food and the seed are for liberal giving. Our generosity should cause men to give thanks to God. This is evidence of our confession to the gospel of Christ. Yet all our giving pales in comparison to God's indescribable gift. How do we find adjectives to describe God giving Christ to us? Our appreciation and description of this extravagant gift by God can only be portrayed by our obedience. God enriches us so we can enrich others, first with salvation, then with all things.

1. The waves are carried by the wind, the wind is carried by the Spirit; no one knows where the waters will take your seed but this we know for sure, you will find it after many days!

2. And you will keep on finding it after many, many days, and still find it after the end of days!

THE TBN STORY

Paul Crouch woke up early one morning. This was crunch time for him. Today would determine the future of the Trinity Broadcasting Network. Paul had no doubt about the vision God had placed in his heart. He had no doubt about the impact of this vision. He had no doubt about God's ability. However, when you are in the heat of the fire looking for a way out, you hear voices.

This is an opportune time for the devil to parade fear and hopelessness with passing time and unfulfilled expectations. TBN was at the very edge. The ministry needed One Hundred Thousand Dollars to stay on the air and the deadline was today.

Paul's mighty weapon was prayer and he prayed. Paul and his wife Jan, a woman of faith who equally carried the vision, prayed. The many partners of the ministry were praying. The reality was that they were in the moment. TBN was in the gas chamber of finances and the hours were ticking by.

Paul could remember his own sacrifice of twenty thousand dollars much earlier in the ministry, and how the viewers responded with a matching contribution to rescue this same vision from another anxious moment. Paul had reason to hope, he had a testimony.

The day started with intensity. Contributions were coming in, but Paul could never be more aware that it was not enough. What difference would a day make? Paul was not prepared to surrender to hopelessness though, although time signaled its disassociation with hope. Hours had turned to minutes. The deadline had now become a mountain. A mountain that was up in the face of everyone who was believing with TBN. A mountain that could not be navigated. A mountain that was quickly closing in. A mountain that was prepared to crash Paul's vision.

Paul sat there in the studio at the place of grave concerns. These were the dying minutes of his efforts to keep the Trinity Broadcasting Network on the air. He needed One Hundred Thousand Dollars. They had managed to raise Sixty-seven thousand dollars after all the time and efforts and sacrifices.

Paul was at the place where faith fights to maintain its distance from fear. The place between resignation and incredulity. The place in the Spirit where your feet fail. Where you know that Jesus had beckoned you out on the stormy seas, you begin to walk on water, then... yes, the place where you need divine intervention. As Paul stood there waiting, not sure what to think it was then he was told someone had come to see him.

There was not much more for Paul to do, so he went to see the person. He had no expectation but he knew God was never late. The individual standing there was a man, small in stature. He was a Catholic. He had something in his hand that he handed to Paul. He said, "I was about to buy a yacht but God told me to give this to you." Paul opened the check. It was a bank draft for exactly thirty-five thousand dollars.

Paul did not have time to tell this stranger thanks. He would kiss his feet later but now he was in a race against time. The minutes were ticking by. It was quickly coming down to single digits. Paul grabbed the check and rushed out of the studio to the bank. He ran the race of his life down the busy streets. It was a race against time.

He reached the bank and looked up at the clock. It was exactly five minutes before closing, five minutes before the axe was to come down on TBN ministry. Many years later, with millions saved through the TBN ministry, scores of stations commissioned across the world; with many ministers raised up, many ministries given global platforms; with millions touched each day and millions more changed, ***the gift of thirty-five thousand by one man, small in stature but big in obedience continues to speak volumes.***

The generational impact of this sacrifice of faith will continue to populate eternity and venerate earth. This man was willing to sacrifice his yacht to be rich towards God. God has multiplied his seed and increased the fruit of his righteousness. ***Although it may not always be visible, and hardly ever immediately visible, every gift perpetuates.***

> ***The story of TBN is personal for millions across the globe, but it is a story that is not complete without the testament of a seed.***

THE CASE OF THE ABANDONED CHILD

"James, Jackie, Wilson, Heather, Munroe… all on board!" the bus volunteer said as she prepared to take another bus load of children to their homes. Bill Wilson observed as the children were numbered and the buses left. This was another exhausting week for him, but very fulfilling.

The children had received all they came for and more today. They were excited and they were ministered to. Bill Wilson operated a high energy Sunday school in the heart of the slums of New York City. He had activities ranging from money grabbing, to motor bikes, to illusions, to… whatever it took. According to Bill, he did whatever it took to get the children out. Bill currently ministers to over twenty-five thousand children in his Sunday School on a weekly basis. He has easily the largest Sunday school in America and the world today.

A tear falls from the face of Bill Wilson. He shakes his head. Every time he picks up a child off the street of New York to bring in for ministry he is picking up himself. Bill Wilson and this ministry would not exist but for the kind act of one missionary.

"Stay here Bill, I will return soon!" Bill could hear the distinct voice of his mother. It was a voice that he loved so much. They did not have a lot but she was always there and that was enough for him. She struggled to survive but she loved him and that was enough.

He watched her leave, knowing she would return soon. She always did. Bill was left alone on a street corner in the city, a small child of just twelve years old.

"Why is mummy taking so long?" Bill remembered saying to himself about twenty minutes later. He realized something must have been drastically wrong as the minutes turned to hours and the hours dragged on into the night. Tortured by the cold night, Bill could feel the pain of hunger in his stomach. He had nothing to eat and he did not dare move in the event his mother would return. He certainly did not want to miss her.

One night passed, then another and Bill fought off the feeling that his mother was not coming back this time. It was too frightening a thought to imagine. Where would he go? What would he eat? How would he survive? "No, I will not go!" He said to himself through the tears and the pain and the hunger. These pangs were even more severe because of his age. Frightened and hungry, this abandoned boy, feeling betrayed, just sat there.

It was there that a Christian gentleman found him three days later. Hundreds of persons had passed him by over the three days. They must have seen this destitute child trapped in his misery as they passed, but no one stopped.

He could recall the kind words of the Christian man. He was on his way to visit his sick son in the hospital but he took the time to care. Bill Wilson gives thanks to God everyday that it is a Christian who found him. He was on his way to give Bill something to eat, and took him to a Sunday School Camp. He paid the full fee for Bill's admission. This is where Bill Wilson met Jesus. This gentleman did everything the good neighbor, the Samaritan, did in the story of Jesus.

"Yes!" Bill Wilson said softly to himself as a faint smile briefly visited his tired lips, "I am who I am today because somebody cared." "Metro Ministries Sunday School is a product of the effect that a Sunday school camp had on me." Bill Wilson thought as he considered the struggles of his ministry and his sacrifices to raise finances. He remembered the time he was shot through the face; he considered the dangers to himself and his staff everyday in the slum of New York City; he remembered the time he found a staff member dead outside his church. "What if the Sunday School Camp had closed its doors because of financial or other struggles? It would have missed this global and generational tree.

I am who I am today because somebody cared- cared enough to pick me up; cared enough to pay my price; cared enough to run a Sunday School Camp; cared enough to persevere. This is what I want these children I minister to every week to say, 'I am who I am today because somebody cared.' This is what I want their children also to say about them, 'I am who I am today because somebody cared.' This is what I want everyone their children will impact to say, 'I am who I am today because somebody cared.'"

Somebody saw Jesus, sitting by the wayside, in trouble and destitute, and stopped to care. Now, look at the impact that Jesus is having in New York City! It is, indeed, the impact of a seed.

"For as much as you do to the least of these, you do it to Me..." *Jesus is presenting Himself in many forms, ministries and persons, waiting for a generous transfer to create a generational impact;* to continue a building He started centuries ago. In accordance with His words, "I will build My church!" God has multiplied the seed of this missionary's kindness and increased the fruit of his righteousness. *We must never get tired of doing good, for although it may not always be visible, every gift perpetuates. In due season we will reap...!*

1. The story of the abandoned child is personal for thousands of children and families in New York City; it is a story that gives credence to the potency and generational impact of a seed.

2. Heaven alone knows the amount of opportunities we have missed to create an impact; history gloriously records the ones taken.

CHAPTER

11

BUILDING A MEMORIAL

He had been doing this for years, loving the poor and giving generously to them. There was nothing he desired more than putting a smile on the face of the destitute. There was nothing that made him happier than seeing the hungry fed. This man was a soldier in command of other soldiers yet his heart was with fighting the battle of the people. He loved people. He loved giving. He enjoyed creating opportunities for people.

There was something else very unique about this soldier. He lived at the time of the death of Christ, where Judaism was very pronounced and discriminatory.

He was a Gentile, yet he loved the God of Israel. He was a dedicated person of prayer and he never missed his daily schedule. Prayer for him was like his food. Sometimes he felt like it was a waste of time, especially when he was around the Jews who had deeded God to themselves, but he kept praying.

At that time he did not know about the vial in Heaven that stored prayers. He did not know that there was a God in Heaven who recorded generosity. He did not know that this God he was praying to treated every gift and act of generosity to the poor as a personal loan to Himself.

Enter the surprise of this man, yes, his name is Cornelius. Cornelius was there praying when he saw an angel of God coming into the room. It was a vision but it was clear as day. It was very real to him, and he trembled. The angel called him by his name. This was exhilarating and amazing yet frightful. In all of this, Cornelius had the presence of mind to ask the angel, "What is it, lord?"

The response was what really brought the reality of Heaven home to Cornelius. Now he knew his living and his giving was not in vain. He recognized that even though he could not claim entitlement to God, he could still get His attention. The prayer and the giving of even a Gentile against a strong background of Judaism, the only recognized authentic religion at the time, would capture the eyes and the heart of God. The angel said, "Your prayers and your giving have come up before God as a memorial."

This lifestyle of devotion and generosity by Cornelius, was to challenge the faith of the most respected leader of the early church, Peter. It would cause Peter to give a defense of himself and his separatist beliefs to the church. It would take Christianity beyond its Jewish roots and culture. It would be an avenue by which God would place His stamp of approval on the Gentiles by giving them the Holy Spirit; this was even before the Jews were prepared to allow them water baptism.

It would remove the differentiation between the Jews and the Gentiles in Christ. It would take the Jews down a pathway that Christ had opened to the Gentiles on the cross, breaking the dividing wall with Christianity. It would pave the way for the church to receive the ministry of Paul, arguably the most accomplished apostle. ***It is clear that a lifestyle of devotion and generosity builds a good memorial before God.***

He was a Gentile, a commander with command of one hundred soldiers. He was assigned to Jerusalem. He was an extremely generous man. He loved to give into projects that were important to the people he was charged to police. He gave from his heart to the pleasure of the people. He knew that nothing was more important to the people of Jerusalem than a synagogue. Their life, their culture, their history and their future was built upon and around their God. He knew this, so he built them a synagogue.

The centurion was also a very compassionate person. He loved people. He loved the nation of the Jews and he loved his servants. It so happened that his servant was terminally ill. It was the time of the ministry of Jesus. The fame of the ministry of Jesus had reached every crevice and corner of Jerusalem. From the palace of Herod to the beggar on the streets. It had not escaped the ears of this centurion.

The centurion was also a very wise man and he had taken time out to study the reports about Jesus. He had come to only one conclusion, Jesus had some divine authority on earth. The centurion loved his servant and did not want him dead. He had a great relationship with the elders of the Jews. He sent for them and said, "Could you please speak to Jesus on my servant's behalf? He is sick and if Jesus does not intervene, he will die."

The elders were happy to return a favor to this centurion who loved them so much. They immediately set out to find Jesus. They, themselves, did not have a great relationship with Jesus because they envied Him. However, they were willing to put these differences aside to speak to Jesus on behalf of this Gentile who was an extravagant giver to their nation.

They came to Jesus and said, "Jesus, please come and heal the servant of this centurion. We beg You. He is a very good man. He loves our nation very much and he has built us a synagogue." Jesus saw the intensity of their desire but He heard something else. He heard the generosity of this centurion calling out to him. He could not resist it. He had built a synagogue. He had given the Jews a place of worship and sacrifice. ***This Gentile had commanded the attention of Heaven by caring for the affairs of Heaven.*** Jesus left immediately and went with them. He went because this is what the Gentile Centurion had requested. His generosity had given him favor and the ability to make a special request of God.

What the centurion did next was most stunning of all. He sent servants to Jesus when He was near and said, "Lord, do not bother to come any further. I am not worthy for you to come under my roof. I am a Gentile sinner. I do not even count myself worthy to come to You. Speak the word and my servant will be healed. I am under authority and whatever my superiors say, I do. I have men under my authority and whatever I tell them to do, they do. Sickness is under Your authority. You speak the word and it must obey Your command; my servant will be healed."

Jesus marveled at the spiritual understanding of this Gentile commander. It was a reflection of the spiritual insight that made him so generous towards God. Jesus commented about him in the presence of all the Israelites. "I have not seen such great faith, no, not in Israel." In other words, this Gentile had surpassed the Israelites in his command of the knowledge of spiritual things, both in faith and, arguably, in his generosity. ***Your generosity will build a memorial with people and make them speak up for you at the appropriate times.***

"You are so beautiful," she said, "I know the right thing for you! Come and see me in three days." Excitement filled the heart of Treleth as she went back home that night. Every woman, especially the widows, in the community got excited every time Dorcas made them a promise. Dorcas was a very talented woman. She was one of the best seamstresses and designers in the village of Joppa. Some of the best and most elegant designs that the women in this community wore were made by her. The best part is that she did it absolutely free.

Dorcas held one belief. She believed that her talent was given to her to be a blessing. She was not rich but she believed that she could use her profession to create a great impact in the kingdom of God. Every day of her life for her was a day to create an impact. Treleth could hardly wait for the three days to come. She could imagine what Dorcas had in store for her. She thought of all the designs she had seen from Dorcas and she fantasized. Anyone of them would be more than enough for her. Treleth was a widow and could not afford to pay for anything like this herself.

"I will go to her now," Treleth said to herself. "No, let me give her some time," she responded. The day had arrived and Treleth struggled with the problem of what time would be the right time for her to go. She did not want to appear too anxious, but she really was. She would at least let the morning past. Early in the afternoon, Treleth turned up at Dorcas' door. Dorcas was ready for her and welcomed her in with a big smile. She pulled out a box from her closet and presented it to Treleth. This was always the best part of it for Dorcas. She loved to see the look on their faces when she presented them with her surprises. She enjoyed the tears and expressions of joy when she surpassed their expectations. This time would be no different. As Treleth opened the box and pulled out the dress, her face contorted.

This was much more beautiful than she imagined. "Why don't you try it on?" Dorcas encouraged. Treleth could hardly get it on, she was so nervous and excited. As she finally put the dress on, her face was a contortion of tears and laughter. As her eyes met Dorcas' eyes, her tears fell freely. She did not need to say more, her tears said it all. She left without saying thanks, she could not find the words but her gratitude was sincere.

This was a typical reaction from every woman to whom Dorcas rendered service in the small community of Joppa. Dorcas loved them all with her talents and they loved her dearly in return.

"Dorcas is dead! Dorcas is dead!" The cry rang out from one end of Joppa to the next. It was a wailing tearful cry filled with pain. It was like a cloud of darkness had fallen on this community in the moment and the tears of every household was soaking the ground. Everyone felt it, deep in their stomachs. It was even worse because her death was unexpected. They brought out the garments Dorcas had made, and just looking at them made her death more unbearable. These garments held memories which, themselves, were alive. The only thing that could ease the pain of these women, the only thing, would be to bring Dorcas back to life; but how?

Someone said, "Peter!" and a ray of hope lit the heart of every woman of Joppa. They knew of Peter's significance. Since the death of Jesus, the miracles he performed were very notable. The anointing upon him was so strong that his shadow had been known to heal many people on the streets as he passed. The good news was that Peter was in nearby Lydda.

"Quickly," one of the leading ladies of the community said, "Let us send two men to get him. He must come!" Immediately they sent two men for Peter and begged him not to delay. Peter, recognizing the urgency of the situation, and that this crisis had affected the entire community of Joppa, set out with the men.

When Peter arrived in Joppa, the widows surrounded him. Everyone had something to say about Dorcas. They showed Peter the tunics and the garments Dorcas had made for them, and Peter understood their grief. Dorcas's generosity had spoken for her. This was an extraordinary woman. Her memorial was her giving, and her impact was her extravagance. She gave her talents and her profession but that was all that was needed to make a notable impact on a community.

Peter put everyone of them out. He then knelt down and prayed. He called Dorcas by the other translation of her name, Tabitha. He said, "Tabitha arise!" This was a time the world would see how Heaven responds to the heart of a liberal giver. Dorcas rose up from the dead.

While she lived, Dorcas had built a memorial by her extravagant giving that could speak for her when she died. ***When you create an impact with your giving, the people will give anything to keep you alive and in memory, or bring you back from the dead if they must.*** The rich but miserly man will fade away in his pursuits, but a generous heart will build a lasting memorial.

"The brethren in Philippi have been a great blessing to me," the apostle Paul reminisced. "They have really cared for me. They have always shown it at every opportunity. I am not even thinking about my needs. I have learnt to be content in all situations. When

I have an abundance I am good and when I don't have enough, I am still very content.

But these people have been very good to me. When I left Macedonia, no church shared with me concerning giving and receiving but the church of Philippi. I am so satisfied with them. Even when I was in Thessalonica they sent more than once to meet my needs. Again it is not that I am seeking gifts or presents for my personal comfort, it is all about them.

If we add the response of God to every act of generosity, then we understand the true character of giving. It is really giving and receiving. When these generous brethren give to me, they are setting up a memorial for themselves before God. Fruits will abound to their account. I cannot discourage them from giving, it is an important part of their discipleship. I would be blocking their blessings."

Paul smiled as he envisioned the work of God among the Philippians' church. "The crop is always greater than the seed," he concluded, "and the promise even greater." Paul committed himself to capture these thoughts and did so in the last chapter of the book to the Philippians that he was writing. He wanted the Philippians to know his heart. He wanted to officially recognize them and to tell them thanks. Paul wanted to memorialize their generosity towards him. He also wanted to assure them that their reward was certain.

---

1. EVERY ACT OF GENEROSITY WILL BUILD YOU A MEMORIAL BOTH ON EARTH AND IN HEAVEN.

2. Search THE EULOGIES THROUGHOUT time, they will tell you what you already know: GOOD DEEDS AND GENEROSITY ARE THE MOST CONVINCING VOICES IN a person's memory.

FORGIVING

When a person understands and adopts the lifestyle of a generous person, a liberal giver, they are said to be pro-giving or for-giving. The question remains though do they really forgive? They have released to others; have they truly released others?

Forgiving is an act of giving. When you release someone, you erase their debt. Whether it is a debt of offence or a debt of money, you have given value to them. ***If you owe someone one thousand dollars and they forgive you, it is the same as someone giving you one thousand dollars to pay your debt.*** If someone owes you a debt because they have hurt you, and you forgive them, you have given to them something of greater value than money; something money cannot buy. ***Forgiveness is similar to tithe, it is not optional; God commands us to forgive from our hearts.***

Joyce sat in her study, soaking in the word of the Lord. There was nothing she loved more than to let the word of the Lord saturate her very being.

"Neither will your Father..." This verse stuck with her and she could not let it go. "Neither will your Father forgive your trespasses."

"Is there really any special circumstance where God will not forgive me of my sins?" Joyce thought to herself. "If I do not forgive those who have wronged me...Wow!" she exclaimed.

Memories of her father flooded her mind that moment and the hurt was as real as at the times of her childhood. She could remember the nights he would silently enter her room as she trembled with fear and trepidation. Hands that were supposed to be gentle, caring and loving, were slithery and cold and rough. Tears flooded her eyes as she remembered the plodding that left her ravished emotionally and in severe physical pain.

Day after day, year after year; "And mother refused to believe me!" she cried. "It hurts! It really hurts!" she whispered through her sobbing. "Neither will your Father forgive…" This was tough. How could God exact such a punishment on someone who has been so abused? How could He refuse to compromise? How could He?

Joyce wanted God, all of God, but how could she give all of herself? How could He be so demanding? Joyce sought answers. Her study took her to the eighteenth chapter of the book of Matthew.

Enter Peter in a conversation with Jesus. Joyce caught her breath out of respect for the Master. Peter was asking Him, "Master, how many times should someone forgive the same person who sins against him?" He had a suggestion, "Should we forgive seven times?" Jesus did not make it so easy for someone to extricate themselves from the compulsion of forgiveness. Jesus responded to Peter, "I say, up to seventy times seven!" This was four hundred and ninety times. Imagine one person, perhaps doing the same thing to offend you four hundred and ninety times and you still forgive them. This was like a life sentence and Jesus knew it. It was clear that His intent was that of complete forgiveness, forgiveness in advance, a forgiveness mindset.

Joyce immediately followed Jesus to a kingdom, His kingdom, the kingdom of God pictured from an analogy of the kingdom of a certain king.

Her tears dried as she saw him. He was tall and gaunt and looking like an average person living above his means. He was dragged before the king and he stood there disheveled and ashamed. The king wanted him to pay the- Joyce gagged at the amount ten thousand talents he owed him. That was millions in today's terms.

"How could the king have been so generous to extend so much to him in the first place? He has a heart!" Joyce thought.

The servant stumbled on his words and stuttered, "Pl.. ll.e..." He had no response. The king saw that he was not able to pay or defend himself. "Sell this man, his wife, his children and everything he has!" the king commanded. "We will use the proceeds to settle his account."

The man fell on his face and immediately found the words that had eluded him. "Please Master!" the servant said falling on his face. Tears were in his eyes as he begged, "Give me time, have patience please, I will pay!" The king felt it for him; he was a man of compassion. He had a heart. He said to him, "You may go. I forgive you everything. Go, you owe me nothing!"

Instead of prolonging this man's pain, the king simply forgave him everything. The expectation was removed. "The king, in his extravagance, had just given the man millions of dollars," Joyce thought. "This was a debt he certainly could not pay!"

The man thanked the king profusely and was extremely happy as he left the king's presence. When he was safely away from the palace he screamed. He could not explain his feeling. It was as if his life was just given to him. He was sentenced to slavery forever and now this sentence was reversed. He screamed again and was smiling from ear to ear as he rushed home to tell his wife.

It was at that moment that he saw one of his fellow servants coming who owed him a few thousand dollars. The laughter was cut from his heart and the ruthlessness that stifled generosity and had kept him poor rose up in him. He immediately took the man by the throat and demanded, "Pay me what you owe me, now!"

His fellow servant fell down and begged him, "Please give me some time, I will pay you." He was very poor and struggling, and this man knew it. He would not listen. He had this poor man thrown in prison until his debt was fully paid. As the prison doors closed on this man he considered his family and wept. Now he had no means of paying or ensuring that they would be fed. In that moment, life seemed hopeless and full of pain and severe heartaches. He was broken and in tears as the reality of his situation sank in.

"This is how we commit people to the prison of our unforgiveness!" Joyce thought. When the other servants of the king saw what this servant had done, knowing all the king had done in forgiving him, they went and told the king of his actions.

The king was very angry, extremely angry. He had this servant brought back to him. He was livid as he pronounced judgment. "You wicked servant!" he said, "I forgave you all your debt because you begged me. You should have had compassion on your fellow servant also, just as I had on you. You shall be delivered to be tortured until you pay me everything."

Joyce heard the voice of Jesus and she woke up, "So My heavenly Father will do, if each of you from his heart, does not forgive his brother his trespass!"

Thoughts rushed at Joyce in that moment as if in a race to enlighten and condemn her.

Thought 1: If this is just like the kingdom of God then who is the king?

Thought 2: God of course. Jesus said, "So My heavenly Father will do…"

Thought 3: What debt has He forgiven us that we could not pay?

Thought 4: Sobs! Sobs! Tears! I am trying to get through here… sobs, tears! You know the answer already don't you. Uncontrollable tears!! Yeah, yeah! Show me the person on earth who can pay for his own sins! Show me the accumulation of wealth on earth that could pay the price of sin! Tears! Sighs! Tears! Holding head in disbelief! Tears! He did not just say, "I forgive you!" He died to bring you your forgiveness. To ensure your debt is cleared!

Thought 5: Wow! Amazing! Wow! Sobs. ***Everything that anyone has done to me pales in comparison to what I have been forgiven.*** The debt that we hold and exact is minute in comparison. Raped, lied on, mistreated, abandoned, double crossed, physically abused… even the sexual abuse of my father who was supposed to protect me, even my mother not listening, even… nothing to compare; nothing to compare!

Thought 6: If we do not forgive these, relatively small, things, although He has already died and forgiven us… wow! He will demand our debts. He will commit us to the tormentors until we pay in full! If God forgave us so much- a debt money could not pay; freedom from the bondage of sin- and we hold others accountable for what they owe us…?

Thought 7: "You wicked servant!" Joyce jumped. The voice was speaking directly to her. It was her own thoughts. Joyce knew what she had to do.

Time passed. Joyce is now a teacher of the word of God with an internationally respected ministry. Her father and her mother are now saved and Joyce is not ashamed to tell her story. Joyce remembers the time she went to her father, hugged him and said, "I forgive you!" The magic of the moment is unforgettable; his trembling; his tears. She knew it, she had just given him back his life.

A gift that a dirty, low down, no good scoundrel needed most was handed to him, and it changed his life forever. Joyce knew this term did not really refer to her father, but to her. She benefited most from releasing him. She was the one the king had singled out as wicked. She was the one who held the small debt, though she was forgiven so much. "Indeed," Joyce thought, "I am the abused girl who has been gifted with life and glory by my extravagant King; I will hold no person in debt; I hold no prisoners."

Forgiveness is necessary for the redemption plan to have its true impact. We must give, we must release money owed, but we must release people. Sometimes this gift of forgiveness will have a greater impact than the gift of money. The redemption plan must reach people who hurt the most for they are the people who have been hurt the most. Many times these debts are held by the most spiritual church members and ardent worshippers among us. Christians who simply refuse to release them.

"Owe no man nothing but love. Do we all owe the debt of love?" ***Unlike the debt of money, no one can pay for their transgressions against you- just as you cannot pay for your transgressions against God- you must release it. This is why forgiveness is the greatest gift anyone can give.***

Did Jesus say, "Leave your gifts at the altar, go make it right and return to offer the gift"? Must the gift of forgiveness precede the giving of the offering for the offering to be accepted? ***It appears God wants us to forgive in advance, to forgive as a lifestyle, to forgive extravagantly.*** Forgive us our trespasses as we forgive…for if we do not forgive…neither will God…!

"Every day is Jubilee in Christ!" Christal said, after hearing Joyce's story. She began to reflect on the Jubilee. "The Jubilee is no more with us but every day is Jubilee in Christ." She could imagine the joy and celebration in Israel as the Jubilee approached, time after time. The Jubilee was the time God had mandated for every debt to be forgiven. Everyone was given a clean slate in Jubilee. It was a time that released the unfortunate and disenfranchised to start again. Jubilee for them was a time to get rid of the effects of bad decisions and bad choices.

Another name for Jubilee could easily be: Forgiven. Jubilee was a time God had scheduled every forty-nine years for men to remove the burden of the bad decisions of fore-parents from the children. Jubilee was a time for which everyone who was in debt waited for. Jubilee was redemptive. As Christal meditated on

Jubilee, she could hear her spirit sing with a perfect definition of Jubilee. ***Jubilee is indeed the extravagant heart of God extended through His righteous laws to man. The blessings of Abraham is the act of taking the forgiveness of God to the nations.*** It is the proclamation of Jubilee for all.

1. SO YOU HAVE NOTHING TO GIVE;
ARE YOU HOLDING A DEBT?

2. SO YOU ARE A GENEROUS GIVER, IF YOU
HOLD A GRUDGE YOU ARE NOT THERE YET.

3. RELEASE PRECEDES EXTRAVAGANCE, FOR
GIVING STARTS WITH FORGIVENESS!

CHAPTER

12

THE GAME - YOUR LIFE; GOD'S STYLE

The voice of the announcer echoed in the hearts of the people, "Are you ready to plaaaay?" We have come to the place where every person gets a chance to assess themselves on the principles of this book, to challenge themselves on the lessons of this book, to commit themselves to the morals of this book.

WE WILL BE BUILDING A LIFESTYLE TABERNACLE OF GIVING FOR GOD. YOUR LIFE; GOD'S STYLE!

Are you ready?

Before you begin building, you must determine whose building you are building. If you are building a hotel for celebrities, you make it luxurious. If you are building a house with projections of low income, you make it as cost-effective and cheap as you can.

Today we look at building a lifetime tabernacle of giving for God. The first thing that you will need in building for God is faith.

Here are some questions you must answer:

Are you a stingy giver or are you generous? How big is the God who will occupy your tabernacle? What sort of structure does He deserve? A celebrity structure? A presidential structure? A "no one like you" extravagant structure? Who is your financier? Can He afford the structure you are building Him?

The announcer then spoke this jingle:

As we proceed you've got to build

According to the picture of the God you have
Is He most awesome and magnificent?
Your gift speaks volumes for your heart
You must know He is and that He will
You can please Him no other way
It is impossible to build for God
If you do not build on faith.

If you can see God, then you can build for God. If He is too small in your eyes, if your giving has been an afterthought rather than an active thought, then pray that God will be magnified in your eyes.

Welcome to the game!

LEVEL 1

The announcer continued:

You now begin level 1. We call it the building plan.

We will be building a lifestyle tabernacle of giving for God.

Your life; God's Style!

Every building must have a plan that can be approved by the Master Builder. It must be signed off by the local government. We know the Government is upon His shoulder. A lifestyle tabernacle for God must be approved by the Holy Spirit, the local Governor.

The voice of the announcer echoed:

What is your plan? Do you want a big tabernacle for the blessings of many, a small tabernacle for the blessings of a few? Or do you want just enough to bless yourself and your family?

The announcer then read this jingle:

Here are the things you've got to know
You can live life in the overflow
A place of exceedingly abundantly more
Where God opens His windows, yes Heaven's door
It's pouring out! It's pouring out!
Your rooms and walls and flooring out
Pressed down, shaken together and flowing out
For nations to be redeemed.

God's style is extravagance! Exceedingly, abundantly, above…! What will your style be?

THIS IS YOUR CHALLENGE QUIZ

Are you a giver or just a liver?

Do you consider what you have, to be yours or to be God's? Do you give and regret or do you find giving happiness? Do you give more than required, or do you rarely remove from tithe?

Is your giving landscape flat at your tithe level, or is it filled with mountains and peaks?

Will you obey if God says…"Yes!"? That amount that makes you say, 'Next! No, not God!'?

Will you build a house of extravagant giving; to allow God through you to reach the dying…world?

THEN THE ANNOUNCER SAID:

This is your choice.

It is easy to be normal.
It is normal to be cursed! (We were born that way)
For those who want extravagance
A place where normal ceases to exist
Where you flow like rivers and can't resist
Where you bless as naturally as how you breathe

> *For you give as freely as you receive*
> *And you make a mark on eternity*
> *You move to level 2; this game is for you.*

YOU HAVE A PLAN; YOU ARE IN THE GAME!

This is the game of building a lifestyle tabernacle of giving for the Big God! Your life; God's style!

LEVEL 2

The announcer started level 2 just as he starts all levels:
We are building a lifestyle tabernacle of giving for God. Your life; God's Style!
Now that you have a plan, welcome to Level 2. This is where we examine your foundation.

Again the announcer reads a jingle:
> *Every building must have a foundation*
> *A giving lifestyle requires*
> *Obedience to the God of creation*
> *You must begin with your tithe*
> *For you cannot have a blessed curse*
> *If you build on a curse it is not wise*
> *For your giving to be blessed*
> *The big question is: do you tithe?*

The voice of the announcer BOOMED as he said:
The foundation for a giving lifestyle is tithing!

NOW FOR YOUR CHALLENGE QUIZ:

Do you pay your tithes consistently?
Have you ever borrowed your tithes?
Do you believe it is right to withhold or to borrow your tithe?

Do you remember to pay the tithes you have borrowed…all of it?

The voice of the announcer rang out in the consciences of the participants; still ringing… in yours.

If you cannot answer this question with a clear conscience, can you make a commitment to tithe consistently right now, from now on?

REPEAT WITH ME:

Lord, I am sorry for robbing You! Please forgive me. You have my commitment never to steal the tithe from You again.

THEN THE ANNOUNCER SAID.

If you are a tither or if you have made the commitment, your foundation is in place.

For you cannot have a blessed curse! You cannot have a blessed offering; you cannot have a blessed life if you are cursed for not paying tithe!

You now may begin building your lifestyle tabernacle of giving on a good foundation. Your life, God's style!

LEVEL 3

The announcer gave every participant the time to recover their breaths. To fully absorb the commitment they had just made; to fully appreciate where they were going. He knew very well that this was just normal Christian life in God's eyes but for many of the participants this was a tough challenge.

THE ANNOUNCER SAID:

You have progressed to level 3 of your lifestyle tabernacle of giving game, congratulations.

Then he began his trademark statement:

We will be building a lifestyle tabernacle of giving for God. Your life; God's Style!

This section has two parts: your treasure, and your measure.

SECTION 1: YOUR TREASURE

Every builder at the outset must make some advance preparation for the building.

The builder must get the materials ready on a timely basis before it is given to the building.

The materials are determined and prepared; the fixtures are selected. They are then presented. They are then used. The process is summarized as follows: Preparation, presentation, offering.

The greater the treasure that is allocated in the building is the more of the heart of the builder that is engaged, and the more he watches over its success.

IN BUILDING YOUR LIFETIME TABERNACLE OF GIVING, YOUR QUESTIONS ARE:

Do you determine or prepare your offering in advance for giving?

Do you present it to God with excitement, knowing He accepts it?

Do you offer it knowing Heaven is participating by the act of receiving?

How much of your treasure will you commit to the redemption plan?

Is your heart fully engaged?

THEN THE ANNOUNCER SAID:

You are now in Part B of Level 3: Your Measure

Every builder at the outset must determine the tools he will employ, based on the magnificence and the size of the plan. How much machinery will be used, as well as manual tools and labor?

How will the materials be distributed?

You must decide the measure you will use for your building.

The truth is, the measure you use will determine the measure of your success. It will certainly be measured back to you by natural and spiritual laws.

Your measure will determine if your building can be finished quickly to allow you to take on greater projects or if it will not be able to be completed in your lifetime!

The announcer then read his jingle:

> *For your building you must decide*
> *The shape the glory and the size*
> *What will be your measure? Tell me*
> *What will be your style?*
> *Will you give with buckets?*
> *Or with spoons and forks and knife*
> *Tractors, cranes, excavators*
> *Or a miserly waste of time?*

Your next question, then, is just as plain as that; do you give full measures?

Or do you give while holding back some portion?

WE ARE BUILDING A LIFESTYLE TABERNACLE FOR GOD. YOUR LIFE; GOD'S STYLE!

An extravagant building will demand extravagant giving. A God-sized building will take a great lot of materials given in full measure. Full measure is a measure that will afford maximum distribution in minimum time!

If your measure is right and is not poor, then you may move to level four.

LEVEL 4 GOD'S VOICE

The voice of the announcer came over the microphone. It was a whisper! It was barely audible.

The announcer spoke again, this time in the same undertones as before!

Everyone strained their ears to hear what he was saying. They were asking each other, "What did he say? Did you hear him?"

The voice of the announcer came over the microphone once again. This time it was very clear and distinct.

For those who have made it this far, welcome to Level 4.

WE PREPARE YOU TO BUILD A LIFESTYLE TABERNACLE OF GIVING FOR GOD. YOUR LIFE; GOD'S STYLE!

I whispered deliberately just now because this level is all about hearing.

Tell me the person on earth that will allow you to build on their behalf without allowing them to have a say?

You are building a tabernacle of giving for God and therefore you must be willing to hear God and follow His instructions.

When I whispered, you strained to hear what I was saying.

You asked each other what I said.

The questions are:

Do you ask God what He desires you to give?

Do you strain to hear what He is saying?

Are you willing to follow His instructions?

To what extent can God give you instructions about your giving?

Can He go as far as- The earth is the Lord's and the fullness thereof, I own everything, you own nothing?

To what extent can God give you instructions about your giving? Can He go as far as- Your son, your only son, the one you... love? Everything!

The announcer was silent for a few minutes. The room was very quiet. Everyone listened intently for what would be coming next. Then it happened. The lights went off, they were in total darkness.

They found themselves in the middle of a field. It was a 4D presentation.

The man in focus was a middle aged man looking wealthy but with the wrinkles and scars of a hardworking man. He had just planted a vineyard and had made it state of the art of his time. He had dug a winepress and built a tower. He did not plan to stay, though. He was about to go to a very far country. He was speaking with six persons who had expressed interest in leasing the vineyard. "We will work the field and give you your due of the output," they were proposing.

"This is what I will do," the farmer said. "I will agree and send my servants to collect my share when the time comes." The farmer signed the agreement with four of them whom he had selected. He then left on his journey. He was very happy. He was very generous to these people. He had made them a good deal. He felt within himself that they were people of integrity.

The farmer arrived at his destination after a number of weeks. He was busy doing his business and preparing for the future of his people. He had generous plans for the persons who had leased the vineyard from him. The farmer was away for some time, and it was time for the grapes to ripen. He sent his servants, three of them, to collect his portion of the produce. He expected his lessors to give him his portion and to be much more generous. He had made them such a good deal with so much slack.

His heart broke, his face drained, the look of disappointment, dismay and anger was evident when the report came to him. These men had beaten one of his servants, killed one and stoned the other. They refused to surrender his agreed portion. Those watching the presentation could see him visibly trying to control himself as he decided to give the lessors an opportunity to redeem themselves. He sent another delegation of servants to the lessors to collect his portion. This time he sent more than before. To his dismay and utter disappointment they meted out the same level of wickedness to these servants, also.

This wealthy farmer decided to send his son. "They will honor my son," he thought. The lessors could see the son of their landlord, with his servants, coming towards the vineyard to collect his father's due. It was then that it happened! When they saw him, they immediately plotted to kill him and steal his inheritance.

As he entered the gate they caught him and pulled him to the middle of the field, below the winepress. It was there that they did the most grievous thing that broke the master's heart; they killed his son.

The lights were still turned off but the questions kept coming across the screen:

Are you holding on to property which does not belong to you?

Are you denying the Owner access to His wealth?

Are you willing to hear and obey the voice of the Owner or do you refuse Him?

Are you willing to honor the instructions of the Owner…the one who owns the earth, everything and every person in it?

The lights flickered on but it lost its glow to a brighter light shining in the hearts of those who were confronted and convicted by these questions.

The announcer said:

God may speak through His servants, God may speak through His Son.

God may speak through His Spirit…a still small voice, a slight impression, yet… you know it is Him.

Do you reject the impression of the Holy Spirit if it is not the most comfortable instruction for you to perform?

If you are willing to hear God, you have graduated to level 5.

LEVEL 5 A GIVING CULTURE

Congratulations to all who have progressed to level five.

This is the level where the game becomes life.

It is the place where you travel near or far, without leaving your generosity behind or in the car, for Generous is simply who you are. In this stage, we no longer prepare you to build a lifestyle tabernacle for God but to be a lifestyle tabernacle for God. Your life; God's style! This stage examines the what, why, where, when, how of giving. You will navigate the beautiful complexity of developing a culture of giving.

THE VOICE OF THE ANNOUNCER SPOKE:

This section is simply filling in the blanks.

We now look at the first culture, a culture of what? Your life; God's style!

It is an art, not just an act

I live to give, but tell me what?

FILL IN THE BLANKS

Exceedingly, AB_ _ D _ NT_Y, M_R_ than is required of me.
Whatever God D _ M _ N _ S of me.
My E _ RT _ _ Y goods and if necessary my L_ _E for others.
E _ E _ R _ _ HI _ G! I own N_ _ HI _ G!
My W_ _ LT_, my T _ _ E, my T _ L _ N _TS,
my S _ R _ NG _ H, L _ V _, a S _ I _ E;
whatever creates an I _ P _ CT.

YOU MAY NOW CHECK YOUR ANSWERS:
Exceedingly, abundantly more than is required of me.
Whatever God demands of me.
My earthly goods and if necessary my life for others.
Everything! I own nothing!
My wealth, My time, My talents, My strength,
Love, a smile; whatever creates an impact.

The voice of the announcer continued:
>	If you get it then you've got it, it is yours.
>	**WE MOVE TO THE SECOND CULTURE, A CULTURE OF WHY. YOUR LIFE; GOD'S STYLE!**

Can you think of five reasons why you should give?
Can you tell me why this is the only way to live?

God C_ _ MA_DS it
Love and compassion DE_ _ ND_ it
The redemption plan RE _ U _ RES it
The next generation N _ _ DS it
Eternity PR _ SE _V_S it

YOU MAY NOW CHECK YOUR ANSWERS:
God commands it
Love and compassion demands it
The redemption plan requires it
The next generation needs it
Eternity preserves it.

The announcer sounded:
>	If you get it then you've got it, it is yours.
>	**WE MOVE TO THE THIRD CULTURE, A CULTURE OF WHERE. YOUR LIFE; GOD'S STYLE!**

> *To place your treasure and have no care*
> *No great concerns and to have no fear*
> *Where maximum returns are received and shared*
> *But how do you know just where?*

YOU ASK: WHERE AM I TO PUT MY TREASURE?

Where I want my _ _ A _ _ to be
Wherever God _ OM_A_ _ S
In the S _ R _ I _ E of its true O_ _ ER
Wherever lives will be R_D_ _M_D
In H_ _ _ EN where M _ _ H and R_ _ T cannot corrupt,
and TH _ _ _ ES cannot steal.

YOU MAY NOW CHECK YOUR ANSWERS:

Where I want my heart to be
Wherever God commands.
In the service of its true owner
Wherever lives will be redeemed
In Heaven where moth and rust cannot corrupt
and thieves cannot steal.

The announcer sounded:

If you get it then you've got it, it is yours.

We move to the third culture, a culture of When. Your life;
God's style!

> *Today, tomorrow, if, but, then*
> *Today we simplify the question of when.*

WHEN DO YOU GIVE?

Whenever there is an O _ _ OR _ _ NI _ Y to C _ E _ TE
an IM__CT
When God IN _ T _ U _ TS me to; when the O _ N _ R
commands it

When I I _ E _ T _ _ Y a N _ _ D; Kingdom _ I _ ST.
All the TI _ E; a river FL_ _S constantly
When I take the next B _ E _ _ H

YOU MAY NOW CHECK YOUR ANSWERS:
Whenever there is an opportunity to create an impact
When God instructs me to; when the owner commands it
When I identify a need; Kingdom First
All the time; a river flows constantly
When I take the next breath.

The announcer sounded:
> If you get it then you've got it, it is yours.
> **WE MOVE TO THE FOURTH CULTURE, A CULTURE OF HOW. YOUR LIFE; GOD'S STYLE!**

> *You know the place you know the time*
> *You know the reason and what is required*
> *But you ask how, the attitude*
> *What is the lifestyle culture of giving for you?*

The real T _ _ASU _ _ of giving is when I find the P _ _ ASU_ of giving. When I give with J_Y not with a heavy heart. When it E _ CI _ _ _S me to bless and to impart.
I will not W _ _T for OPP _ _TUN _ _ IES to come, I will look for OPP _ _TUN _ _ IES or C _ _ATE some.
I will give as if I believe someone's L _ _E depends on it, that the next GE _ _RA _ _ON needs my sacrifice.
I will give as an act of W _ _ S _ _P to God. I will give to put God and gold in their proper P _ _SP _ TI_ E.
I will always S _ E Jesus, F _ _ L Jesus, H _ _R Jesus. I will see Him in PE _ _LE: His redemption, His FOR _ _ _ _ NESS; the true PO _ EN _ IAL of my gift.

I will consider myself BL _ _ _ ED with Abraham to be a CON _ _IT of the blessings of Abraham. I will see an EX _ _ V _ G _ NT God, and be an EX _ _ _ V _ G _ NT child of my Father God.

NOW YOU MAY CHECK YOUR ANSWERS:

The real treasure of giving is when I find the pleasure of giving. When I give with joy not with a heavy heart. When it excites me to bless and to impart.

I will not wait for opportunities to come, I will look for opportunities or create some.

I will give as if I believe someone's life depends on it, because the next generation needs my sacrifice.

I will give as an act of worship to God. I will give to put God and gold in their proper perspective.

I will always see Jesus, feel Jesus, hear Jesus. I will see Him in people: His redemption, His forgiveness; the true potential of my gift. I will consider myself blessed with Abraham to be a conduit of the blessings of Abraham. I will see an extravagant God, and be an extravagant child of my Father God.

THE ANNOUNCER SAID IN CLOSING:

Jesus had a free spirit. He was a gift that kept on giving. Everywhere He went, He was doing good. He not only was but He is, the gift that keeps on giving. He is still giving salvation, healing, comfort, power to become sons, and… whatever you ask in faith.

For all those who have completed the game, you are winners in principle. Go and translate this into a winning lifestyle.

I leave you to seriously consider, meditate upon and seek the revelation of this instruction of Jesus in the thirtieth verse of Luke six: Are you ready? *Give to everyone who asks of you. And for the person who takes away your goods do not ask him back for it!*

> *1. YOU DID NOT CHOOSE ME, BUT I CHOSE*
> *YOU AND APPOINTED YOU. (SELECTION)*
>
> *2. THAT YOU SHOULD GO AND BEAR FRUIT. (REDEMPTION)*
>
> *3. AND THAT YOUR FRUIT SHOULD REMAIN. (PERPETUATE)*
>
> *4. SO THAT WHATEVER YOU ASK THE FATHER IN*
> *MY NAME HE MAY GIVE YOU. (EXTRAVAGANCE)*

JESUS TAKES IT VERY PERSONAL

Matthew had a lot on his mind. On a normal day, it would take him hours to digest the loaded statements he hears from his Master every day. But most of his days were not normal, he would be chewing on the food for days. Matthew found it very useful to take notes, it afforded him time to review.

Today, a statement that Jesus had made was locked in his mind and refused to be dislodged. It kept gnawing at him. Every time he saw a person in need, every time he passed a sick person, every time he heard of someone he knew who was incarcerated, it kept coming back, time and again. "Did Jesus just make it impossible to serve Him without serving others?" he said to himself. "What Jesus is asking is not difficult, it is very easy. What we lack is motivation." He thought. "We are so preoccupied that we ignore the call to be generous. We often forget that Jesus Himself needs us."

Matthew went back to his notes and read, "As often as you do it to one of the least of these, you do it to Me! Jesus takes it personally," he said to himself. "Oh no; it is much more! Jesus is saying, 'You cannot separate Me from a need; from an opportunity to minister, from an opportunity to be generous.'"

Matthew gulped as he read his notes. Jesus was decreeing punishment and rewards for those who fail to act and for those who act. It was clear Jesus did not see these acts of generosity as optional but as an obligation. Matthew decided to read his notes very carefully to ensure that he did not miss anything.

Matthew remembered Jesus, in all His authority, standing on the Mount of Olives. There was a hint in His appearance that He was physically drained. "Well perhaps I think this was so, because I knew Him, and I knew His tight schedule," Matthew thought. Whatever His physical state was, every word He spoke revived and refreshed Him. It flooded Him with energy and kept Him going on and on, sometimes for hours without losing His intensity. Matthew could hear the authority in His voice coming from the notes as if Jesus was there speaking at the moment. He closed his eyes and he could see Him there, not speaking from the Mount of Olives but coming in His glory:

The heavens were filled with angels, over one hundred million of them. Ten thousand by ten thousand, perhaps billions. Jesus came and sat down on His throne of glory. It was a magnificent sight. It is exactly as Jesus had said in the notes Matthew had recorded. All the people of the nations were gathered before Him and He was separating them. He was placing some on His right hand. He called these sheep. He placed some on His left hand. He called these goats.

Matthew could hear His voice, commanding, full of authority and tempered with love. He said, "Come, you who are blessed of My Father. Come and inherit the kingdom prepared for you before the world was founded." Jesus was speaking to those on His right, the sheep. The angels were worshipping respectfully. It was clear to Matthew that redemption was not an afterthought. God had it all worked out, even before He made the world.

The rationale of Jesus for selecting this group and rejecting the other sent shivers down Matthew's spine as he observed. He said, "I was hungry and you gave Me food, thirsty and you gave Me drink, a stranger and you took Me in. I was naked and you clothed Me, sick and you visited Me, in prison and you came."

It is normal for a king to be this generous for an act of generosity to him. He recalled King Ahasuerus' reward for Mordecai.

It became clear though that this generosity being rewarded was not generosity to the King Himself, but generosity to third parties. Those considered sheep asked, looking confused, "Lord, when did we see You hungry and give You food, thirsty and give You drink, a stranger and took You in? When did we see You naked and clothed You, sick and visited You, and, in prison and came to You?"

Jesus looked at them compassionately as He enveloped them in His love. "As much as you did it to the least of these; to the least of individuals, you did it to Me." Thoughts began to flood the mind of Matthew just then. "It is all about generous and compassionate service. To feed the hungry, give drink to the thirsty, accommodate the stranger, clothe the naked, visit the sick and imprisoned. Awesome! Jesus is not here with us but we have Him every day. He is all around us. We can minister to Him in many different ways. As much as you do it to…" Matthew laughed.

Immediately the laugh was cut off and the reality sunk in. He was brought back to the moment by the voice of Jesus addressing the goats on His left. He could see the angels herding them to take them away to everlasting punishment of fire. It was never prepared for them but for the devil and his demons. They would be sharing the punishment of the devil and his demons. The punishment determined was bitter and severe.

Matthew wanted to know what their charge was. "What could they really have done to deserve this?" He heard the voice of Jesus reading out their charges. They had rejected Him. They saw Him in need and ignored Him. Matthew heard Jesus say, "I was hungry and you gave Me no food, thirsty and you gave Me no drink, a stranger and you did not take Me in. I was, naked and you did not clothe Me, sick and you did not visit Me, in prison and you did not come to visit Me."

Matthew thought, "Utterly deserving! Anyone who does this to a King also does it to His kingdom and to all His subjects. They are an enemy of this kingdom. Ignoring a king in need is just like attacking the king and his kingdom. They strike a blow to the very heart of the kingdom from which they benefit. Utterly deserving!"

While this was absolutely true, Matthew never saw that Jesus was looking at it in the reverse. Matthew was brought back to reality again when he heard the bitter, almost tearful pleas of the people being condemned. Certainly, they would have responded better if they had seen Jesus Himself in need. "These charges were really trumped up," they appear to be saying. They said, "Lord, when did we see You hungry and refused You food, thirsty and refused You a drink, a stranger and refused to take You in? When did we see You naked and did not clothe You, sick and did not visit You, in prison and did not come to You?"

They had a strong legal argument. They all were trembling uncontrollably at the punishment that was determined against them. They waited to see how this King, sitting in judgment would respond to their appeal. His voice was cold and final. He had no love or regard for them. He was dismissive, as if they disgusted Him. "As much as You did not do it to the least of these, to the least of individuals, You did not do it to Me."

The apostle Paul would later receive a revelation of angels presenting themselves in the form of men to test the obedience of kingdom people. He asserted that when we minister to those in need, sometimes we are ministering to angels without knowing it. What we know for certain is that everytime we minister to someone in need, we minister to Jesus Himself, the King of angels.

Matthew covered his face. This scene is one he did not ever want to remember. The look of dismay and distress on the faces of the many millions who were being led away was frightening. The tears that wet the faces, the screams, the trembling, the patches appearing on the trousers and skirts, the…aw!

Matthew's heart shook. "All this because they did not live generously!" He thought. As far as Jesus is concerned, whatever we do to a citizen of His kingdom, we do to Him, the King, and we do to His kingdom. Extravagant giving is normal living. Living generously can be nothing but the standard lifestyle.

The administration of the blessings of Abraham is the very breath of life. Redemption is everything. This was designed before the beginning, and generous distribution of the blessings is necessary to propagate it. Redemption is everything. It was the start of the story before the beginning and it will be the end of the story.

God is preparing a people to live with Him and His angels and it is being expedited on the generosity of the people He is preparing. Those who refuse to be generous towards Him will share the same punishment as, and with, the devil and his fallen angels.

Matthew could remember Jesus telling him and the other disciples, "Freely you receive, freely give!" This would certainly become his new mission statement. "Freely receive, freely give!" Matthew said aloud as he opened his eyes and was transported back to the current time.

FREELY RECEIVE, FREELY GIVE

---

*1. FROM THIS TIME FORWARD, we relate
to NO PERSON according to the flesh
2 Corinthians 5:16.*

*2. GIVING IS EASY WHEN WE EMBRACE THE CHRIST AND THE
CHRIST POTENTIAL IN EVERY PERSON WE MEET.
THE TRUTH: Jesus is who you are really dealing with!*

MY FINAL PRAYER

"Tell them to stop, tell them to stop!" The poet laughed as he dramatically related this story of Moses and the tabernacle to the audience. "We have enough, and even too much; restrain the people tell them to stop!"

The poet started again from another angle:

Why don't you tell the people, take it slow
No tell them to return and go
It is too much; we need no more
No more, no more; return, no more!

Have you ever seen
Anything like this that has ever been
Offering refused and being turned back;
We have too much we accept this not?
Instead let us all lament
This happens too frequent
Pastors, ministries and ministry networks
Constantly asking and begging for more
Missions everywhere closing their doors
The richest weak, the richest poor
This poet is in tears
For the resources are all here
But the miserly and the thieves
refuse the kingdom its resources to release.

The poet then took a passage from the CWDS Bible, the Caribbean Worship and Devotional Study Bible. The passage was from Exodus chapter thirty-six. The poet read the rhythmic relation of facts presented in a prayer to the gentle tune of his piano to close his presentation:

It happened then; Lord, let me live, To see once more God's people give, Till they are restrained and we say, Stop! The kingdom has more than enough. To see skilled men take up their part And put their hands to Kingdom art, Till God's commands, as written down, Are all complete; the work is done!

EXODUS 36

1 "And Bezalel and Aholiab,
and every wise-hearted artisan in whom the Lord has
put understanding and wisdom, to know how to do all
types of work for the service of the sanctuary, the church
shall do all God has commanded." ************
2 It happened then, all that were wise Gathered with
Bezalel and Aholiab; Everyone in whom the Lord placed
wisdom, And whose heart was stirred to do the work.
3 They then received from Moses' hand, the
offering brought from their own land;
An offering free, from willing hearts,
More every morning Israel brought.
4 And all the craftsmen to do the work came,
Each for the work he was assigned,
5 They spoke to Moses, saying, "Tell Israel stop!
Moses, we have more than enough. "Much more
than is needed for the work at hand;
Much more than is needed for God's commands."

6 They were restrained, from that same hour; To hear the cry,
We need no more! Rather, Moses caused it to be proclaimed,
"From bringing let the people be restrained;
Let neither man nor woman offer any more to the work."
The people were restrained from giving more,
7 for the material they had was sufficient, and yet too much.
8 Oh, see them work! All that in artistry were wise…

As God commanded, the work progressed,
Busy men, all giving their best.
It happened then, Lord, let me live To see once more God's
people give. Give of their time, give of their strengths,
To kingdom work, to purpose bent. Give of their all,
till they are refused, Give of a positive attitude.
Lord, let me see God's people work, Till we all see
a finished course Till the Father receives a perfected
Church Yes, until our Redeemer returns!

"Simon, son of Jonas, do you love Me more than these?"
These words rang through the morning like the sound of a bullet,
piercing the concentrated quietness of an examination hall. The
knowledge of who was asking the question added greater significance to the question. It was Jesus. The fact that Jesus had just
risen from the dead, and had proven His divinity beyond question,
made His words even more awe-inspiring. The marvelous catch
of fish before them made the atmosphere already charged with
energy, miraculous. This question for Peter, however, was personal
if not self-condemning. He had, not many days before, denied any
knowledge of this Man whom he said he loved so dearly. Could it
be that this is why Jesus was questioning his love?

Peter thought about the question. Jesus had said, "More than
these!?" He was talking about the fishes. Jesus had earlier miraculously and extravagantly filled their nets with large fishes. The fact

that the nets did not break was another big miracle. Such was the catch. The fishes were right there before them as a stark reminder of the awesome power that was in their midst.

They had toiled all night doing what they did professionally, but without success. Yet with just one word, Jesus had given them the success of a lifetime. Now Jesus was asking him if he would put Him above his professional success. If he loved Him more than the proceeds of his labor that he had toiled so hard all night to obtain. Peter said to Jesus, "Yes, Lord; You know that I love You." This was the easy part. It is always easy to say we love Jesus, it is much harder to prove it with sacrifices. Jesus stated the action He required of Peter. He said, "Feed My Lambs!"

Jesus was asking Peter to let go of His success and be a blessing. He was also asking Peter to use His success to be a blessing. For many persons, this is always a very difficult question to answer. When God gives to us extravagantly, do we make Him more important than His extravagance? Can we put His desires above our own cravings?

Jesus was not finished. He asked Peter a second time, "Do you love Me?" This is a question that needed to be properly ventilated. It needed to go deep into the inner crevices of the heart to see if there was any holding back. It needed to make a statement to the spirit that would never be forgotten, "Kingdom first!"

Peter responded, "Lord, you know that I love You!" Does Jesus know you love Him? How does He know? Does He know by your actions or your words? Jesus told Peter how he could conclusively prove his love for Him. He said, "Tend My sheep. I give to you success but will your success be your life's pursuits, or will I?" Will you look beyond the success to the redemption plan? Will you use your success to tend My sheep? Will you be extravagant to Me as I have been extravagant to you, withholding nothing? Will you love Jesus more?

Jesus heard Peter both times before, "You mean more than this world to me. I wouldn't trade You for silver or gold. You are my everything." Jesus asked him a third time as if He was not convinced, "Do you love Me?"

Peter was a little annoyed. Why did Jesus not believe Him? He said to Jesus, "You know all things, Lord. You know I love You!"

Jesus replied, "Feed My sheep!" For Jesus, the proof of our love is in our regard for His flock. Our love for Him can only be truly expressed on our brothers whom we see every day. We will also have to face the choice between His heart, which is the redemp-tion plan, and the wealth He has given into our human hands. *The redemption plan must always be given priority over the wealth, but the greatest blessing is to have the wealth serve the redemp-tion plan. The greatest treasure in life is to use the treasures of life to express your love for Jesus Christ and for His heart.*

Whatever Jesus gives to us is a tool by which we can say, "I love You!" It should not be a wedge to come between us and God. As Jesus read Peter his death sentence, Peter was resigned. He was not just willing to surrender everything to express his love for Jesus, he was willing to die also. He would eventually be crucified upside down in his relentless pursuit of the heart of Jesus. *Peter realized that his wealth was only truly his when he gave it away. He also realized that his life was only truly his when he gave it* away.

My Prayer:

> *It happened then, Lord, let me live*
> *To see once more God's people give.*
> *Give of their time, give of their strengths,*
> *To kingdom work, to purpose bent.*
>
> *Give of their all, till they are refused,*
> *Give of a positive attitude.*

Lord, let me see God's people work,
Till we all see a finished course
Till the Father receives a perfected Church
Yes, until our Redeemer returns!

---

1. NOW WE KNOW WHAT BIRTHDAY
PRESENT TO GIVE TO JESUS,
what is really on His heart.

2. NOW WE know HOW TO DEMONSTRATE WE LOVE HIM,
REALLY LOVE HIM; truly love Him MORE THAN ANYTHING,
MORE THAN all THE TREASURE HE GIVES US.
IN HIS OWN WORDS: "FEED My SHEEP; ATTEND
TO My FLOCK;" APPROPRIATE your catch 'His
blessings' TO THE REDEMPTION PLAN.

---

1. YOU DID NOT CHOOSE ME, BUT I CHOSE YOU. (SELECTION)

2. THAT YOU SHOULD GO AND BEAR FRUIT. (REDEMPTION)

3. AND THAT YOUR FRUIT SHOULD REMAIN. (PERPETUATE)

4. SO THAT WHATEVER YOU ASK THE FATHER IN

MY NAME HE MAY GIVE YOU. (EXTRAVAGANCE)

EPILOGUE

t was a beautiful new day in Jerusalem. The sun settled on the house of God. The rays were like an inkhorn that wrote the words JOY. Heaven was smiling on the house of God and it was reflected in the fields all around. They were brimming with abundance like never before. It was amazing because they did nothing above what they were doing previously. They plowed with the same plows; sowed the same seeds, but this time…this time the ground responded as if it had just come alive from a long sleep. It was producing so much. The days of not enough had turned to the days of more than enough. The days of lack had changed to abundance. Benjai could never remember the days his farm laughed with him that way. He sat with his family reflecting happily and his wife said something that brought it all together, "Honey, Hezekiah has done such an awesome job. He has brought heaven to us once more."

Benjai nodded in agreement and then stopped, "Honey, it is not just Hezekiah. It is us. It is our giving. He commanded it; we gave. Look at how God has responded."

The days had changed since the years when the sun angrily went through its paces seeking to burn as much as it could in the few hours it was allowed each day. It would suck every moisture from the day that the night offered little relief for. The crops had no cry for mercy; they simply burnt. This was to change. The king Hezekiah had just led the people in keeping the Passover in a manner that was unprecedented since the days of Solomon. The priests and the Levites, however, were returning to their fields. Their appointed place was in service to the Lord at the temple. They were to maintain the house of the God, all its standards and

to offer sacrifices for the people. They would have happily carried out their duties but they were hungry. They could not sustain themselves and their families and serve the people in the house of the Lord simultaneously. Hezekiah was troubled. "This is not right. The portion of the priest and those who serve the commission of the Lord is appointed by the Lord from the people. The people are not giving. The spiritual life of the kingdom is being restricted by the giving of the people," he thought aloud.
 "I must do something about this."

Benjai received the command with mixed feelings. His was elated at what the Lord was doing through this blessed new king but, initially, he was reserved and somewhat trepid at this new command to give tithes and firstfruits. His family was barely sustaining themselves. To pay a tenth of this limited supply made him struggle. He loved his king but not this much. He loved the Lord but questioned the relevance and application of this law. Was it not archaic? It was his wife who broke the ice, "Honey if God says it I would rather not eat than be disobedient. Let us honor God above ourselves. For too long we have relied on ourselves and dishonored Him. Let us change that. He is loving and faithful. He won't let us starve."

It was just four months after that heaps of food were stacked up in the temple of the Lord. Where there was lack before, there was now abundance and excess. Hezekiah came to inspect and was baffled. He had questions to ask. 'What is happening here?' The response was enlightening and encouraging. Azariah, the chief priest said to Hezekiah, "Since the people began bringing the offerings into the house of the LORD, we have had enough to eat and abundance of excess, for the LORD has blessed His people. This enormous heap of supply is what is left after we have received."

The giving of the people not only changed their attitude to giving and to the things of God, it changed their economy and the economy of the country. The people had changed.

Since they started giving to the kingdom of God they found the missing ingredient in their prosperity. Those who were struggling stopped struggling, those who were surviving were saving and those who were prospering were multiplying wealth. God had blessed the people. The only thing that changed was their giving. There was more than enough provision for the work of God. Everyone became so successful that their bank accounts were brimming. Those engaged in full time ministry service were provided for. Missions were fully supplied and there was so much left over. Hezekiah banked the excess. He also took the faithfulness of God to bank from that day. Giving that supplies the work of God in the earth never diminishes the people. Just the satisfaction of seeing the death of Jesus on the cross avenged should be satisfaction enough for lovers of God. God however is no man's debtor; He will never allow anyone to outdo Him. He always responds. Giving was the avenue for God to lavish His goodness on His people. It was the check book necessary to withdraw from the abundant supply of heaven's central bank. If we allow God to use us to supply His kingdom, then God will bless us so that our supply will be memorable and His kingdom will never lack. We supply His work, He supplies us. We care for His heart, that none should perish, He cares for our heart. We put the kingdom first, He attends to all the others things we are interested in. That is his design for the kingdom.

The time for struggles is over when you understand kingdom is a win-win. When you set your heart to becoming an administrator of kingdom resources, the King sets His heart on you. You demonstrate capacity by giving from what you have, even when it seems insufficient for your own needs. Kingdom acknowledges your capabilities above your gifts. When kingdom sees your heart, it supplies you based on your capacity and faithfulness. This result is an increase in your seeds, your capacity to give and an abundance of fruits; your impact and personal supply. It does not stop there, while you live good in the most satisfying, rewarding and fulfilling job on earth, the awards in heaven are astounding. God not just gives you a star, or calls you a star performer, He makes you shine like the stars eternally.

CWDS BIBLE NOVEL EXPLANATION AND DISCLAIMER!

The Bible Novel series takes real Biblical experiences and places them in hypothetical situations, settings and conversations to give readers an imaginary yet real-life experience of what may have taken place in the moment and minds of the characters. Every pastor, every minister, every Bible teacher uses their own stories, drama and style to teach the same stories and lessons of the Bible we so love. They are all unique but as long as the lesson is consistent with the word and the spirit of the word, they are spot on. This Bible novel series is no different. Any person may use their own imaginary and expressive backdrop, venture into deeper depths of creativity and style of delivery that would be so different from the author of this series and they would be perfectly accurate, as long as the lessons and the Word of God remain the same. WE DO NOT CLAIM KNOWLEDGE OF, OR A PROPHETIC REVELATION OF THE BACKGROUND SETTINGS AND CONVERSATIONS CONTAINED IN ANY OF OUR NOVELS, except where it is directly from the Bible. Although these are called Bible Novels, they are in fact a collection of short stories, some unrelated, but are tied together by the general theme of each book. The Bible Novel is an unapologetic portrayal of the attributes and heart of God who is the main character, consistent throughout every book and throughout the series.